THE EARTH KNOWS MY NAME

THE EARTH KNOWS MY NAME

Food, Culture, and Sustainability in the Gardens of Ethnic Americans

PATRICIA KLINDIENST

Beacon Press, Boston

BEACON PRESS
25 Beacon Street
Boston, Massachusetts 02108-2892
www.beacon.org

Beacon Press books
are published under the auspices of
the Unitarian Universalist Association of Congregations.

Portions of the prologue appeared in "Are We in America?"
Los Angeles Review no. 1 (2004).

09 08 8 7 6 5 4 3 2

This book is printed on acid-free paper that meets the uncoated paper
ANSI/NISO specifications for permanence as revised in 1992.

Composition by Wilsted & Taylor Publishing Services

Library of Congress Cataloging-in-Publication Data

Klindienst, Patricia.
The earth knows my name : food, culture, and sustainability
in the gardens of ethnic Americans / Patricia Klindienst.
p. cm.
ISBN 978-0-8070-8571-4 (paperback : alk. paper)
1. Gardeners—United States—Interviews. 2. Farmers—United
States—Interviews. 3. Ethnic groups—United States—Biography.
4. Gardens—United States. 5. Traditional farming—United States.
6. Immigrants—United States—History. 7. Klindienst, Patricia. I. Title.

SB455.K55 2006
635.092'273—dc22 2005030607

FOR THE GARDENERS

ESPECIALLY
MASKA AND MARIO PELLEGRINI

A l'alta fantasia qui mancò possa;
ma già volgeva il mio disio e 'l *velle,*
sì come rota ch'igualmente è mossa,

l'amor che move il sole e l'altre stelle.
—DANTE, *Paradiso* XXXIII

At this point power failed high fantasy
but, like a wheel in perfect balance turning,
I felt my will and my desire impelled

by the Love that moves the sun and the other stars.
—Translated by Mark Musa

FOR THE GARDENERS

ESPECIALLY
MASKA AND MARIO PELLEGRINI

A l'alta fantasia qui mancò possa;
ma già volgeva il mio disio e 'l *velle,*
sì come rota ch'igualmente è mossa,

l'amor che move il sole e l'altre stelle.
—DANTE, *Paradiso* XXXIII

At this point power failed high fantasy
but, like a wheel in perfect balance turning,
I felt my will and my desire impelled

by the Love that moves the sun and the other stars.
—Translated by Mark Musa

To change ideas about what
the land is for is to change ideas
about what anything is for.

ALDO LEOPOLD
A Sand County Almanac

CONTENTS

PROLOGUE
Vanzetti's Garden

Whenever the people whose stories you are about to read asked me why I wanted to talk to them about their gardens, I would tell them this story. It's how I earned their trust, and why they shared so much with me.

I told them how I grew up in a huge extended family that spoke a richly embroidered tongue, an English made to lurch and sing and wail by the Neapolitan dialect it was stitched onto. My mother's people—Natales, Iannaconis, Piambinos, and Pescatores—were cooks and tailors, casket makers and seamstresses. My mother's parents, who grew up in Caserta, met in the Italian enclave of Hoboken, New Jersey. They came over separately in steerage in the first decade of the twentieth century, the epic period of European immigration to America. My grandfather, Antonio Natale, traveled with his brother, Stefano, in 1907. My grandmother, Virginia Delia Miggliaccio, came with her brother, Amadeo, in 1908. They left from the port of Naples and steamed into New York Harbor past the Statue of Liberty, landing on Ellis Island, where, after the long and anxious wait to be processed, they struggled down the ramp with their baggage to take their first steps on American soil.

I told the gardeners how I didn't inherit my Italian grandparents' language except for a few choice expressions. Growing up, I heard exactly one story about my grandfather's life in Italy—how he saved a crust of bread from his lunch on a hike into the mountains and was glad to find it in his pocket on the long, hungry walk back. I knew nothing at all about what it had been like for my grandparents and their brothers and sisters to leave their families in Italy and cross the Atlantic to begin the difficult process of becoming Americans. Our past was a blank. We were so new to America that we seemed to have no history.

All of this changed on the afternoon of my father's funeral, when the innocent wish to preserve what was left of our family stories brought to light a photograph that connected my family with one of the greatest betrayals of ethnic Americans in the twentieth century—the trial and execution of Sacco and Vanzetti for a crime they did not commit. These two Italian immigrants were avowed anarchists who had fought for the laboring class's right to a just wage and decent working conditions. Their real crimes were their ethnicity—as Italians, they represented the largest group of the "darker races" of immigrants arriving in America at the time—and their politics, which frightened many in 1920, when America was still in the grip of the Red Scare.

Violet, my mother's youngest sister, handed me a small black-and-white photograph, its surface scratched and stained, then waited expectantly for my response.

"Who are these people?" I asked her.

Obviously, they were Italian Americans, this small group of children sitting on the wide wooden stoop of a fine house on a bright summer's day. But whose? There had always been so many of us.

"What do you mean, who are these people?" Violet said.

"Don't you recognize us? That's your mother." And she pointed to the dark-haired girl in the center of the group.

I'd never seen an image of my mother as a girl before, so I stared and stared. *She was so beautiful.*

She sits on the stoop of her parents' summer home on Bay Avenue in Atlantic Highlands, New Jersey. Elegantly dressed in the long, slim style of the twenties, she is flanked on her right by her brother Joey (Giuseppe) in knickers, on the left by her sister Nancy (Nunziata), who would die young.

"That's me," Violet said, pointing to the child dressed in a little sailor's suit, her hair cut like a boy's, one knee crossed over the other, an apple in one hand.

Set apart from the beautifully dressed Natale children sits an Italian man with a mustache, wearing a chef's hat and an apron. Joey mugs for the camera; the cook looks grim.

My mother, Esther (Esterina), and Nancy hold up newspapers. Nancy, whose daily shouts some sports scores, looks tentative. My mother has a look of mild derision in her eyes, as if she is thinking, *What has this to do with me?* and holds her paper stiffly upright, as if following an order from the person with the camera. Clearly, she is not reading. It is we, who would see this image on some future day, who are meant to read the huge banner headline across the front of the *Hoboken Daily Mirror:*

BRANDEIS DENIES SACCO'S APPEAL

"When was this taken?" I asked my aunt. "What do you remember about Sacco and Vanzetti?"

But no one in the room that day, including my mother, could tell me. Their blank faces only deepened the mystery. I knew that Sacco and Vanzetti had been put to death and that their trial and execution had been a cause célèbre, but I didn't know why or when.

The absence of memory among my mother's generation, and

my own failure of recognition, soon propelled me across America to collect the stories of ethnic Americans for whom the making of a garden is a way of keeping memory alive and protecting their cultural heritage from everything that threatens their survival as a people.

Back home, I showed the photograph to a reference librarian at the public library in the small New England town where I now live. "Come with me," she said, leading me into the stacks. She pulled out a small paperback, *The Letters of Sacco and Vanzetti,* and handed it to me.

I dated the photograph from Vanzetti's last letter, written from the Death House of the Massachusetts State Prison in Charlestown. It was August 22, 1927. My mother was twelve. She would turn thirteen exactly one month later—and decide to change her name, hoping to disguise her ethnicity so that people would stop calling her things like dago, wop, guinea. On the afternoon she was wearing her stylish dress and elegant shoes, Bartolomeo Vanzetti, a fish peddler whose Italian neighbors testified that he had sold them eels for their traditional Christmas Eve supper on the afternoon he was supposed to have committed the robbery and murder for which he and his friend Nicolo Sacco, a shoemaker, had been condemned to death, wrote to H. W. L. Dana, a Harvard professor who had become a passionate advocate for justice in the case.

Dear Friend Dana,

. . . I am writing now because it seems that nothing and no one is going to stop our execution after this midnight . . .

Yesterday, Judge Brandeis repelled our appeal on the ground of personal reasons; to wit, because he or members of his family are favorably interested in our case, as demonstrated by the facts that after our arrest Rosa [Sacco's wife] and her children went to live for a month in the empty house of Justice Brandeis in Dedham, Mass.

. . . The Defense Committee, the Defense, our friends

> *here, Rosa and Luigia [Vanzetti's sister] are working frantically day and night in a desperate effort to avoid our execution, and they fail second by second and our execution appears always nearer and unavoidable. There are barely 12 hours to its moment, and we are lost...*

In New Haven, I spooled through hundreds of pages of the *New York Times* in the basement of Yale's Sterling Memorial Library until I found the headline for the morning of August 23, 1927:

> SACCO AND VANZETTI PUT TO DEATH EARLY THIS MORNING;
> GOVERNOR FULLER REJECTS LAST-MINUTE PLEAS FOR DELAY
> AFTER A DAY OF LEGAL MOVES AND DEMONSTRATIONS

Less than twelve hours before Sacco and Vanzetti were put to death in the electric chair, while thousands of people stood in vigil outside the Death House, which was guarded like a besieged medieval fortress, my illiterate Italian grandfather, who was Vanzetti's age and had come to America the same year Vanzetti had come, posed his children on the front steps of their summer house and took their picture. Not only was my family's past not a blank, it had been shaped by the tragic force of history.

"Sacco and Vanzetti," the novelist John Dos Passos wrote, "are all the immigrants who have built this nation's industries with their sweat and their blood and have gotten for it nothing but the smallest wages it was possible to give them... They are all the... factory fodder that hunger drives into the American mills through the painful sieve of Ellis Island." And in their passion for justice for the working class, Dos Passos added, they stood for "the dreams of a saner social order."

The Sacco and Vanzetti case, Edmund Wilson noted gravely, "revealed the whole anatomy of American life" and "raised almost every fundamental question of our political and social system."

In the aftermath of the tragedy, the Italian ethnic community turned in on itself. Silence closed over the wound.

My mother learned to be ashamed—of her name, her black wavy hair and dark eyes, her olive skin, her parents' accents, her very name—*Natale,* from the Latin word for birth and the Italian word for Christmas. She vowed that she would never marry an Italian—only an American—so that no one would ever laugh at her again. She would put it behind her. But forgetting did not protect her; it only robbed her of a context for her shame.

Now when I studied the photograph, I could feel the pressure of history behind the silent image of my mother on the front porch of the house I visited all through my childhood—Grandpop Natale's house, where he made us pastina with pats of butter for lunch when we'd walk over from St. Agnes Elementary School, and gave us red wine diluted with a little water in jelly jars painted with oranges and strawberries. For so long, all I had of my Italian heritage was the memory of food: my grandfather's thin-crusted pizzas—bizza, to us; the pastries my beloved great-uncle Giro, the casket maker, would bring when he came down from the city to play the horses at Monmouth Track; my mother's thick red sauce, her pasta e fagioli on Friday nights; and a little red glass pepper, a charm against the evil eye, that she gave me when I was in my twenties. Now I had something more.

My Italian grandfather had not wanted this moment of America's betrayal of the immigrant to pass unrecorded, and now his silent act of witness had come to me.

But what could I do with it? The more I learned about the case, and of the history of injustice toward ethnic Americans, the darker it all became. For a time I felt it would sink me. I returned to the letters Sacco and Vanzetti had written in prison and began to read them through from the beginning. That's how I found Vanzetti's garden.

On October 7, 1926, just two weeks before Sacco and Vanzetti's eighth and final attempt to win a new trial was rejected by Judge Thayer—though someone else had confessed to the crime and two FBI agents assigned to the case had sworn affidavits stating their belief that Sacco and Vanzetti were innocent—Vanzetti answered a letter from a woman named Mrs. O'Sullivan, who had written to thank him for a gift he had sent her. From the way he responds, I see that she must have expressed her hope that he and Nicola Sacco would be granted a new trial and then described her family's farm in Kansas.

"Dear Friend," Vanzetti's reply to Mrs. O'Sullivan begins. "Your letter of the 1st of October was handed to me the day before yesterday. I am grateful for all you are doing in our behalf, and glad that you appreciate the little pen-holder."

Next he answers her hope with his own frustration and despair. "Your letter voices your hopes and optimism on the good outcome of the case. Would it be as you believe," he begins, "—but I cannot share your good expectations . . . Only the thunders of a mighty world-wide agitation and protest could induce the enemy to free us. In Europe it cannot be done; in America it is not done—to explain why, would drive me crazy."

Then, without pause, Vanzetti moves from anguish to peace, from despair to joy, as he describes his father's gardens in Italy. His mother had died when he was a young man; grief over the loss of her had impelled him to emigrate to the United States.

"You speak of wheat farms...," he writes. "My Father has plenty of good land and a beautiful garden... As for our garden, it takes a poet of first magnitude to worthy speak of it, so beautiful, unspeakably beautiful it is."

The catalogue of what they grew is astonishing. Acres of corn, wheat, and potatoes. Mulberry trees for silkworms. Vegetables, some for market, the rest harvested and stored for their family—onions, garlic, red and yellow peppers, carrots, spinach, cabbages, fennel (*anicettes*), tomatoes, parsley, lettuce, asparagus, cucumbers. Next the fruits, including grapes for wine: "We have fig trees, cherry trees, apple trees, pear trees, apricot trees, plum trees, peach trees, rhubarb shrubs, and three hedges of grapes—two lines of black and one line of white."

And then Vanzetti pushes beyond the edges of the cultivated fields. For him, the garden includes its grassy paths and the meadows beyond, comprehending a great web of relationships that includes the wild with the cultivated, all on an equal footing.

> And the singing birds there: black merles of the golden beak, and ever more golden throat; the golden orioles, and the chaffinches; the unmatchable nightingales, the nightingales overall. Yet, I think that the wonder of the garden's wonders is the banks of its paths. Hundreds of grass leaves of wild flowers witness there the almighty genius of the universal architect—reflecting the sky, the sun, the moon, the stars, all of its lights and colors. The forget-me-nots are nations there, and nations are the wild daisies.

If his friend were to walk in his father's garden, Vanzetti writes, a "rainbow cloud" of pollinators would rise up with each step she took—"the king wasps, big velvety . . . and the virtuous honey-bees . . . the hedge's butterflies and the variated armies of several genuses of grass eaters, the red conconcinas, the meadows gri-gri." She would be enveloped, he told her, by the sound of the "multiphoned vibration of wings."

What power does a garden have that a condemned man can turn from anguish to rapture in remembering it? Even in his extreme circumstance—he was allowed only one hour a day to walk outside—Vanzetti relished the aesthetic and sensual satisfactions of a garden. To dwell in the garden, even in memory, is to experience ecstasy—to be ravished, as the flower is ravished by the velvety bee. The garden offers solace, consoling him in his loneliness and grief.

But the energy in the details of Vanzetti's garden suggests that the garden, as he understood it, means far more than this. A moral universe is mapped here, one that transcends intolerance and injustice. Remembering the garden, Vanzetti returns to what it means to work the land, where the harvest offers a just reward for his labor. The garden reminds him who he is and who his people are. To walk the garden's paths, even in memory, surrounded by clouds of insects, singing birds, and drifts of wildflowers, restores to this man stripped of his freedom—a man in exile, stateless, soon to be robbed of his very life—a place in a vast and intricate community that reaches well beyond the human. Here in his father's garden, Vanzetti is a citizen of the land. Remembering his place in the community of living things in the garden provides him with a sense of coherent meaning, distinct from the chaos and tumult of the legal battle raging around him.

If a garden holds this power for the gardener in a moment of extremity, might it hold this power at all times, but we just don't see it?

Garden metaphors have always been used to describe the experience of migration. The titles of two classic studies of the American immigrant experience, Oscar Handlin's *The Uprooted* and John Bodnar's *The Transplanted,* reflect our tendency to conceive of immigrants as if they were plants, not people. But this makes them the objects of history, at the mercy of huge impersonal forces—war, persecution, poverty, famine. What if I reversed this metaphor? What would become visible if I focused on the immigrant as a *gardener*—a person who shapes the world rather than simply being shaped by it?

For three years I traveled the United States, visiting the gardens of ethnic Americans whose stewardship of the land is an expression of their desire to preserve their cultural identity from all that threatens their survival as a people. I told them about the photograph, about my family's loss of our heritage, about Vanzetti's vision of the garden. When I asked whether they thought a garden could be about justice, every one of them said yes. Then they told me their own stories, and in this ritual exchange of narratives we forged a bond.

I asked how gardening was traditionally practiced in their homeland, what compelled them to leave, and how they adapted their garden traditions to the United States. As I listened, I came to understand that I was hearing a people's history of America and the making of Americans. I began to see how gardens map worlds. They hold within them the human side of the story of how and why plants migrate with people. I began to ask very simple questions about things that no longer felt obvious to me. What are seeds, that people carry them thousands of miles to an unknown land and treat them as if they were kin? What have we forgotten about food that people of traditional cultures remember when they regard a meal as a ritual offering?

Very soon, I realized that I had to include the stories of other ethnic Americans, people whose ties to the land predate the drawing of our national boundaries—Native Americans, African Americans, descendants of the Spanish settlers who followed the conquistadors—and the last of America's colonial people, Puerto Ricans.

Like immigrants, all these people have endured the loss or suppression of important elements of their traditional culture, including their religion, ceremonial dress, and mother tongue. Their personal stories have rarely, if ever, been included in books about gardens, though they have helped to shape American land, culture, and cuisine for centuries. Using seeds inherited from their ancestors and techniques passed down over generations, all of them create gardens that are a form of living, embodied memory.

The focus of nearly all the gardens described in this book, from the ten-by-twenty-five-foot plots of an inner-city community garden to a four-acre field of Asian vegetables, herbs, and fruits, is food—food as a form of deep cultural memory, food as a source of sustenance that answers many hungers—for beauty, for connection to a place, for a sense of community. For these gardeners, men and women, young and old, rich and poor, urban, suburban, and rural, to garden is to claim a portion of

American soil as their symbolic home, even when they can never hope to own any land.

Many of the gardeners talked to me about the spiritual power of the act of gardening. The land is said to "speak," and the gardener learns, from wisdom passed down orally through generations, how to listen for its voice and respond with reverence. With this, a second reason for collecting these stories emerged. I began to understand that in preserving and restoring their own culture, these gardeners are also conserving and restoring the land.

I came to see the ethnic gardener as both culture-bearer and citizen, not only of "the lovely organism of America," as Aldo Leopold once put it, but of the larger, more encompassing community—"the land," as Leopold described it in his classic work of environmental ethics, *A Sand County Almanac*. Since all ethics begin with a sense of community, a "land ethic," he argued, "simply enlarges the boundaries of the community to include soils, waters, plants, and animals, or collectively: the land." To live by this ethic means we take our place "as plain members and citizens" rather than as conquerors or masters of the land community. This is what I had no name for in Vanzetti's all-encompassing catalogue of the plants and creatures with whom he shared the world of his father's gardens in Italy.

In keeping alive their heritage, ethnic gardeners also keep alive a wisdom about our place in nature that is all but lost to mainstream American culture. In this, the garden can be a powerful expression of resistance, as much a refusal of one set of cultural values as an assertion of others. This, I felt, was a little-noticed or little-understood aspect of the contribution of ethnic peoples: in refusing to assimilate fully to mainstream American values, ethnic gardeners keep alive, and offer back to us, viable alternatives to the habits of mind that have brought us to our current ecological crisis. The irony of the pressure to assimilate, then, is that it not only robs people of their heritage and their dignity, it robs the dominant culture too, impoverishing us all.

In *The Unsettling of America,* Wendell Berry warns that our ecological crisis is a crisis of character, inseparable from the irrational waste that defines our agriculture. He brings to the urgency of our debate over how we might restore ourselves and our land to health the essential question of culture. *Who are we?* he asks. What vision of America can we call upon now to restore our sense of obligation not simply to our native land but to the earth?

E. O. Wilson brings to this question the long view of an evolutionary biologist. In "The Environmental Ethic," the closing chapter of *The Diversity of Life,* he too offers us a warning. "Our troubles," he argues, ". . . arise from the fact that we do not know what we are and cannot agree on what we want to be. The primary cause of this intellectual failure is ignorance of our origins . . . Humanity is part of nature, a species that evolved among other species. The more closely we identify ourselves with the rest of life, the more quickly we will be able to discover the knowledge on which an enduring ethic, a sense of preferred direction, can be built."

Wilson describes our disregard for the intricate ecosystems that sustain us as an "amnesiac reverie." A long forgetting defines us.

Where might we begin the work of remembering who and what we are? The simple answer I offer here is, in the gardens of ethnic Americans.

Who are the gardeners whose stories you are about to read? From dozens of interviews, I have selected fifteen gardens to write about. The stories of the people who created these gardens will, I hope, resonate with the experience of many other Americans, including the one in five among us whose parents or grandparents came here as immigrants and the one in ten of us who is of foreign birth.

My idea of the garden is broad and runs counter to the strict distinctions observed in most garden writing—the separation of ornamental or formal gardens from cultivated landscapes devoted primarily to the growing of food, which are usually treated like less cultured kin.

Some of the people I spoke with refer to the land they cultivate as a garden, while others call their landscapes farms. But the distinction has little to do with the size of the piece of land in question or what is grown there. The "farms" are often smaller than the "gardens": one family calls the intensively planted land behind its house a farm, while another refers to its four acres of vegetables, herbs, and fruits as a garden. One inner-city community garden made up of thirty-odd small plots bears the name La Finquita, Little Farm, more because the men who first created it are all retired migrant farmworkers displaced from their rural homeland than because of what they grow.

I offer these stories of people keenly aware that they straddle two cultures in the hope of changing the way we think, see, and write about making gardens. Each chapter is an independent narrative. You can open to any one of them and begin reading without losing the thread of the whole, though the book is clearest if you read the chapters in sequence, as the parallels and echoes among the stories accumulate.

The book opens and closes with stories that reach back to the European conquests of America—the Spanish conquest of the Southwest and the English conquest of the Northeast. Both show how corn passed from the conquered to the conquerors, and how its sacred meaning was transformed as it was adopted into the foreign culture.

Two family gardens in the Rio Grande Valley of northern New Mexico open the book. At Tesuque Pueblo, a group of Native Americans hoping to restore their land and their people to health are renewing a thousand-year-old garden tradition that was two family gardens away from being lost. Forty minutes' drive north, a Hispanic family whose ancestors came with the conquistadors has embraced its heritage on the land after the pressure to assimilate to Anglo culture nearly persuaded its members to let it go. The Indians, adapting ideas from leaders in the international movement to promote sustainable agriculture, and the Hispanics, through the Santa Fe Farmers' Market, keep their local cultures alive through contact with the world far beyond America's borders.

The stories of two islands, one off the South Atlantic coast, one in the Pacific Northwest, both fragile ecologies and places where ethnic peoples have waged historic struggles for the right to own and keep land, come next. On St. Helena Island, South Carolina, the gardens of two Gullah elders reflect both the enduring legacy of their African ancestors and the sacred place of land in their emergence from slavery into freedom. And on Bainbridge Island, Washington, a Polish American vintner and a Japanese American berry farmer wage a passionate fight to preserve the largest and oldest remaining farm on the island—a farm nearly lost once before, when the Japanese family who worked it was rounded up and taken away to Manzanar, one of ten "relocation centers" constructed in the desert for Americans of Japanese descent after the bombing of Pearl Harbor in December 1941.

Both the idea of America as the land of refuge and the far older idea of the garden as a sanctuary are given new life in the story of the Khmer Growers. For these survivors of the Pol Pot regime, who rent a four-acre field from the town of Amherst, Massachusetts, it is work that heals—hard work in the garden, all day, every day, even though they still bear the scars of years of forced labor, starvation, and torture.

The stories of two Italian gardeners, one from the north of Italy who lives in California and one from the south who lives in New England—one who fled as Mussolini was coming to power, one who came here just after Mussolini's defeat—capture two distinct ways of transmuting the memory of self-sufficient rural village life in the garden. Their stories, more than any others, capture the power of the experience of migration and the complex negotiation with memory, identity, and loss that is an inevitable part of coming to America.

The next chapter tells the story of a woman who, barred by social custom from working the soil in India, finds not only freedom of conscience in coming to America but the chance at last to plant her own garden. In her tiny backyard in a dense suburb of Los Angeles, she has used the skills she learned from her family's gardener and rural villagers to create a Punjabi garden filled with rare and beautiful fruit trees, flowers, and herbs. Among them is a tree held sacred in India, both for its extraordinary healing properties and for its place in the story of an emperor who renounced war and turned India onto the path to peace. But the neem tree she has planted is also the subject of a heated legal battle that pits the rural poor of her native land against wealthy transnational corporations and the government of her adopted homeland.

Next come the stories of the gardeners of Nuestras Raíces. By way of small garden plots created on vacant lots all over the blighted industrial city of South Holyoke, Massachusetts, members of a Puerto Rican gardening association have lifted a community up from dejection and despair. From one garden and a loose band of gardeners, many of whom are retired migrant farmworkers, Nuestras Raíces has expanded to include over a hundred families in seven community gardens. Through the gardens—and their greenhouse, community kitchen, and ethnic restaurant—these members of a disenfranchised minority are creating a model of a truly sustainable local economy.

The book closes with the story of a Yankee farmer in Stonington, Connecticut, whose land came down to his family as a result of America's first war of extermination, the notorious Pequot Massacre of 1637. Now, as he contemplates the end of three centuries of harvesting this land, which has never left his family, he is returning seeds of sacred Indian corn to the tribes from whom his English ancestors first received them. The story of the loss and return of the seeds of the most sacred plant in the oldest garden tradition of America has much to teach us about the role of gardening in the restoration of justice for people and the land.

"It is inconceivable to me that an ethical relation to land can exist without love, respect, and admiration for the land, and a high regard for its value," Aldo Leopold wrote in the concluding paragraphs of *A Sand County Almanac*. By value, he of course did not mean economic value but "value in the philosophical sense." If you asked the gardeners interviewed for this book if they are philosophers, they would most likely say no. But every one of them lives by the ethic our most eloquent environmental philosopher outlined as the best hope for the land. Their knowing love of the land they till is their birthright, a portion of their cultural inheritance. One of the most important gifts they offer America is the refusal to let it go.

THE EARTH KNOWS MY NAME

1

RENEWAL

Four Sisters Garden and Monte Vista Farm

TESUQUE PUEBLO AND ESPAÑOLA, NEW MEXICO

Tesuque Pueblo

At first the dogs don't see me. They wrestle and nip at each other, take off across the empty plaza, tumble in a heap, and come up covered with dust. Then they lie down panting, only to begin the game over again in a minute or two. When they do find me, sitting on Clayton Brascoupé's back porch wondering where everyone is, they spring up and race over, pummeling me with dusty paws, licking my face, crowding into my lap to sniff my clothes, my neck, my hair. As fast as they came in a happy, yelping clamor, they grow bored and run away again. I stand up and dust myself off. Did anyone see that? Only one placid dog lying in a nearby doorway surveys me with a calm regard.

Except for the dogs, I am alone in the chill of a desert morning in the plaza of Tesuque Pueblo, the smallest and one of the most traditional of the eight Pueblo communities east of the Rio Grande in northern New Mexico. The sun is about to come up over the mountains. Sangre de Cristo, the Spanish named them—Blood of Christ—for the red-gold stain on their flanks at sunset, not for the blood the conquistadors spilled when they came north from New Spain in the sixteenth century, searching for Cibolá, one of the fabled cities of gold.

Ten miles north of Santa Fe, I find myself in another world, where the connected adobe dwellings, like the earth of the bare plaza, are the color of cocoa. There is nothing here to accommodate me, the stranger. The plaza is the inside, the center, of a distinct world. It offers none of the visual cues of mainstream America to help me orient myself—no streets lined with wood-framed houses, no green lawns, no asphalt driveways, no garages, and no conventional landscaping. Here, land is not private but communally owned. Here, to garden is to continue one of the oldest forms of cultivation in America. Here, where the sun is about to light up the cross on the adobe church in the northeast corner of the plaza, members of each of Tesuque's two moieties, Summer and Winter, perform the ancient dances—the Corn Dance in June, the Animal Dance in November.

As I slap the dust off my pants, I wonder how I'm going to find Clayton. A Mohawk married to a Tewa woman of the pueblo, Clayton Brascoupé has lived at Tesuque Pueblo since the 1970s. He is now the director of the Traditional Native American Farmers Association, an intertribal group devoted to helping Native growers of the Southwest maintain and pass on their traditional crops, land, and way of life. We were to meet so I could see Four Sisters Garden, the Brascoupé family's garden.

While I ponder my situation, I study the tall stalks of corn Clayton has planted just outside his door. Tendrils of bean vines climb them to reach the sun, while the thick, hairy leaves of squash plants cover the ground at their feet. The earth is so hard and dry, it seems impossible that this traditional interplanting of the "Three Sisters," a reflection of Clayton's Iroquois ancestry, should grow at all. But that's the point of my having come here—to see how the Tewa, like the Zuni and the Hopi, are blending indigenous traditions of planting the high desert with innovative ideas from leaders in sustainable agriculture.

Indian gardening and farming have suffered a decline. Native Americans of the Southwest are so intimately linked to the foods their ancestors ate millennia ago that once they adopted a mainstream American diet, as they have in recent decades, they suffered an epidemic of adult-onset diabetes. To become self-sufficient again on the harsh land of the high desert of northern New Mexico, where Pueblo Indians have farmed and gardened for nearly a thousand years, is to restore both the people and their land to health.

Clayton's corn is a sign of his lineage and links him to his wife's people as well. Iroquois white corn came east with the Algonkin peoples from whom they are descended a millennium ago. And in Tewa, the language of Margaret Brascoupé's people, the word for food, translated literally, means "white corn meal." For the Iroquois as well as the Tewa, corn is the mother of the people.

For the Europeans who came to conquer them, it had a different meaning entirely. When Coronado led his expedition north from New Spain in 1540, the sun glinting off his breastplate etched with an image of the Virgin Mother of God, he found no fabulous cities. What the conquistadors found instead was "something we prized much more than gold or silver," as one of the tired and hungry soldiers recorded—Zuni gardens full of "plentiful maize and beans," and domesticated turkeys "larger than those in New Spain." The European invaders demanded the food, without which they would have starved, as "tribute"—one of the many rituals of subjugation the young and arrogant Coronado imposed.

In 1680, angry with the violent suppression of their religion and with the demands for tribute, the Pueblo Indians, led by a man named Popé from San Juan Pueblo, rose up to drive the Spanish conquerors from their homeland. After setting fire to the church in the plaza, the warriors of Tesuque joined seven thousand other Pueblo Indians as they moved toward Santa Fe, eight miles to the south, destroying colonial settlements and killing missionary priests along the way. When word of their approach reached the city, the bell in the small adobe church of San Miguel rang out in warning.

For nine days the Indians encircled the city, cutting off the water supply. On the tenth day, the Spanish survivors fled, taking with them the small figure of La Conquistadora, the Virgin dressed as a Spanish queen which the Franciscan superior of the missions had brought with him when he came to New Mexico in 1625.

The Spanish left behind a land and a people changed by their coming. Horses, sheep, cows, and pigs, grazing animals Native Americans had never seen before, had transformed their traditional agriculture, as had the thousand irrigation ditches they had been forced to dig when pressed into slave labor. These ditches, called *acequias,* and the introduction of metal tools made it possible to cultivate the fruit trees the Spanish introduced—peaches, apples, cherries, pears, grapes, and apricots—and foreign vegetables like asparagus and lettuce, and the chilies brought by the Mexican Indians who traveled with the Spanish.

Following the Pueblo rebellion, Popé—one of eleven men who had been whipped before his own people by a Franciscan who had punished him for practicing his native religion—traveled from pueblo to pueblo, urging the people to "burn the seeds which the Spaniards sowed." He exhorted them to return to planting "only maize and beans," the crops of their ancestors. The practice of Christianity and the use of the Spanish language—including their baptismal names—were to be expunged.

But there could be no simple return. The people, and their land, had been changed by 150 years of contact.

Two gardens, one at Tesuque Pueblo and the other forty minutes north, in the Española Valley, reflect the ironies of conquest and mutual adaptation as the descendants of both the Pueblo Indians and the Spanish colonials renew their ties to the land.

"Any garden to me is sacred," Clayton Brascoupé explains as we sit in his office. The stuffed head of a javelina he killed with a traditional bow and arrow is mounted on the wall behind him. His braids hang well below his shoulders. He speaks slowly and thoughtfully and will not be hurried.

"Most of the villages here have been farming the same place for eight hundred to a thousand years," he says. "When I talk to older farmers or gardeners, I hear that the land speaks to them. And they speak to the land. They'll describe what the land is telling them—what should be planted here, what shouldn't be planted, if the land should be left alone—they learn all those things just from walking around."

The elders read weeds, indicator species that "tell you what nutrients are there, what isn't there, what should be there," as Clayton puts it. "I've seen farmers pick up soil, smell the soil, taste the soil," he says. "It's a way of communicating. It's a way of reading the soil and speaking to the land. The older farmers I've worked with knew all of that. They had years and years and years of experience practicing it, and the knowledge that was handed down to them orally from their elders. All that could be lost in one generation."

As much to himself as to me, Clayton adds, "They will find people in their communities to pass it on to. They will."

Clayton uses the words *listen, speak, communicate,* and *community* again and again as he tells me about the movement to restore traditional Native American gardening to Pueblo communities before the wisdom of the remaining elders is lost.

He has been gardening since he was a boy. "I grew up in a community called Tuscarora Indian Reservation, in western New York, outside of Niagara Falls. I'm a Mohawk."

The Iroquois Confederacy originally included five peoples: the Oneida, Seneca, Mohawk, Onondaga, and Cayuga. There are now Six Nations in the confederacy, with the addition of the Tuscarora of South Carolina.

"My mom and dad, my brothers and sisters, the occasional cousin, all lived in a very small home. Our grandmother had a big influence on our lives, on me. Anthropologists like to say that the Iroquois are matriarchal, you know—that women are a leading factor socially. Our grandmother wielded a lot of authority in the home." Her name was Sarah Doctor, and Clayton remembers her as a source of wisdom.

The intergenerational household Sarah Doctor presided over reflects the legacy of communal life in the Iroquois long house. "Materially, she didn't have a lot. Back in the early fifties, I think people outside of our communities probably would have considered our nation poor, they would have seen us as living in poverty. But I never felt that. We didn't have a lot, but we were loved. It was all there. Everything that we needed was there.

"My grandmother spoke Mohawk, Cayuga, Tuscarora, and English. The smaller we were, the more we were able to understand." Clayton remembers his aunts and uncles telling him stories that explained why these languages were not passed on. "There were whippings in school. Children were tied to immovable objects in dark closets. My parents discouraged us from speaking the languages to protect us. There was a stigma to eating our own food, so we ate one kind of food at home and another at school. I think that's why a lot of people kept their gardens—they could have the food they wanted. Gardens were safe—gardens weren't scrutinized.

"As we got a little older, we began to see social dividing lines. We were being persuaded to become more 'American,' whatever that means. I guess we were to give up our identity as humans." Members of the Six Nations of the Iroquois Confederacy call themselves Onkwehonweh, the Real People. Though their lands cross two national borders, they do not refer to themselves as American or Canadian.

"The garden was a way of preserving our identity. Especially if the garden contained the seeds that were given to us by our elders. It meant we kept that relationship to the earth." The garden became a form of resistance to assimilation.

"The original garden is in the Iroquois story of how the earth was created," Clayton explains. "The Iroquois didn't actually *make* the world," he adds, pausing to laugh, "although some of them think they did—and we do claim a lot of things—but that's not one of them. The original garden was actually a grave. You know, it was dug deep. Instead of seeds being planted in this garden, it was the body of one of our original mothers.

"The grave wasn't one that you would envision today, where a person would be laid out horizontally. In the past our people were buried as we are found in our mother, curled up in a ball. So the original garden wasn't rectangular, it was circular, and from it emerged these plants, this array. Out of this grave a garden emerged, our plants," Clayton says—the corn, beans, and squash traditionally cultivated by women and the tobacco used in ceremonies, which was planted and tended by men. "Today they call it intercropping. I'd never seen it, ever, when I was growing up. People knew about it, people talked about it, people referred to the story, but I never saw one person do it." The story, but not the practice, of the traditional Iroquois garden had endured.

"I was born in 1951, when gardens and farming were commonplace. If you didn't have a garden, you didn't eat as well. A lot of people were still making what you would consider a living by farming. Some had cows. Some had chickens, some had pigs. Not everybody had all of those things. But it was a farming community, so you didn't need to—you could barter for whatever you needed. We grew potatoes, tomatoes, and cucumbers. Some corn, but not a lot."

Clayton was about nine years old when he started working the land. "I started working on commercial farms at the age of thirteen," he says—potato farms, chicken farms, farms that grew only tobacco, and vineyards, where he learned how to prune and how to keep a greenhouse. "I worked on commercial farms and I worked on Native American family subsistence farms. And I began to see a difference.

"There was one Native American farmer in particular that I worked with who really inspired me. His name was Mike Boots. He's passed away now. He had a place on Akwesasne," the Mohawk name for a small reservation on an island in the St. Lawrence River. "The Mohawk territories straddle New York on the United States side and Ontario and Quebec on the Canadian side," Clayton explains. "There's a pretty good-sized island in the middle of the St. Lawrence called Cornwall Island, with two bridges, one connecting to the Canadian side, one to the States side. Mike Boots was dedicated to his very large garden on the island." It was Boots's love of the land as much as his skill that made this the place where Clayton too learned to love working the land.

"I used to walk quite a ways to get there before seven o'clock in the morning. It was so peaceful," Clayton says, "so calm. We worked hard all day. I enjoyed that. We got dirty," he adds, smiling. "And that was enjoyable too. I tell people now, 'You know, when you farm, your hands are dirty at the end of the day, but your hands are clean.' With organic farming, the ethic it takes to maintain that type of farm, there's an integrity to that. So your hands are clean. You haven't poisoned the water, you haven't poisoned the food chain. You haven't maliciously hurt birds or insects."

But Clayton didn't learn that on commercial farms. "I was exposed to pesticides, herbicides, fungicides, all of those things working commercial farms," he says. "I have residues from those days in my body yet.

"The messages that were coming to me and all the younger people in the Iroquois communities in western New York were that we needed to continue to farm. We needed to continue to plant our old, traditional varieties of the corns, the beans, the squashes. Oral traditions passed down in Iroquois communities, and also in my wife's community, the Pueblo communities, told us that we should be doing these things. Back in the fifties, the elders were saying that we had to protect our fields. They said that we should not get involved in chemical agriculture, the spraying of pesticides and so on.

"I listened really carefully, and I began to understand what they were telling us. If we eat this diet that was described in oral tradition telling how this land was created, how the spirit of the earth—her being—came with the corns, beans, and squash, we're eating a balanced diet. And if we plant these things in the prescribed manner, we are also taking care of the land, our first mother."

Clayton was introduced to the Iroquois way of gardening just as Cornwall Island came under assault, not from a nation intent on colonizing this time, but by national and transnational corporations. "Since I left, Akwesasne has suffered horrendous ecological problems. They're out of dairy farming now because of air pollutants that fell on the grass. The cows would eat the grass and die."

Peter Matthiessen devoted a chapter of *Indian Country* to the destruction of Akwesasne and the violence that almost engulfed the Iroquois Nation in its standoff with the State of New York when the Native Americans tried to defend their land. Beginning in the fifties, with the building of the Moses-Saunders Power Dam on the St. Lawrence River, which generated cheap hydroelectric power, corporations began locating heavy industry on or near Iroquois land. Reynolds Metals, General Motors, Alcoa, and Domtar pulp mill (a division of Reed International) began to release toxic waste, poisoning the water, the air, the ground—and the Iroquois people. It was ash and fluoride from the Reynolds Metal plant that poisoned the cows. As the cattle ate grass coated with ash, they began to grind down their own teeth. As toxins entered their bloodstream, their bones weakened. They began to starve.

"In 1959, when Reynolds began its operation," Matthiessen wrote, "there were five times as many cow barns on Cornwall Island as there are now: the Indians say that the starving cattle, disabled by bone afflictions, lay down to graze, and crawled from one place to another" before they died. The fish began to disappear and the bees vanished entirely as wild game and gardening declined and conifer forests began to die.

Clayton left Akwesasne just before the ravages of industrial pollution destroyed Mike Boots's land. He began traveling across the country, from one Indian community to another. This was when his real education began, his apprenticeship on the land.

"I visited other Native communities. I started looking at other ways of doing agriculture. I made myself available as a farmhand. Then I moved out West, and I did the same thing, because I didn't know much about the type of farming that's being practiced out here." Then he met Margaret.

"I made myself available to my father-in-law and to some of my wife's uncles. When we started, there was only a handful of elderly men still gardening at Tesuque. Margaret was eighteen and I was twenty-one. This was in 1974."

The radical spirit of the early 1960s, including the revolution in race relations achieved by the civil rights movement, awakened in ethnic peoples across America a fierce new awareness of their right to retain their cultural heritage, whether in religious ceremonies, language, dress, or food. By the early 1970s, as public awareness of the dangers of industrial agriculture increased, organic gardening was enjoying a great resurgence. People once again became interested in growing their own food. The peace movement that helped end the war in Vietnam in 1975 introduced a generation to the politics of engagement and inspired the rewriting of our national myths of origin.

The Native American rights movement of the 1970s and 1980s, which included tragic episodes of repressive violence, was a part of this extraordinary resurgence of the democratic impulse. And when Clayton Brascoupé began to encounter representatives of the new environmental ethic—people who understood that agricultural restoration had to include cultural restoration as well—the tiny community of Tesuque Pueblo, with about four hundred and fifty inhabitants, was linked to an international movement that affirms rather than denies the wisdom of ancient traditions.

"There's an elder Japanese farmer, Masanobu Fukuoka, who wrote this book called *The One-Straw Revolution,*" Clayton says as he hands me a well-worn paperback he found on a bookrack in a train station. The title, derived from the saying of a Japanese elder—"Treat every piece of straw as precious and never waste a step"—intrigued him. One straw, Fukuoka saw—one straw at a time—could bring about a revolution. Live in relation to the land this way, and many things will change.

Fukuoka's ideas startled Clayton. They resonated with everything he had heard growing up with Iroquois elders in western New York. Clayton takes the book back and begins to read aloud from Wendell Berry's introduction. "'We cannot separate one aspect of life from another. When we change the way we grow our food, we change our food. And when we change—or lose—our food,'" Clayton continues, looking up at me, then down at the page again, "'we change society, we change our values.'"

At the close of World War II, Masanobu Fukuoka retreated to a mountain, giving up his position as a plant pathologist in Yokahama. He left the lab to return to the land, where he invented a form of no-till agriculture that enriched the soil and produced staggering yields with less labor and less water than conventional methods of rice cultivation. "The ultimate goal of farming," Fukuoka teaches, "is not the growing of crops, but the cultivation and perfection of human beings."

The spiritual dimension of Fukuoka's practice was in harmony with the stories Clayton had heard from his elders.

In 1992, when the founders of Native Seeds/SEARCH, an organization devoted to the collection, preservation, and distribution of heirloom seeds of Native American foods, sponsored a conference on traditional Native American farming in Gallup, they hoped to address the collective crisis facing Indians of the Southwest. Forty-three Native American farmers, some in their teens, some in their eighties, came with their families to talk about the loss of their agricultural traditions, the degradation of their environment, and the weakening of family and community ties that seemed to go with them. It was there that the Traditional Native American Farmers Association, TNAFA, was formed. Clayton was one of its early program directors.

"Traditional Native American agriculture can mean a lot of things to a lot of people," Clayton explains. "Some people will describe it as planting the old varieties of corn, but behind a horse and plow." But both the horse and the metal plow arrived with Coronado and the conquistadors. "That's their version of traditional agriculture, their own mindset," Clayton says. "There are other techniques that have arisen recently. They're not new forms of agriculture, but old forms being reexamined.

"I've taken some workshops with John Jeavons. He's with a group called Ecology Action, out in Willits, California. He's a wonderful person. He's an advocate of double-digging and bio-intensive agriculture. They've taught this method throughout the world successfully."

At their experimental farm in Willits and through their seed catalogue, "Bountiful Gardens," Jeavons and his small crew at Ecology Action are having a profound effect on the lives of the rural poor in every part of the world. "How can we revitalize our extraordinary planet, ensuring life and health for the environment, the life-forms of a myriad of ecosystems, humankind, and future generations?" Jeavons writes in the opening of his classic how-to manual, *How to Grow More Vegetables*. "The answer is as close to each of us as the food we consume each day," he teaches. "We farm as we eat."

As Jeavons explained his method during a workshop, Clayton says, "I realized that he was outlining the oral tradition I'd heard when I was younger." Jeavons's method, modeled on the four-thousand-year-old Chinese tradition of sustainable agriculture, begins with deep soil preparation, or double-digging, after which you cultivate only the top two inches of the soil. The method includes the use of compost to nourish the soil; closely spaced planting, mimicking nature, to preserve moisture and suppress weed growth; and the interplanting of crops whose nutritional needs complement one another—like the traditional Iroquois planting of corn with beans, a legume that fixes nitrogen and so returns nutrients to the soil, and squash, whose ground-hugging vines and leaves both cool the soil and help it retain moisture.

Jeavons's is a system of miniaturization, especially useful for people with small plots of land. Once established, the biointensive method of gardening actually restores the soil as much as sixty times faster than nature does. By comparison, industrial agriculture destroys topsoil eighty times faster than nature can replace it. Biointensive gardening leads to less water consumption—conserving the most precious of natural resources in the desert—and a greater yield relative to the area under cultivation. In many ways it is, as Clayton says, close kin to traditional Native American gardening.

Clayton made a similar discovery of shared values in the mid-1980s, when Bill Mollison, the Australian who introduced permaculture to the world, came to Santa Fe to do a workshop. "A couple of Anglos kept saying, 'Oh, you've got to go see Bill Mollison.' I told them I might. You know, a lot of times people come to our communities from outside with 'the answer.' So in a polite way I was being evasive, hoping they'd leave me alone."

But the eager Anglos didn't go away—they arranged for Clayton to get a scholarship. When he heard this, he figured he'd show up, listen to a little bit of the morning program, get a nice lunch, and leave. "I ended up staying all day and going back the next day as well."

"Permaculture," Mollison explains in his *Introduction to Permaculture,* "is a design system for creating sustainable human environments. The word itself is a contraction not only of permanent agriculture but also of permanent culture, as cultures cannot survive for long without a sustainable agricultural base and land use ethic. On one level, permaculture deals with plants, animals, buildings, and infrastructures (water, energy, communications). However, permaculture is not just about these elements, but rather about the relationships we can create between them by the way we place them in the landscape."

Mollison's ideas echoed those of one of Clayton's most influential teachers. "One of the elders that influenced me was a gentleman who's passed away now. His name was Philip Deer—he was a Creek out in Oklahoma. He taught me that if we learn to listen to our mother, we can also listen to the elements—like the winds—and the winds can talk to us and teach us things. The water can do the same thing. The stars. The moon. We just have to be able to learn.

"I had the greatest respect for him. He lived the words that he spoke, Philip. This is what our people did. They studied nature, they learned how to listen. Nature was their university. I thought, if Bill Mollison from Australia was this close to Philip's teaching, then there's got to be something valid here. As a people, we have to relearn how to work with the natural elements, natural forces, in order for human beings to survive. Philip had said this.

"Bill Mollison was saying what I heard coming out of our own communities. I thought about it for a very long time. It still seemed like something from outside. But the more I studied it, the more I saw that the concepts had been instilled in our communities from generations back. Permaculture was already a part of our communities. So I based my teaching on this."

Every summer for the past ten years, Clayton has taught a course called "Traditional Agriculture/Permaculture Design: Indigenous Solutions for a Sustainable Future." "We use Mollison's syllabus, but we teach from a knowledge base of our own communities," he says. "Newer technologies, like solar power, fit within our philosophy. The Hopi and Navajo have also adapted permaculture to their communities. It's all about sustainable culture and communities. So we're looking at what a lot of other people are doing and integrating what works with our land and our communities and our people."

Someone knocks on Clayton's door. The interruption makes us realize that we have talked so long that we must leave right now if we are going to see the gardens at the pueblo before sundown.

The community's gardens have been planted on a large shelf of land between the Tesuque River and the highway that divides the flatlands from the hills. As we walk down to the Brascoupés' garden, I notice that there are no signs or fences, no visible dividing lines among the gardens, though everyone knows whose field is whose. The land here belongs to everyone, and will be passed down to everyone who comes after them.

"We have a family-size garden," Clayton explains. Four Sisters Garden covers about two acres. It is named in honor of Clayton and Margaret's four daughters: Winona, who is named for blue corn; Peen Tsawa, whose name means "blue mountain"; Phoye, which means "yellow autumn"; and Povi, which means "flower." The six of them and one son-in-law share the garden.

"All of my kids garden and save seeds," Clayton says, obviously pleased. They plant their garden using traditional digging sticks, or dibbles. Three teams of two can plant two acres in half a day. They walk side by side, one opening a hole with the dibble, the other dropping in the seeds, then covering them with soil.

The open-pollinated, heirloom varieties of seeds come from Native Seeds/SEARCH, which distributes them free to Native American growers. "They provide the palette," Clayton says, "and we, the farmers, we're the artists. We paint the land."

Though they always grow corn, beans, squash, and melons, the varieties change from year to year as they experiment. This year they're growing four varieties of squash, pinto and Iroquois red beans, peas and gourds, and an old variety of watermelon, 'Moon and Stars,' an African American cultivar long known to

Pueblo gardeners. Close by, Clayton has planted *Nicotiana rustica,* an indigenous strain of tobacco used in religious ceremonies. We walk slowly down rows of corn four feet tall, listening as the deep green leaves rustle in the hot afternoon wind.

"You start with good thoughts, good intentions, prayers," Clayton says when I ask how they begin each planting season. "Once you begin the seasonal cycle, taking care of the earth, it should be on your mind every day. You complete the process. It becomes a responsibility for taking care of the earth. So each day you have to be aware of what you started and where you want to take it.

"This is Hopi blue corn," he says, running a long green leaf through his fingers. "It has a shorter growing season than other heirloom corns. It's good in a year when the water supply is uncertain."

New Mexico was in a deep drought for six years beginning in 1996. In 2001, Clayton says, they bottomed out. "People were breaking locks on the irrigation system to get water." If it had gotten any worse, he says, people might have been killed. This year the drought seems to have broken. They've finally had good rain.

The corn is intercropped with beans and peas, but not in the way the Iroquois would have done it in the Northeast, where rain is plentiful. "The corn is picked at the end of September," Clayton explains. "The peas then take off up the dried stalks. Leaving the dried stalks and leaves in the fields shelters the peas and pinto beans from the wind and frost."

Pueblo gardens were described in some of the conquistadors' chronicles as slovenly—weedy and without order—which they saw as a reflection of the Indians' moral character. A more discerning chronicler who was not looking for moral analogies recorded the way one year's healthy crop could be seen coming up through the stubble and straw of the previous year's, needing only a little hoeing and moderate irrigation to help it along.

What this chronicler describes sounds strikingly like the no-till or "do nothing" method Fukuoka rediscovered in the 1970s.

The blue corn is grown for making piki bread, Clayton tells me as we stand in the cornfield. "My wife and daughters use an ancient way of processing it. Piki is a very thin bread, high in iron and calcium. The technology for making it is only found among the Pueblos of New Mexico and the Hopi in Arizona. It's a local corn and a local bread."

The making of good piki bread is an art. Pueblo women kneel before a large flat stone balanced above a hot fire in a stone enclosure. When the stone is hot enough, the experienced piki-bread maker mixes the ground blue corn meal with juniper ash and spring water, scoops some up, and then, with one swift move, lays a thin coating over the surface of the rock and quickly peels it off. She then rolls it, like parchment, one leaf within another. Each generation of Pueblo women teaches the next how to make it.

"In the fall, we pull the corn and put it away for the winter," Clayton explains. He has shown me photographs of his grandchildren learning to remove the seeds from the corn. "The harvest of the corn," he says quietly, "is that the end or the beginning of the cycle?"

I remember the moment that question came to me. It was the summer I planted my first garden and realized that seeds were one of the most important parts of my harvest. It felt as if I'd been initiated into a fundamental truth, something so simple and obvious that I wondered at my lifetime of ignorance before I had a garden.

"If we walked up into those hills," Clayton says, gesturing to the east, "I could show you the remains of thousands of gardens."

The sky, which has been a deep blue bowl all day, has filled with huge mounds of billowing clouds. They lay purple shadows on the flanks of the Sangre de Cristo Mountains. The air begins to cool a little as we turn and slowly walk back. We talk about how hopeful and promising the new restorative gardening movements are in their reverence for the wisdom of ancient practices and traditional cultures. Clayton returns to Fukuoka, Jeavons, and Mollison.

"These people have taken the time to observe natural systems—they've begun to talk to the land," he says. "The land began to speak to them, the plants began to speak to them. And they began to listen. So they began to communicate back and forth. So I realized that this type of agriculture is universal, because the mother is speaking to us. The mother has always spoken to us. But we haven't listened. Like all children, we don't listen, we know it all. As human development goes, maybe we're just barely getting out of our teens. We're maybe just now beginning to listen to her."

As the sun starts to set, the light on the fields turns gold and the clouds flush rose.

"When my family is out here working, everyone stops to watch the sun set," Clayton says. They take a few minutes and just stand still. He adds, "Okay, I tell them, now we're gonna get paid."

Española

"We've been in this valley since the seventeenth century," David Fresquez says as we sit in the living room with Loretta, his wife, and their daughter, Jennifer.

By the time I found their house, the sun had risen high and the heat was intense. The Fresquez family had already finished the morning's work in the garden out back and taken refuge inside. Later, after I leave, they will venture out again to harvest for the farmers' market. Sometimes, David says, they've been known to be out there picking basil guided by the glow of flashlights.

"Everything was farming here," David explains. "Once when I was hunting I found letters from the early 1800s in a little cabin in the north here, and I read them. They were always talking about the land—the weather and the land, that was it. It was always the land. Always, always the land." His voice slows as he repeats the word *always, always*, emphasizing the bond between the old Hispanic families and the land of Española Valley.

"When Loretta did her family tree, it was the same thing," he adds. "This one's a farmer, that one's a farmer. I know my family's the same way."

"We were raised to be close to the land," Loretta says quietly. She is a reserved woman. It will take hours, and the exchange of stories, for her to speak of what her garden has given her.

David Ramon Fresquez is descended from a miner named Jan Frishz, also known as Juan Fresco, who was born in 1570 in Flanders. Frishz emigrated to New Mexico in 1617, coming up from Mexico City to explore for minerals. The story goes that when he and two other Flemish miners traveled back to Mexico City and brought mining equipment up to Santa Fe, it was destroyed by envious colonial settlers. Frishz returned to New Spain and did not come back to Santa Fe until 1625, when he traveled north with the wagon train carrying Fray Alonso de Benavides, the Franciscan superior of missions, who brought back with him the small wooden statue of the Virgin that became known as La Conquistadora. This time Frishz stayed, marrying a Spanish woman and eventually becoming mayor of Isleta. Over generations, the name evolved from Frishz to Fresqui to Fresquez.

Loretta's roots in this valley reach back to the 1700s through her father, Salomon Jaramillo, and her mother, Maria Espinoza. She grew up surrounded by a beautiful orchard and ate from her family's extensive garden. Every generation of David's and Loretta's families has lived off the land. It was only with their generation that the tie to the land was almost broken.

I met the Fresquez family at the Santa Fe Farmers' Market one Saturday morning, waiting my turn to speak to them as they stood under a white tent with a sign that read MONTE VISTA ORGANIC FARM behind them. A chef in a starched white tunic had gotten there before me, and he was deep in conversation, laughing and talking as he chose what to cook that day from their display of beautiful vegetables and fruit. I could see baskets of potatoes—red, gold, blue, white, and purple; firm heads of red-striped garlic; gorgeous, fat tomatoes—red, yellow, and orange—plus red and green chilies, of course, and neat bunches of deep green herbs. Arranged near these were bags of crisp greens, bowls of strawberries, plates of sliced melon, and bouquets of brilliantly colored dahlias.

The Santa Fe Farmers' Market is resplendent on a Saturday morning in summer. The smell of roasting chilies wafts through the air. You can watch as a man turns the round cage of a chili roaster mounted in the bed of a pickup. Cloth-covered tables are spread with displays of tomatillos and arrays of melons or squash. Ristras of garlic and chilies hang from cords strung across the booths. Organic farmers bring fresh chickens and eggs. Others offer artisanal cheeses and breads. There are growers who offer only mesclun or stunning bouquets of flowers. I see, and sample, jams and jellies and stop to admire the elaborately woven wreaths of dried flowers. Everyone offers a chance to taste the produce. The competition is stiff, the clientele sophisticated. Farmers drive in from all over northern New Mexico to participate in the rich, communal life of this market.

Every Saturday and Tuesday, the Fresquez family makes the drive down from Española, a small town situated in the green expanse of valley between the Sangre de Cristo Mountains to the east and the Jemez range to the west, home to many of the old Hispanic families. It's a rural community and fairly homogenous, in contrast with the moneyed and often rootless mix of people in Santa Fe. The market has the power to connect these communities, which are separated by the wide gulf between those who grow food and those who buy it. And as David, Loretta, and Jennifer's stories will teach me, growing food also has the power to restore and renew an ethnic heritage effaced and nearly lost to assimilation.

"If somebody wants to know my family's background," Jennifer says with energy, "my short version is we're Mexican. If anybody wants to hear more, then I have to explain the whole New Mexico situation."

Jennifer is a student at the Culinary Institute of America in upstate New York, which for her is a natural extension of growing up in a family that has always grown its own food. But leaving New Mexico has also meant traveling to a part of the country where few people understand her ethnic heritage. "When people try to guess what I am," she says, "they usually guess Italian or Greek, something like that—for my brother too. Neither of us is bilingual, we're monolingual, so we have that too. People have all these preconceived ideas about what we are, who we are."

First of all, Jennifer says, the Spanish spoken in their region is archaic, based on a very old form of the language that developed in isolation and has been preserved in the rural communities in the northern Rio Grande Valley. It's radically different from the Spanish spoken by Puerto Ricans or the Mexican Americans from California or Texas she has met in her travels.

"Other Latinos don't understand why I don't speak Spanish," she says. "They think it's a willful assimilation. So I have to explain about my parents being punished for speaking their own language."

"Punished?" I ask.

"They wouldn't let us speak Spanish when we were little." David, who has been sitting quietly, watching Jennifer, suddenly begins to speak. "In our school system. It made me ashamed to speak Spanish when I was a kid. I wouldn't say things. I knew the word in Spanish, but I wouldn't say it because I was ashamed. 'Only English, only English, only English,'" he says, imitating the tones of a scolding Anglo teacher.

"I'm still ashamed," Loretta says with surprising candor.

The pressure to assimilate extended to anything that identified them as ethnic Americans, including food. "I wouldn't have dared to take tortillas to school," Loretta says. "We were so ashamed to let other people know we were eating tortillas. Oh,

God! You can't let anybody know that." She took sandwiches made with white bread instead.

"White bread was exotic," Jennifer says, laughing.

At home, real food came from the land and they raised it themselves. "During the war my father worked in the shipyards in San Francisco," Loretta says. "He was away a lot, so my mother was alone with the children. She used to plant a big garden. We lived off that." Loretta grew up canning hundreds of jars of fruits and vegetables.

"My mom's family garden," Jennifer remembers, "was such a magical place. All the cousins feel the same way. We all remember my grandfather with his straw hat."

Loretta smiles as Jennifer speaks. Shame and the memory of shame fade in the presence of the rich, sensual memories of the garden.

"My mother's parents had a beautiful orchard," Jennifer says. "It was much bigger than what we have now. They had apples, cherries, pears, peaches, apricots. The trees were all concentrated around the ditch. They didn't like us to be too close. That particular ditch was deep, people used to drown in it." The ditch—an *acequia*—was centuries old. "I remember my grandfather irrigating from that ditch," Jennifer continues. "It was exciting to see all the water coming in. The ditch was on a hill and the garden was lower, so the water would flow down into it. My grandfather would be directing the water where he needed it. You only have a certain amount of time. There are gates all over the property. It's interactive—it's not like turning on a switch or opening a faucet."

She pauses, radiant, then adds, "It's funny, because you don't realize that's not how people get water everywhere in the world. The relationship we have with water is very important to us. The ditches are very important. Irrigating from the ditches means people have to share. Everyone's responsible."

The cleaning, maintenance, and regulation of the thousand ditches in northern New Mexico is done by neighbors who form an association of shareholders, or *parciantes,* which is governed by a *comisión* of three members. The word *acequia* can refer both to the ditch and to the association of landholders whose land is irrigated by lateral ditches that branch from the larger main ditch. Each *parciante*'s share of water is assessed according to the size of his field. In exchange for water, each shareholder must offer work—cleaning the ditch with his neighbors each spring—or money in lieu of work. The ditch manager, elected by the *parciantes* and the *comisión,* is called the *mayordomo.* Up north, where David and Loretta have just bought a larger piece of land so they can grow even more to take to market, David has been elected *mayordomo.*

"Whenever I think about New Mexico," Jennifer says with emotion, "it's one of the things that's always been there and will always be there, the ditches. It's what makes us, us.

"That, and having my grandparents, and running wild in the orchards—I think I was very lucky to grow up with all of that. And here, at my parents' place, being part of growing food from start to finish, harvesting something I planted, I think, *This came from me.* That's really a beautiful feeling. It's sad that mainstream Americans are losing that—or have lost it," she says, pausing. Then she adds, "Or never had it at all."

"I remember how my grandfather's cellar smelled of apples," Loretta says. She has been watching intently as Jennifer speaks, moved and pleased. "For a long time I could conjure up that smell." Conjuring smell, conjuring memory, Loretta conjures a sense of time and place, a sense of herself as a person undivided, connected through the generations of her people to the land.

David, who has been smiling and nodding as Jennifer describes the life of the ditch, is roused to his own associations by Loretta's memories. "My grandfather and father, they used to grow a lot of corn and chilies—and pumpkins," he says.

"That's a lot of what our cuisine is," Jennifer explains. "It's built around those things."

"And the blue corn meal . . . ," David puts in.

When I ask if their traditional cuisine is very different from Mexican cuisine, they all speak at once. "Oh, yes!" they say, excited, happy. Food is their favorite topic—the bridge that carries them over a river of loss.

"And it's not Spanish either," Jennifer says, insistent. "It's a mix of the foods of the Indians here and some Mexican things. A lot of it, I would say, has more to do with the Pueblo Indians.

"All our dishes are based on the regional chili, which is the long green Mexican chili. We eat it two ways. We eat it fresh, as roasted green chili. Then we have what we call red chili, hot, they're ground, and then we make a sauce out of them. That was what people did in the winter. They had their red chilies. Now we can have green chili all year long because we can freeze it. So we roast the chili and then we freeze it.

"You always want to have enough chilies to get you through the year. You have to dry the chilies, then take all the seeds out. Then you have to rinse each one off, because stuff gets in there, you know—spiders and dust. Then you dry it for a month and a half. And then you take it to the mill. There's still a mill in Española," Jennifer says, "or you can grind it yourself."

Jennifer remembers how Loretta's mother always hung her ristras of drying chili in her enclosed porch.

"I think Jennifer's preserving our heritage more than we are, you know," David says, "because she goes back and she wants to learn from my mother how to do things."

"I ask her how to cook traditional dishes from this area," Jennifer says. "We have a lot of traditional dishes that people still eat that are very, very old. Like around holidays—Lent, Easter, Christmas. During Lent—you know, we're Catholic—there are all these foods that are very symbolic. You eat this at this time, you eat that at that time—"

"You push it back, you know. Try to suppress it," Loretta breaks in, her thoughts emerging in fragments. "You miss those things. I find myself longing for..."

"For what?" I ask.

"Foods—like what my mother used to cook. The Lenten foods, I really miss them. Panocha. That's sprouted blue corn pudding. We used to grow our own blue corn," Loretta says. "My mother used to sprout hers behind the stove."

"My mother makes it every year," Jennifer says, with great affection, "then she mails it, packed in ice, to my brother and me wherever we are. It's a lovely thing. I'm just so excited when it comes. I share it with my friends. They wait for it too. This is the only time of the year we eat it. We serve it with cream or ice cream."

Hopi blue corn, sacred to the Pueblo Indians, was adopted by the Spanish as a food with symbolic meaning, to be eaten on the holiest days in the Christian calendar, the days from Holy Thursday, when Jesus had his last meal with his friends, until Easter Sunday, the day of resurrection. Like the piki bread Margaret Brascoupé learned how to make from her mother and has taught her daughters to make, panocha, also made from blue corn, connects Loretta with her mother and her daughter. Sprouted blue corn pudding, ritually pure food, is something Loretta can claim, and pass on, with love. It is untainted by shame.

Hearing about it makes me want some. It sounds as if they have a renewed sense of how much their heritage means to them, I say.

"Now more than ever," David agrees. He has a story about his longing for the old food ways too and tells his own blue corn story.

"I remember when I was five, six, seven, I'd walk to school, about a mile and a half, two miles, and when I'd get back from school, I'd stop at my father's aunt's place. She lived on my grandparents' farm in a separate room attached to the side, by herself. One room, that was all. There was a bed on one side and a stove on the other. Lala, I think her name was. And you know, when she cooked a rabbit, she used every part of that rabbit. The lungs, the liver, everything would go into a stew. She used to make a wonderful meal. And they had pigs. Pork was pretty much the staple—the hocks, hams, bacon, everything. They used to make chicharones. It's bacon, but it's thicker. They'd cut it into one-inch cubes, then they'd render the fat, then store it in a five-gallon bucket with a lid.

"We'd come from school and she'd have fish and blue corn tortillas and she'd add those chicharones, the little bacons—oh, and they were so good! To this day, I cannot find one person who can make a tortilla like that. Because the corn was so intense. I've been trying myself. I bought the blue corn last year. And I don't know what it is, whether it's the techniques, the right mix of water, salt—"

"It's not the recipe, it's the technique," Jennifer says, breaking in.

"Maybe your grandmother knows?" I suggest, turning to Jennifer.

"My grandma knows," she says, meaning David's mother, who still lives nearby. "In fact, I had this conversation with her last week, because I went over to her house. She had roasted chilies that day, and you need fresh tortillas to go with them. She doesn't make tortillas very often anymore, but she did that day. You can have the recipe, but it's the technique—you have to do it every day for ten thousand days in a row to get them to taste like my grandma's."

"My mother used to make them with one hand," Loretta says, "and she'd roll with the other. She could make them real fast. Then she would slap them on the top of the stove."

All three of them start talking about the sound of Loretta's mother making those tortillas, remembering that slap.

"Life is about taste," David says, and then we all stand up and head out the back door to see their garden.

"We don't really have a traditional garden," Loretta explains as we walk. "We don't grow traditional food."

"We grow what we like to eat," Jennifer explains. "But we

don't grow chilies, or the corn. We don't have very much land. Those things are very land-intensive—chilies, corn, squash. You need acres and acres of land."

Outside the kitchen door is their patio, with work sheds to one side, and beyond that the garden begins. The land is a flat rectangle, with a raised berm above the irrigation ditch that marks the southern edge. They use every inch of space, so even the narrow strip of raised earth between the ditch and the fence sprouts flowers and herbs.

"Look at these apples," David says of a single tree beside the irrigation ditch. "I never put anything on this land, and look at this fruit." He cradles a bright red apple in his weathered palm.

The garden is laid out in long, neat rows with wide paths of grass all the way around it. A wall of dahlias—hundreds of them, a feast of color and texture—crosses the front of the garden. Most of them are as tall as we are, some taller. David begins to choose his favorites, gathering a bouquet for me.

"I started most of the farming here," he says as he selects from his prolific blooms one by one. "So I thought to myself, I've always loved tomatoes, melons, the sweet stuff. And I love flowers, so I started to grow dahlias, and tomatoes, just Romas. I had the tomatoes all ready to dry and thought, well, I'll just sell a few, make a little bit of money. So we went over to the farmers' market in Santa Fe and I sold all my Romas. So that's where it all started, you know. It started with the tomatoes."

Five years ago, after twenty-three years working at Los Alamos National Laboratory, David got laid off. "That's when I got into growing big-time. We started doing plots and plots of potatoes, tomatoes, onions, garlic, and I always had flowers. We had all these beds here in front full of dahlias."

"You know what people always say to us about the dahlias?" Jennifer says. "They say, 'Oh, we love dahlias—my grandmother used to grow these.' "

They're so obviously a team, these three, and they love being part of the market.

"It's the people," Jennifer says.

"Every week, you meet new people," David agrees. "People from all over the world. You form relationships."

"And experimenting with new foods," Jennifer says. "We've tried a lot of different things. This year we're growing twelve different kinds of potatoes. American consumers, they know red potato, russet potato—that's their whole knowledge of potatoes. So part of it is educating people, talking to people about the things that we grow."

"And then we've met so many restaurant owners and chefs," Loretta says, "and they like our produce. So the more they like it, the more ideas we get about foods and what to grow and how to grow them. And on and on it goes."

"You learn so much," David says.

The world comes to them in the market, and now, as they've begun to travel through Europe together, they go out to the world, visiting local markets in Italy, France, and Spain, talking to growers, sampling their food.

"We love food," Jennifer says. "Not just traditional foods, but we love all food. When we went to Europe last year, it was great, because we got to try all this different food. We got to talk to a lot of people. People there really appreciated that as Americans we were so interested in tasting food that was foreign to us. Because that's not what typically happens, I guess, when Americans travel abroad.

"One thing I really loved about Europe," she adds, "is that they understand what food is—it's central to their culture. They eat in big groups, multigenerational groups. Dinner goes on for a long time. It'll be ten o'clock on a Tuesday night! That's how food should be—it should be part of your relationships with people, especially your family. Then people go out in the evenings. They stroll. There's *movement,*" she says with emphasis. "That's when people in America are home watching TV. Americans are very lonely," she adds quietly.

I nod, remembering the huge gatherings of my mother's Italian American family—all the aunts and uncles, cousins, nieces, nephews. There were always older people, always babies. And always lots of food. Stories, controversy, laughter. And then, when the family unraveled, the silence, the loneliness. When I miss my family, I make pasta.

"You know, people have a natural affinity to come together over food," Jennifer says. As we walk, Loretta begins selecting tomatoes for me to take home. She hands them to Jennifer, who cradles them in her arms. "But the way we live our lives now is going away from that. America has no food culture. The farmers' markets are filling that void. I think the market in Santa Fe has done an exceptional job."

At the market, the Fresquezes have become teachers. Young Anglos, new farmers committed to growing everything organically, are eager students. They're hungry to learn and respectful of David and Loretta's experience.

Loretta steps into the flower house, one of the four hoop houses, two for flowers and two for vegetables. She wants to show me the tuberoses they've just started growing. The scent is enveloping, intoxicating. They'll go fast at the market in Santa Fe.

David's passion for tomatoes means that they grow a hundred varieties of tomatoes—a thousand plants—keeping notes that run to seven pages on their size, flavor, and color, weeding out the ones they don't like. Just as Jennifer said, they also have an amazing array of potatoes—ten thousand plants' worth. And five thousand onion plants—Vidalia, Spanish, and Italian—grow near five thousand garlic plants, including the beautiful mottled red French variety I saw at their market display, with six hundred leeks nearby. They've begun experimenting with dehydrating the garlic and making it into powder. The palest jade green, it's sweet and mild, nothing like store-bought garlic powder.

Four long rows of mixed greens—'Green Forest,' 'Galactica,' 'Lola rosa,' mizuna, and claytonia—are sold in two ways, as individual heads and as part of the Fresquezes' own mix, which is rinsed four times and includes beet tops, spinach, and arugula.

There are D'Avignon, French breakfast, and Easter egg radishes, a hundred eggplants, strawberries, raspberries, and beds of asparagus, broccoli, and carrots.

When David was growing up, his family grew only one variety of melon—*melones mexicanos,* as he knew them. Now, through Jake's Melons, a mail-order seed company, his family experiments with French and Italian varieties in addition to local ones. "My family didn't have the means that we have," he says. "The rest of the world is giving me their best."

And then there are the pumpkins. The array is astonishing. The standard orange variety is dwarfed by enormous bright red-orange specimens with deep, even seams. There are pumpkins in jade green, blue-green, dark forest green; some with specks, some half green and half orange, and others a strange metallic golden brown. Round, squat, puffed like pillows with depressed centers, indigenous and exotic, they all display nature's profligate variety. Is there one they love most?

Oh, yes: it's called Tio, for Loretta's uncle, Eudoro Jaramillo, who gave them their first seeds. No one has any idea what the actual name of the variety might be, but with its green skin and sweet, soft flesh, it surpasses all others. The Fresquezes sell fresh pumpkin by the slice at the market, where they invite people to taste their produce, to try new things.

This year, David says, they harvested twenty tons of pumpkins from their four hundred plants. It doesn't seem possible that all this could grow on a little more than one acre in what is essentially their backyard. They have learned to load the land with as much as it will bear without depleting the soil, using no chemicals and wasting no water.

Monte Vista Farm represents both a leap forward—a new international impulse, as David, Loretta, and Jennifer reach out to the world beyond their valley and beyond the borders of the United States—and a release from the experience of being defined as strangers in their own land. David and Loretta Fresquez have never lived anywhere but this valley. They both grew up within five miles of this garden. Their parents and grandparents, generation upon generation, lived off the land. The pressure to assimilate that led David and Loretta not to pass on their language—a choice that was not a choice—finds redress here, where they create a wide, embracing world together and take it to market in Santa Fe.

I watch as Loretta fills Jennifer's arms with tomatoes of every color and size, all of them still warm from the sun. David leans into his dahlias, disappearing as he reaches to cut deep purple, warm peach, soft pink flowers for me to take home. Finally Jennifer can't hold any more tomatoes and David's free hand can't close around any more stems.

"I never dreamed that we would be doing this," Loretta says. "Everybody grows a garden, you know? Big deal. But now we eat, breathe, and sleep gardens. Everything we do is defined by our work here.

"People couldn't believe it when I gave up my job." Loretta decided to retire early from her own job at Los Alamos and join David in the garden full-time. "'Do you like farming?' people ask me. 'Isn't it a lot of work?' What was my job?" she says with feeling. "I wasn't doing anything good for anyone." She was just earning a wage. "Here we're making an honest living doing something we truly enjoy from the heart. We're teaching other people the importance of good food. I never realized how much I knew until now. And we're keeping our heritage by keeping our food. It's a way of life for us, our food."

"When I'm out here," David says, "just working the land, I'm so happy, so content. Just being here. Especially in the morning. When you're out here just working the soil and putting seed in the ground and picking up the harvest, you know, you feel like you could live forever..."

Monte Vista, they call this place—mountain view. From where they work, you can look up and see horses grazing in the near distance. Your eye can travel across the valley to the mountains, east and west, where huge dramas unfold every summer afternoon, especially in this monsoon season—dark roiling clouds, bolts of lightning, dark chains of rain connecting heaven and earth, and then, an hour later, the rainbows, vast arcs of color spanning the ridges, every band electrified, lit up against the dark sky. You can stand here, dry and safe, musing among the vegetables while bees ravish the flowers, and watch the ridgeline where huge forces contend.

"When there are birds sitting there on the wires watching us while we work," Loretta says, sweetness filling her voice, "I truly think it's my parents. Especially the meadowlarks—they sing so beautifully—and I think how happy they are with what we're doing. Now I understand the value of the skills they taught us. To be close to the earth—that's what we grew up with, that's what I'm about. I never had words for it before. It's part of who I am. I've completely acknowledged that now."

2

FREEDOM

The Gardens of Two Gullah Elders

ST. HELENA ISLAND, SOUTH CAROLINA

"Have you been to see the Emancipation Tree yet?" Ralph Middleton asks me.

I have come to St. Helena, the largest of the Sea Islands off the coast of South Carolina, to talk to Gullah elders about their gardens. Right away I learn two things. First, that any question I ask about gardens will elicit an answer about "the land." Second, that no one can understand this community descended from enslaved Africans without encountering the history of slavery and the failed promise of emancipation, when the seeds of true racial equality might have been planted. That history begins with the tree. Ralph Middleton fully expects me to go see it before we meet again, so I do.

In this landscape, where legendary storms wipe out homes, wash out sandy roads, take down trees—live oak, pecan, sea pine, palmetto, and pear—where fields of ripening crops and every flower or bush that cannot survive a salt flood perishes, old live oaks invoke the spirits of ancestors. One among them is considered the most sacred: the tree where, on New Year's Day 1863, Abraham Lincoln's Emancipation Proclamation was read aloud to the blacks of St. Helena Island, telling them that now they were truly free.

It stands on a small rise at the edge of Route 21, the two-lane highway that crosses the island, with a pleasant brick house behind it. Its huge trunk supports enormous spreading limbs hung with Spanish moss. While written history records the drama of the formal ceremony Brigadier General Rufus Saxton of the Union Army arranged in Port Royal, Gullah oral history preserves the quieter story of a local gathering of those who could not make the journey to the mainland. "They came in from all corners," Ralph Middleton tells me. "Most of them had to walk."

Someone from the Union Army read the text aloud to them. Lincoln proclaimed three things that New Year's Day. First he announced the liberation and protection of slaves in states currently in rebellion against the federal government (followed by a list of those parishes and counties, state by state, where the slaves owned by families loyal to the Union would not yet be free). Next he asked the freed blacks for peace, a stay against retaliation for the long cruelty, and urged them, where they could, to work for pay. Finally he invited all the freedmen who could to serve in the Union Army, which was in need of soldiers.

When Ralph was a small boy in the 1930s, there were still elders in the community, men like Sam Polite, who remembered hearing Lincoln's words read that day: "On the first day of January, in the year of our Lord one thousand eight hundred and sixty-three, all persons held as slaves within any State or designated part of a State, the people whereof shall then be in rebellion against the United States, shall be then, thenceforward, and forever free." Emancipation set free four million women, men, and children.

The blacks of St. Helena who gathered beneath the great live oak had enjoyed an informal freedom as "contraband of war" since early November 1861, when Union gunboats steamed up

Port Royal Sound and fired on Confederate troops stationed at Hilton Head Island. The "big gun shoot," as Gullahs know the battle, lasted exactly one day. When word reached the planters of St. Helena that the Union had taken control of the Sound and were heading up the Beaufort River, they fled, some rising up from tables set with their finest china, silver, and crystal, leaving their dinners uneaten. The Union troops who landed on the mainland and entered Beaufort a few days later found to their astonishment that it was empty of white people but for one planter, who was stone drunk.

Ten thousand slaves had been left behind. Though their masters had tried to scare them with stories about what the Yankees would do to them (harness them like beasts to carts or ship them off to the infamous sugar plantations in Cuba), most refused to leave. Many hid so they wouldn't be forced to accompany the masters' families as they headed north for Charleston. Some were shot by masters incensed by their disobedience.

The people of St. Helena were among the first to be freed, the first to be offered the chance to buy land, and the first to study in a school for free blacks, the Penn School, founded by the Philadelphia abolitionist Laura Towne in 1862. They soon became one of the most closely studied African American populations in the country. Lincoln himself took a keen interest in how the Sea Island blacks were making the transition to freedom. Representatives from Europe, Latin America, India, and Africa regularly visited the Penn School, which was considered a model of rural education for the disenfranchised.

Now, 145 years later, the community of St. Helena Island is the largest stronghold of Gullahs who still live on their ancestral lands. In the decades since historians demonstrated the living connection between the Gullahs and West Africa, particularly Sierra Leone, clarifying how enduring their culture truly is, Sea Island Gullahs have been engaged in an increasingly difficult struggle to hold on to their land. Since the bridges that link the Sea Islands to the mainland were built, many communities with a black majority have been displaced by resorts, gated communities with golf courses, condominiums, and private beaches. The culture of tourism threatens the survival of one of the most significant African American communities in the United States.

The stories of two gardeners determined to pass on their land to future generations—Ralph Middleton, who returned to the island in retirement after forty-five years away, and Otis Daise, who has never lived anywhere else—bear witness to a stunning act of cultural endurance. Their stories begin and end with gardens.

It is already ninety degrees by 9 A.M. when I turn down Martin Luther King, Jr. Drive and see Ralph Middleton, a tall, dignified man of seventy-nine, standing alone in the shade of a great live oak. He calmly waits, lifting one hand in a slow wave as I pull into a long driveway lined with oyster shells pressed into the sandy earth. His smile is warm and welcoming as he reaches out to shake my hand, his voice deep and quiet as he introduces himself.

"Indigo is the main garden now," he says quietly as he guides me to a large rectangular garden bed that runs along the wooded edge of his property, ten acres that have been passed down through the family since emancipation. The indigo garden is full of tall bushy plants with bright green oval leaves. "It gets about eight feet tall. The flowers are dark blue, very small. I try not to do anything to it, because we're experimenting to see how it performs on its own." Indigo is not easy to grow. It prefers not to be transplanted but is sustained by the spread of its seed. On Ralph's land, it comes back strong every year.

"This is very rich soil," he says, and leans down to show me. Lifting away a patch of grass, he gathers up some earth. "It's sandy loam, but it's very rich." I lean down beside him and take some in my hand too, admiring its fine tilth.

When he releases the soil from his hand, Ralph's gesture is

reverent. He stands up slowly and turns, inviting me to walk back to the house. "After slavery, most blacks stayed on the land here. We feel that we are part of the land," he says in his deep, calm voice. "This is where we've been, where we've worked, for generations. You know your grandparents and great-grandparents planted here. We have memories about the land, about what they did here. So it's important. It's sacred." For Gullahs, the land is freedom. It is the ground of their dignity and the reason they have endured.

"Most of us are poor," Ralph continues. Though he speaks in the present tense, it is his childhood he is remembering, for he and his wife, Lisa, are prosperous now. They live in a beautifully constructed wood frame house built by Ralph's great-uncle, Benjamin Boyd, who was a revered teacher of carpentry at the Penn School decades ago. "We were so poor," Ralph adds, laughing lightly, "that we didn't even notice the Depression."

I turn to look at him, and he smiles. The Gullahs were not only that poor, they were that self-sufficient as a community.

"Many of us had to make it on the land when we didn't have any other jobs here. This was our source of life for years. That's why we don't like to see fences. We hate gated communities, most of us do, because everybody here was raised to feel free to walk anywhere, and you respect it, that freedom."

There is no fence around the Middletons' land. You see very few fences anywhere on Gullah land on St. Helena Island.

"Here, you respect a person's land," Ralph explains. This is a tradition that never needed stating until their island attracted the attention of developers.

Ralph never uses the word *property* or *mine* in speaking of this place. His habitual use of *you* for *I*, like his tendency to speak in the plural, suggests the importance of the Gullah community over the individual.

Gullah is the name of both the people and their English-based Creole language, which contains elements of many African languages. By emphasizing the African rather than the English vocabulary and grammar within the language, enslaved Africans could communicate among themselves while concealing their meaning from their masters. They were experts in the art of "code shifting," speaking their language one way with white folks and another with blacks.

No one knows for sure whether the word *Gullah* refers to a place (Angola, some think) or a people (perhaps the Gola of Liberia and Sierra Leone). Lorenzo Dow Turner, a black linguist who studied the Gullahs for fifteen years beginning in the 1930s, recording and analyzing their songs, folktales, and everyday speech, was the first person to bridge the worlds separated by the African diaspora. He demonstrated that Gullah was profoundly influenced in its grammar and structure by African languages and contains thousands of African names and words. His race and his gracious manner gave him access to intimate aspects of Gullah culture, like the private "basket name" every Gullah child was given at birth, for use only within their community—an assertion of their African heritage in opposition to the master's gesture of stripping slaves of their birth names as the first step in making them chattel. Gullah basket names, like the actual sweetgrass baskets their newborn children nestled in—"fanners" made for the winnowing of rice—reflect the endurance of ancient African traditions.

The Gullah language is so close to a language currently spoken in Africa—Sierra Leone Krio—that when President Joseph Momoh of Sierra Leone came to the Penn Center in 1988 and greeted the community in Krio, some elders wept as they realized they could understand him. For so long they had been told that their language was no more than a broken and degraded form of English that their ancestors had acquired from their white masters under slavery.

It is in keeping with the Penn Center's contemporary role in the community that it was the place where the Gullahs learned that their African cultural heritage had survived 250 years of separation. Since Emory Campbell became the first Sea Island Gullah to serve as director, Penn has been at the center of the movement to preserve and restore traditional Gullah culture.

When Ralph Middleton was growing up, Penn Center was still a school. Its mission included helping Gullahs remain self-sufficient on the land while encouraging them to adopt English so that they might assimilate to mainstream culture. Like his father and grandfather before him, Ralph was fortunate enough to be educated at the Penn School for twelve years at a time when many Sea Island blacks could not go to school at all.

"Most of the community schools only went up to the sixth grade," Ralph explains. "It was important to get into Penn, because that was the only place you had to go. At first it was just academics, in Miss Towne and Miss Murray's days. Then, around 1900, it changed to include trades. Gardening was year-round. In the summer they taught us to strip the corn blades to strengthen the ears. We'd dig potatoes. We'd have a row a quarter of a mile long, and we'd go along with a horse and plow. We had a dairy. We had silos where we stored fodder for the animals, horses and mules. And we had chickens, of course. In the spring we had what was called Planting Week, and then in the fall we had Harvest Week. It was part of our curriculum. They would teach us new ways to plant, new things to plant.

"The teachers would come out to each family's garden. Rossa Cooley and Miss House, they'd ride out on their horses. The main thing was to see how you were getting along in your home garden. Miss Cooley was still there when I graduated. It was her last year. She and Miss House really took an interest in the people here—they knew every child by name, they knew every family."

When Rossa Cooley, Penn's second principal, arrived, there was no garden at the school. She set to putting one in and turned it into a classroom. She decided that teaching a rural African American community to memorize the kings and queens of England, to study the Magna Carta, and to solve abstract problems in mathematics would never train them for a life of dignified self-sufficiency. Forty years after Laura Towne proved that the newly freed blacks could be educated, the community needed a different kind of school.

Under Cooley's direction, Penn became a working farm. The entire cycle of cultivation, from preparing the soil for planting to sharing a meal with friends who helped harvest the food, became part of the curriculum. Students trooped outside to mark the land they would help dig to make the gardens. Mathematical problems were now concerned with measuring out plots and calculating yields. Science began with soil and light and water, how seeds grew, how corn is pollinated, why all nutrients should be returned to the soil, how to get the healthiest harvest from the land and preserve the surplus for winter.

"Our object was to bring island life into the classroom—into the little world of teaching too much bound up in the printed word," Cooley wrote in her 1930 memoir, *School Acres*. But the family fields exerted a pull on the students that could not be ignored. "The crop often called the children to the fields at the same time our old Liberty Bell called them to the classroom," she wrote. Penn "had that paradox of an agricultural school seemingly in conflict with the farming community it served." So Cooley adjusted the school day and year to the rhythms of the Gullahs' fields. The knowledge of how to cultivate land, she knew, was "their true Magna Carta." "Education," she declared in her 1926 book, *Homes of the Freed*, was "to teach power, not technical skill."

Planting and Harvest Weeks, as Ralph remembers, were a time when children stayed home to help with the family gardens. The teachers came to them, riding island ponies they'd given names like Jubilee and Wonder.

Ralph left Penn in 1945 to join the army. Once the war ended, he went on to get his B.A. as well as an M.S. in social work from Howard University. Fifty years after he left the island for the first time—and encountered a world that had no idea there was a place in America where blacks had owned their own land for five generations—he now tends a garden that holds within it the memory of the African origins of his people's culture.

Indigo has not been grown on St. Helena Island for over two hundred years. Since 1995, Ralph Middleton has been growing it from seeds given to him by an African American artist, Arianne King Comer, who studied textile arts in Nigeria. King Comer moved to St. Helena when she learned that indigo had once been widely cultivated here. Her home and studio are part of the Penn Center campus, just down the road from Ralph's place. Together with a visiting artist from Nigeria, Arianne prepares indigo dye in the traditional African way, using a mortar and pestle to pound the leaves harvested from Ralph's garden. The beauty of her cloth has brought her recognition and respect. She has begun teaching children in the community about the African origins of indigo cloth and often takes classes to Ralph's garden to learn about the plant that played a pivotal role in the evolution of the island's culture.

For thirty years beginning in the 1740s, indigo became a successful cash crop, second only to rice in the low country, the region that includes the Sea Islands and the flat, fertile coastal plain that extends inland for forty to fifty miles. Since the Sea Islands lack the freshwater swamps and tidal rivers necessary for the large-scale cultivation of irrigated rice, island planters hoping to duplicate the success of rice on the mainland with their own lucrative export crop eagerly turned to indigo, which does not require irrigation and thrives in the loose, sandy soil. The discovery that indigo would flourish there transformed the culture of the Sea Islands, as planters brought in great numbers of enslaved Africans required for the large-scale production of indigo dye, which is labor-intensive at every stage.

The introduction of indigo to South Carolina is traditionally attributed to a young female slave owner, Eliza Lucas Pinckney, who was born in 1722 on the Caribbean island of Antigua, where her father served as lieutenant governor. Educated in England, she moved with her family to a plantation on Wappoo Creek, near Charles Town, where her father hoped the climate would be easier on his wife's health. But it wasn't, and when he was called back to Antigua, Eliza, by all accounts an extraordinarily accomplished young woman, assumed control of the family's plantations at the age of sixteen. Her youth, her gender, and her indigo have made her the stuff of legend.

"When talk of indigo began," historian William Gaillard Stoney writes in the introduction to his 1938 volume, *Plantations of the Carolina Low Country,* "Governor Lucas sent packets of seed to his daughter and was also able to find to help her a man experienced in the trick of making the dye, a task of great delicacy. Any fair planter with the average gang of hands could make the weed, but training and organization of master and men were extremely necessary once the mass of green leguminous stuff was cut. The quality and price of the manufactured dye varied widely and it took a split-second judgment as to just when to stop the 'steeping' or the 'beating' of the liquor and when to let in the lime-water that precipitated the 'mud,' as each step might settle the question whether you got something that remained truly little better than mud or the fine purple, the fine copper, or the most-to-be-desired fine flora of the trade . . . Eliza Lucas," he concludes, "with the aid of her assistant and the cooperation of a neighbor, Andrew Deveaux, did a very great deal towards establishing the new crop."

Though tradition leaves little room in the story of indigo for anyone but Eliza Lucas, who has been called "America's first great agriculturalist," small details scattered among historical accounts suggest where to look for the missing pieces. Who, for example, was the "man" Governor Lucas sent his daughter, whose expertise, as Stoney acknowledges, was "extremely necessary" to the training of both master and slaves?

In her 1896 biography, based on Eliza Lucas Pinckney's letters from the period, Harriott Horry Ravenel is careful to note that Governor Lucas sent not one, but three men to help his daughter learn the complex art of making dye. Though nearly all scholars refer to the passage in Ravenel's text where she mentions all three, most acknowledge only the first two, brothers named Nicholas and Richard Cromwell, overseers from plantations in Montserrat, a center of French colonial indigo production. Nicholas Cromwell arrived in 1741 and built the brick vats on Wappoo Creek that made it possible to produce the first indigo dye in South Carolina. Some version of Eliza Lucas Pinckney's famous account of how Nicholas Cromwell "made a great mistery of the process" and intentionally spoiled the color because he "repented coming" to help the American colonies compete with his own country must have reached her father soon after the making of the first inferior dye occurred because Governor Lucas sent Nicholas's brother, Richard, to replace him. In 1744, when four years of experimentation with the crop finally yielded a successful harvest, Eliza wrote to her father that Richard Cromwell had produced "17 pounds of very good Indigo, so different from N[icholas]-C[romwell]'s, that we are convinced he was a mere bungler at it."

"The truth," Ravenel adds to this account, is that both Cromwells "were traitors," and neither made excellent dye. It was not, she wrote, until Governor Lucas "sent out a negro from one of the French islands" that "the battle was won." Whoever this black man was, his name, his origins (was he a free black or a slave?), and his pivotal role in the economic, political, and cultural life of South Carolina have been all but erased.

Among the lingering injustices of slavery has been the distorted history of who shaped the landscape and culture of the South. None of the three cash crops that made South Carolina so wealthy—rice, indigo, and cotton—was indigenous to the United States. For so long, the question of who made their large-scale production possible was answered by historians who relied on the accounts of white planters and their descendants, who tended to take the credit themselves. The enslaved, whose African cultural heritage, it was assumed, had been expunged by the experience of slavery, were said to have provided little more than brute strength. In *Black Rice,* Judith Carney, building on the work of a generation of scholars who have been rewriting the history of slavery, reverses this model. By focusing on the African side of the Atlantic slave trade, Carney demonstrates how the evolution of rice cultivation in South Carolina depended upon "the diffusion of an entire cultural system" indigenous to the Rice Coast of Africa, where rice had been grown for millennia. White planters in South Carolina, whose early attempts to grow rice failed, were at first completely dependent upon their African slaves for the agricultural and technical knowledge of how to grow and process rice.

Though no one has done for indigo what Carney has done for rice, the story of white planters eager to produce a cash crop but ignorant of the proper methods of cultivating or processing it suggests how to restore balance to the story of Eliza Lucas and indigo, and so provide a context for Ralph Middleton's indigo garden.

Statistics on the production of indigo vary, but most historical accounts show that after 1745, when South Carolina exported 5000 pounds of indigo dye in the form of dried cakes, the numbers rose with stunning speed. By 1747 the figure had risen to 150,000 pounds, and by 1775, South Carolina was shipping over a million pounds of indigo a year to England. In the three decades leading up to the Revolution, colonial planters received a bounty of six pence for every pound of indigo shipped to England when access to dye from the French West Indies was cut off by hostilities between Britain and France. The bounty system worked so well that shrewd low-country planters who invested in indigo could double their wealth every three to four years. As a result, "the province," Stoney records with relish, "expanded as it had never done before." Many of the great Palladian mansions of Charleston, the most fashionable city in the South, were made possible by indigo, as were some of the great plantation houses along the Ashley River fifteen miles inland, including Drayton Hall and Middleton Place, with their magnificent gardens, and the early plantations of St. Helena Island. None of this could have been accomplished without African slaves, whose numbers ballooned in this period.

The success of indigo is directly related to the establishment of a black majority community on St. Helena. In 1720, as the census data Peter Wood cites in *Black Majority, Negroes in Colonial South Carolina* demonstrates, before indigo was introduced, there were 150 whites and 42 enslaved Africans in St. Helena parish. By 1760, as indigo production soared, slaves made up three quarters of the population. Many of the Africans brought to South Carolina in this period came from areas where people would have been proficient not only in the cultivation of rice but also in the growing of cotton and indigo as part of an indigenous cloth-making tradition like the one Arianne King Comer observed in Nigeria. As Johann David Schöpf, a German visitor to South Carolina observed in *Travels in the Confederation, 1783–1784*, it was not the white planter but the skilled slave who was commonly the head-man in the dye-making process. As with rice, the seeds, the technology, and the knowledge necessary to the large-scale production of indigo dye all came to South Carolina as part of a system of "ecological imperialism," as Alfred Crosby calls it, in which colonial planters appropriated the agricultural traditions and exploited the knowledge of those they enslaved.

Ralph Middleton's indigo represents a new kind of garden on St. Helena, a form of heritage garden that reconnects the pieces of a tradition torn apart by the Atlantic slave trade, when Africans for whom the production of indigo, like the growing of rice, was part of an honored heritage were compelled to share their expertise with the colonial planters who enslaved them. Indigo links Ralph to generations of his forebears who worked the indigo plantations of the Sea Islands. And it reaches farther back, restoring a severed tie to their ancestral homeland in Africa.

It's Saturday, early morning, and the breeze coming off the Beaufort River tempers the heat as I walk along the waterfront park to the farmers' market, where Otis Daise has spread his table with baskets of fresh produce. Otis's pickup is parked nearby, the tailgate down, holding boxes of cucumbers, zucchini, and potatoes. His onions, with their long green stems and big panicles of white flowers still attached, make a great show at one end of his crowded display.

People have already begun to stroll slowly from one table to another in the shade of overhanging trees. It's impossible to talk with Otis here, so I scrawl his phone number on my pad and later, when I call, he gives me directions to Orange Grove Community, down past the Penn Center at Land's End.

A live oak shades the front of the house Otis built with the help of his father-in-law in 1970. Yuccas he dug from the beach years ago hug the base of the mulberries, and white oaks protect the approach to his door. Just beyond them grows a row of evenly spaced bushes covered with red roses. A fire-blackened tub rests on a table beside one of the sheds that dot the side yard. Out back, the sea breeze lifts a line of neatly hung laundry.

Otis comes out to meet me, grinning as he extends a hand. Dressed in camouflage pants, a yellow polo shirt, and sneakers and wearing a red baseball cap that says *Grandpa,* he is so trim and fit that he looks far younger than his sixty-six years.

"I have about ten acres of my own. It's all right here," he says, "straight across. These are the original acres." He opens his arms wide, gesturing left and right. "I've got a market garden out back. And I got five acres I bought across the road. Then I got the four fields I rent other than my own. I go to the waterfront, the farmers' market, make money. I give my neighbors a lot of stuff too." Otis's rent helps his neighbors pay their taxes.

Welcoming me inside, Otis brings me a tall sweating glass of icewater, sits down, and begins. "I was born and raised right here. My mother, grandmother, sisters, and brothers, all raised right here. My great-grandmother, she started it off. She was a Smalls, Jane Smalls. All this land was hers originally, from 1861. My mother keep it up. And then me and my brother and sister keep it going. Now it's me keep it going, since my oldest brother died.

"Back in the forties, a storm destroyed the house and everything, took out all the fruit trees. They rebuilt, but that house gone now too. Most of the trees from old times, the fruit trees—all them, you know, they gone.

"I raise five kids on this land. My wife died back in '72. I put all my kids through school. Two married an' gone. But I got my son here and I got two daughters live here. I got nine grands.

"All of this come from the land. History, history. Two of my grandsons, they work in the fields with me. When you look back over your shoulder and you see your grands helping you, it make you feel good. I try to teach them, you know, how to follow my footsteps. You got to be a leader, because if you be a leader, they tend to follow you. You train 'em right, they'll do good. But if you stagger, stagger, stagger, they gonna stagger too." He shakes his head, then says it again. "They gonna stagger too.

"We're six or seven generations on this land. We all speak Gullah. My children and grandchildren, they all know Gullah.

"I love my land. I love right where I'm at," Otis says, pointing to the ground beneath the house we sit in. "I know my neighbors, they love where they at too. You got to love your land. Just like you love your husband or wife. You've got to love it."

Each time he repeats the word *love,* it sounds different. Sometimes it's one long curving note, other times an exclamation. Typed out, Otis's words lie flat, lined up in orderly rows. They convey nothing of his authority over language. Growing up in a rich oral tradition, his standard English, a second language, is adapted to the grammar of Gullah. His voice rises and falls in quick shifts of pitch and timbre. His range spans octaves, and he uses every note.

"My great-grandparents, they give me this, I didn't have to buy it, so that's why I love it so much. We work hard, selling cans and doin' this and that, try to keep the land, so when I come up, it was here for me. Now, when I go, I'm gonna leave it to mine. I stress to them over and over, pay your tax. 'Cause I work hard. Just keep it. If they don't keep it, it's gone. And that's all over this whole island."

The strength of Otis's urging, his shift from "we work hard" to "I work hard," suggests how anxiously older Gullahs now watch the young.

"When I come up, in my old house, we used to go outside morning time, we didn't have to come back in for lunch, because we had everything. We had fruit trees—peach trees, fig trees, walnut trees, pecans. We had orange, apple. We had figs, we had walnuts, we had grapes, anything we want out here to eat. And we had the outside pump to get the cool water. Everybody had a flower garden too. We had all kind, sunflowers, lily, tulip. You name 'em, we had 'em. My grandmama work it. I used to work some of 'em too.

"That was good times, comin' up. For me it was. You never wanted for nothing. The whole family been together. Sometimes they got to call us to come in 'cause we play all night. That was the enjoyment.

"We'd take the corn to the mill and grind it. We used to get the grits, the cornmeal, and the flour. We used to put the peanuts on the housetop to dry. We made our own peanut butter. We raised our own hogs. We used to have our own chickens, get the eggs. In the fall, we used to kill a hog and cure it with salt. We had a smokehouse. Everything we grow, we had 'em to eat.

"Everybody shared. It change, I'd say about twenty, thirty

years ago. When all the old-time people died, it changed. My mother's generation. Them old-time people, they used to pray and sing in the fields. Got the hoe goin', and everybody got a tune, songs like 'Take Me to the River,' 'River of Jordan,' 'Do Lord, Do Lord.' They used to go along like that and then they make up songs too. All that gone. Right now, if a neighbor move in, if you don't live with them, you don't know if you neighbor is sick. See, them old-time people, when they get up in the morning time, they used to say, 'You go over there and see who got a need.' You know, like that. You got some meat, you got a chicken, you got some rice, you share."

Otis leans toward me. Every word he speaks next he says with his hands too. "If you got," he says, extending his hands toward me, palms up, "I got." He pulls his closed hands back to his chest. "And if she got, you got." He turns and points to an invisible woman beside him, then back to me. "But now everybody like this," he says, hugging his crossed arms to his chest as if cowering in fear. "Now everybody is so alone, what they got they ain't share. And that's bad."

The thought of it makes us so sad that when Otis says, "Want to see my fields?" we're both on our feet before I finish saying yes.

"My whole family eat from this garden," Otis says as we stroll along the edge of the garden behind his house, where he grows okra, butter beans, pigeon peas, peanuts, watermelons, eggplants, white potatoes, cucumbers, tomatoes, squash, and more. "These peanuts. You know how they grow, don't you?"

No, I don't. This is the first time I've ever seen peanuts growing.

"That's the leaves," Otis says, pointing. "The peanuts be in the bottom. The bushes turn. Then you pull 'em. When I was comin' up, you make your own peanut butter. We go in the wood and cut the tree and make the mortar out of hickory wood. We used to make the pestle out of hickory wood too. Put that peanut in that and get the oil."

We walk by rows of squash and watermelons. Fat green

cantaloupes ripen in the hot sun. Beans and peas are coming along well.

"I wish you come last week," Otis says, chewing a toothpick. "I had some white potato out there," he says, indicating a long stretch of clear earth, weed-free and ready for replanting. "They was so pretty." The way he says it makes me wish I'd been here to see them.

Tomato plants, leafy and dark, span several rows. Nearby, cucumbers ripen on the vine.

"I make my own pickles," Otis says. "I can my own tomatoes."

"In that tub near the shed?" I ask.

"Yeah, that be the best place, outside."

Near the peas, I see zucchini vines with beautiful open blossoms. "Have you ever eaten squash flowers, Otis?"

He takes his toothpick from his mouth and turns to look at me, incredulous. "You eat the flowers?" His voice rises, *flowers* breaking in two, one note high, one low.

"Sure," I say. "You dip them in egg and milk, just as you do the okra, then in the flour, and then you fry them. They're delicious."

"That's how I like my okra too." Otis puts his toothpick back in his mouth, then walks on, shaking his head.

We drive deep into the community, where Otis shows me a field of beans, peas, and okra, then another with cucumbers, squash, and watermelons. He grows nearly everything from seeds he harvests every year.

"You can save all the seeds," he says. "Once you buy it one time, then you plant it, then you don't have to buy it anymore. I save okra seed, bean seed, potato seed, peanut seed, corn seed, watermelon, cantaloupe."

"How long do you think it's been since you had to buy a seed?" I ask him.

"I say it's thirty years . . . ," he begins. He looks down, thinking, then he looks up at me, smiling and shaking his head. "Whew!" he says. "I save my okra seeds all my life."

Okra. African word for an African seed. Okra is like kin, its place in Otis's life reaching back so far that it has no beginning. Of course he still uses it to make soup.

We're still talking about food as we turn down the road heading back to the house, passing a huge field stretching to a stand of live oaks in the distance, planted thick with a dark green leafy crop.

"What's growing there, Otis?" I ask.

"That's just tomatoes."

"That whole field is just tomatoes? Who owns it? Someone from the island?"

"Yep, that's all just tomatoes. They get the Mexicans to come in and work it. All I know is their name is Six L. They a big company. They got fields all over."

As we walk along the edge of Otis's newly planted field, birds hidden in the cool foliage of the big trees start to sing. We look over the windrow at the field a hundred times the size of the one we're standing in, planted with nothing but row after row of tomatoes, with a wide, cleared aisle of dirt on either side. A yellow cooler stands on a post at the edge of the dirt road. Every now and again we see a Mexican fieldworker's head as he stands up.

"Nice and quiet here," Otis murmurs, turning to look at his own field. "Peaceful too. I love fieldwork."

A breeze comes up and we stand side by side, quiet, listening, just looking at the neat rows of seedlings.

"So hot the stuff ain't growing. No water. Need some rain." Otis looks the length of the field. "It coming, though."

"Do you irrigate, Otis?"

"No," he says—a long, deliberate exhalation. "I just wait on the Lord's rain."

It was a stupid question, really—there are no pipes, no pumps in sight to suggest that he does. It's just that without realizing it, I've registered the fact that the crops in the commercial grower's field are ten times the size of Otis's. The white PVC pipe bringing irrigation water mixed with fertilizer, a technology called fertigation, stretches the length of the countless uniform rows.

"Right across the street from your house, right here beside your field, with just this hedge between you, you've got this big industrial farm operation," I say.

"Yeah," Otis agrees. "And I'm the little farmer on the other side," he adds, and laughs. "They work hard for they money," he says, thinking of the Mexican workers. "They don't spend it. They send it home to they families. They nice people to be around."

Otis's thoughts turn to his own field. "You come back about another three months, this whole field will be clean." He sweeps one hand lengthwise in the air. "I going to dig it in September. Then I'll make sweet potato pie. Candy yams.

"When you finish with this, you go into collard greens and cabbage in winter. That grow September to January. January, you start back with this again. So it's a constant thing. I ain't get a break from last year, and I still going. But that's farming. You go from one to the other. Hard work. But I like what I do. You got to like what you do."

As we head back across the road to Otis's house, a handsome teenager wearing a straw hat strides slowly toward us. "That's my grand," Otis says with pride. "That's the one that help me in the field, Oti the Third. Oti, come here," he says affectionately. After Otis introduces me, I ask if I can take their picture.

"Okay, Oti." Otis puts his arm around his grandson's shoulders and says something to him in Gullah. Oti takes off his hat and lowers his head, then looks up at me, smiling.

"Two farmer," Otis says, and they look straight into the camera.

"The present and the future," I add, releasing the shutter.

"He might be the future, if he don't go in the army." Otis turns and gives Oti a look. Oti smiles, but he's not saying anything.

It hangs over everything here, the question of the future of the land. I wonder if Oti has any idea how rare it is in America to be the seventh generation of a family to work the same land. Or if he understands how important this land and these fields are to the history of his people.

Otis Daise's gardens map the history of Africans becoming Americans as well as the Africanization of American culture. It was in the gardens of Ralph Middleton's and Otis Daise's ancestors that three garden traditions and three cuisines—African, Native American, and European—were blended to create one of the most distinctive culinary traditions in America. It was also in their gardens that the enslaved blacks of St. Helena prepared themselves for freedom.

Of the plants slaves are known to have cultivated, there are only three that Otis Daise doesn't grow—tobacco, sorghum, and benne (sesame). The seeds of the original African American gardens—okra, yams, peanuts, watermelons, pigeon peas, and other African foods that Otis still grows—came with the slave trade and were cultivated in the slaves' small allotment gardens —"provision gardens," as they are known. Judith Carney calls them "the botanical gardens of the dispossessed." Their history has yet to be written.

Until I visited St. Helena, I knew very little about the gardens that were granted to the slaves, one of the four kinds of cultivated land that might be found on a big plantation in the South. The largest areas would have been the master's extensive fields planted with a single cash crop—rice, indigo, and cotton being the three most important in South Carolina. Then there would have been kitchen gardens to serve the master and mistress's table. The wealthiest planters and their families might also have had formal gardens filled with ornamental trees, shrubs, and flowers.

All four kinds of cultivated land were created and maintained primarily by slaves. But only one type of garden has endured, the slaves' provision gardens. Provision gardens offered them a place apart from the oppressive work of the master's fields, and the task system offered them time. Well established on low-country plantations by the eighteenth century, this system assigned fieldwork according to age and gender. A "task" was a quarter acre. Since their labor was regulated by tasks, not time, once they had completed their assigned work, slaves had time for their own work, including their provision gardens.

In giving slaves a measure of autonomy and self-determination, the task system also allowed them to demonstrate their solidarity. When their own tasks were done, they could help others who were tired or sick, saving them from a whipping. Sometimes this meant they didn't get to their own gardens until after dark, when they would hoe and weed by the light of the moon or a pan of grease set on fire.

From the master's point of view, provision gardens offered important benefits. They relieved some of the economic burden of providing for the slaves, and they discouraged runaways, because, as masters noted, slaves tended to become deeply attached to their gardens and their animals.

But in this, as in so many things, enslaved blacks operated in accord with their own quite distinct understanding of their situation. Keeping a garden and some livestock meant they could participate in trade, earning and saving money. It was common for slaves to sell their produce, sometimes even to their own masters. The making of a garden offered them important immaterial benefits as well, including the symbolic power to shape a portion of their world. Bringing life from the earth restored agency and a sense of purpose. Growing traditional African foods from seed preserved a link to their homeland and their ancestors. Having the means to feed loved ones supported the family structure that slavery so often broke down. Cultivating a garden meant they could grow herbs to use in traditional medicine and flowers for beauty. In all these ways, gardens could heal and empower.

When emancipation came, many low-country slaves not only

had money to buy land, they had seeds passed down for generations. Most important, in their gardens they had kept alive a love for the land that even the dehumanizing experience of slavery could not expunge.

❦

Today the making of gardens remains as significant a cultural and political activity as it was for the Gullahs' ancestors under slavery.

"If you work the land, you keep the land," Otis Daise told me the afternoon we walked his fields.

"Lose the land and you lose the culture," Ralph Middleton says, completing Otis's warning, during our long visit the next day, when he shows me the original deed to his family's ten acres.

"These are the descendants of my great-great-grandfather," he explains as we lean over a print out of the Middleton family tree. The name Richard "Dick" Middleton stands alone at the top in large capitals. "They just took the name from the Middletons," Ralph adds quietly, referring to one of the wealthiest and most powerful slaveholding families in South Carolina, one of whom—Arthur Middleton—signed the Declaration of Independence.

"We were slaves on Wadmalaw," Ralph continues in a matter-of-fact tone. Wadmalaw Island lies just south of Charleston and north of St. Helena. "We came here around 1866 and bought land in the Corner Community." After emancipation, the Gullahs renamed each of the plantations a community.

The men who bought the land that has come down to Ralph and his heirs were brothers. But because they were slaves, their stories are nearly impossible to recover. The white man who sold them the land, however, can be traced. "This man came down from Massachusetts and bought the land off the tax sale," Ralph tells me. "Then he sold it to whoever wanted to buy it. When people heard that they were selling land to freed slaves here, they came down from Wadmalaw. This is how Richard Middleton had a chance to buy land on St. Helena."

He hands me a clear copy of a handwritten deed dated February 5, 1866.

> Know All Men by these Presents. That I, Edward S. Philbrick of Boston, in the County of Suffolk, and State of Massachusetts. In Consideration of Fifty five Dollars, paid by Richard Middleton of St. Helena Island, in the District of Beaufort, and State of South Carolina, the receipt whereof is hereby acknowledged, do hereby grant, remiss, release, and forever Quit claim unto the said Richard Middleton a certain piece or parcel of land, situated on the said St. Helena Island ... According to this plot of the U.S. Tax Commissioners for South Carolina, containing Eleven acres of land more or less, Being a portion of the tract of land formerly known as the Corner place ... and sold to the said Grantor by ... U.S. Tax Commissioners for the State of South Carolina, as per Tax Sale Certificate No. 19, dated March 9th 1863 ... To have and to hold the above released premises, with all the privileges and appurtenances to the same belonging to the said Richard Middleton, his Heirs and Assigns, to his and their use and behoof forever.

"So few blacks had a chance to buy land," Ralph explains as we try to imagine the moment when the deed was signed. "But we were lucky in this area. When the Freedmen's Bureau people came down here, they started the Port Royal Experiment. When the slaveholders left, the land went up on tax sale."

In *Sea Island Diary, A History of St. Helena Island,* South Carolina historian Edith M. Dabbs tells the story of the representatives of the Freedmen's Bureau who came to St. Helena in 1862—some traveling with Laura Towne, the founder of the Penn School—ostensibly to help the newly freed slaves make the transition to freedom. They bought many of the abandoned plantations, with the understanding that the land would be sold to the blacks within a year for the same modest price they had paid the federal government for the confiscated land. Edward Philbrick was one of them. A white man born and raised in Boston, Philbrick graduated from Harvard in 1846 and worked as a civil engineer for years before arriving on St. Helena in the spring of 1862 as part of the Port Royal Experiment. Having donated a thousand dollars to the experiment and paid for his own passage to St. Helena, he was rewarded for his generosity with the position of superintendent on the largest plantation on the island, Coffin Point.

As a plantation superintendent, Philbrick was expected to hold the land in trust. He was to recruit freed slaves to work the land for pay, with the promise that in one year they would be able to buy a parcel of their own. When he became the overseer of eleven plantations, owning nine outright and renting two, he held title to 810 acres of land planted with Sea Island cotton, the finest cotton in the world. Another 1500 acres were planted in food for the 933 freed blacks who lived and worked on what was now his land. Philbrick owned more land on St. Helena than even the richest of the slaveholding planters had owned, and more blacks worked on his lands than had ever worked for one master under slavery.

A year later, although he had promised to sell the land to the freedman at the same price he had paid for it, Philbrick instead began selling off whole plantations to Massachusetts friends and business associates who came down to St. Helena to try their hand at raising Sea Island cotton. Having paid $1 to $1.25 for land he then sold for up to $12 per acre, "Edward Philbrick," Dabbs adds pointedly, "became a very wealthy man."

Though the blacks of St. Helena rose up in protest, addressing their grievances directly to President Lincoln, when Richard Middleton signed his deed two years later, Philbrick was still selling confiscated plantation land to freed slaves for ten times what he had paid for it. Given the extent of his holdings, there must have been scores of land transactions like the one Richard Middleton's deed represents.

As a result, the failed promise of emancipation is still mapped in the pattern of land distribution today. Members of the black community own small parcels of land—the same ten acres their ancestors bought after emancipation—while a small white minority holds the large ones.

Commercial tomato fields deep in Gullah communities are part of this legacy of racially determined landholdings. These industrial farms have been carved out of large parcels of land passed down through white families. How do these industrial farms figure in St. Helena's future as a black majority community?

"Tomatoes are the cotton of the latter part of the twentieth century," Dana Beach, an environmentalist with the Coastal Conservation League of South Carolina, says when I ask him what these fields mean. "Cotton was not a local product, and the planters didn't even deal with the United States. They engaged in some trade with the Northeast, but most of their trade was with Europe. That's why they thought they could be their own country." Like the cash crops grown on the old plantations, "tomatoes are a boom-and-bust crop," he adds.

Dana has seen what the commercial growers of tomatoes do to the land on St. Helena. To prepare their fields, they cut down all the trees, then scrape off the topsoil and sell it off-island. What's left serves as a mere substrate for the production of a chemically dependent crop watered with millions of gallons drawn from the local aquifer, for which the commercial growers pay nothing.

The Mexican migrant farmworkers who harvest the tomatoes are paid between forty and forty-five cents per thirty-two-pound bucket. They have to pick two tons of tomatoes to make fifty dollars in a day. Out of that, they have to pay rent and buy food. They receive no benefits of any kind.

Cam Lay of the Clemson University Agricultural Extension Service agrees that tomatoes are a boom-and-bust crop. He likes to quote John Walpole of Anchorage Plantation on Wadmalaw Island, a grower who recently opted for the one-time windfall of selling his family's old plantation to real estate developers and who summed up the situation in a single pithy phrase: "I can make more money planting Yankees than I can planting tomatoes."

If it comes down to a choice between tomatoes and Yankees on St. Helena, though, tomatoes are clearly the lesser of two evils. At least the tomato fields are green and open. The alternative would bring condominiums, golf courses, and gated communities, with the chemicals it takes to support their lawns, the runoff from newly paved roads, and all the demands for goods and services their occupants would want. Property values would go up, raising taxes so that even more Gullah families might lose their land, as they have on Hilton Head Island, once also a traditional Gullah community but now one of the most famous elite resort areas in the world.

However goofy the pitch, real estate ads for land in Beaufort County, including the discreetly worded advertisements for some of the old slave masters' houses, like Tombee, make it clear that the marketing of St. Helena to wealthy white outsiders depends on a willed oblivion to history.

"Welcome to St. Helena Island," the Island Realty Web site begins, below a color photograph of sunset over a low-country marsh.

> Isolated by the hauntingly beautiful physical barriers of tidal marshes and saltwater creeks, the sea island of St. Helena, near Beaufort, South Carolina, evokes a warm feeling of stepping back into time and nature... Meandering rivers and tidal creeks blend with tree shrouded and dusty roads which hearken back to a kinder and more gentler time when St. Helena's great plantations produced some of the finest cotton in the

> world—Sea Island Cotton. Even today St. Helena still maintains a 19th century aura. History and wildlife abound. Come and experience what life was and what it can be. Come to St. Helena Island!

It's as if the Gullahs were already gone, and with them the awkward and inconvenient history of slavery.

On my last day in South Carolina, I drive north, toward Charleston. There is one more kind of cultivated landscape I need to see—a slave master's garden. I have chosen Middleton Place, created by the family from whom Ralph's ancestors took their name. There, the formal eighteenth-century gardens made possible by the success of rice and indigo have been restored to their pre–Civil War distinction through the efforts of direct descendants of the family. The old rice fields are still there too, and the old rice mill.

Henry Middleton, for whom Middleton Place is named, was the third generation of a family of wealthy planters. In 1741 he married Mary Williams, heir to the property that now bears his name. "Already of independent fortune," William Gaillard Stoney writes in *Plantations of the Carolina Low Country,* "marriage and management would make the first Middleton of Middleton Place one of the province's richest men." By the time he was elected president of the First Continental Congress in 1774, Henry Middleton owned fifty thousand acres of land, twenty plantations, and eight hundred slaves.

Middleton Place in the days of Henry Middleton comprised 200 acres. It is the site of the oldest landscaped gardens in America. Soon after taking up residence, Henry Middleton began to plan the gardens after the style of Le Notre, the great French landscape architect who designed the gardens at Versailles. Stoney considered this "the premier garden of the thirteen colonies." Even now, it is ranked as one of the greatest gardens in the world.

The land Mary Williams brought to her marriage with Henry Middleton is striking for its elevation, a rarity in the low country. Rising a quarter mile above a great curve of the Ashley River, it overlooks a long sloping bluff that reaches down from the original house site to the tidal rice fields below, commanding a stunning view of the river and the marshes beyond. The two most striking features of the landscape on the river side of Middleton Place are the terraced hillside sculpted from the bluff, with soft green steps suggesting the wide marble stairs of a great European house, and the lakes shaped like a pair of butterfly wings that lie at its base.

Nothing in the literature I am given for my self-guided tour suggests how I am to deal with the most salient fact about the creation of this entire landscape—acres of formal gardens, two long reflecting pools, a labyrinth of garden rooms, one opening into another; a long, meandering path leading to the white statue of a wood nymph who leans down to tie the ribbons of her slipper, her head framed by clouds of blue hydrangea blossoms. According to family legend, it took one hundred slaves ten years to carve these features from the land.

I know from the little map I carry which path will take me to the rice fields, which are, the map says, right beside the butterfly lakes, for which Middleton Place is famous. After several minutes, the path leads me out onto a narrow strip of grass between the demonstration rice field and the lakes. Spring-green blades of rice have sprung from the rich mud of mounds raised above the water, which pools in the channels below. Standing still in the full sun even for a few moments, trying to take in what I see, makes me lightheaded. Sweat runs down my face, stinging my eyes; it forms rivulets that course down my arms and legs and stain my clothes. How could anyone work in these fields in such heat?

The labor involved in transforming river bottomland into irrigated rice fields like these was nothing short of staggering. Using shovels, hoes, and baskets, slaves moved many tons of earth, reshaping the land and redirecting the flow of water on a vast scale. The banks built to hold back the Ashley River are taller than the men who built them. Once the banks had been constructed, the land had to be carved into geometrically shaped fields separated by handmade dikes and irrigation canals. Floodgates, or "trunks," controlled the inflow of fresh water at high tide, suppressing weed growth and irrigating the rice, and then the outflow at low tide, which kept the crop from drowning. The floodgates were called trunks because in their earliest form they were actually hollowed-out tree trunks with removable plugs, a technology for water control that had evolved as part of West African rice culture, which the slaves introduced to South Carolina. The huge project of transforming the landscape along the lower reaches of the Ashley River and redistributing its mud took several years, as Henry Middleton learned the art of rice cultivation from enslaved Africans.

The digging and cleaning of the dikes and canals of the irrigation system was called mud work. The slaves hated it. They hacked at weeds, mosquitoes swarming around their heads while alligators and water moccasins swam in the murk around their legs. "No work can be imagined more pernicious to health," Alexander Hewatt, an eighteenth-century South Carolina historian, wrote, "than for men to stand in water mid-leg high, and often above it, planting and weeding rice." As they worked in the rice fields, "the scorching heat of the sun" would render "the air they breathed ten or twenty degrees hotter than human blood."

Standing here in the fierce heat, I realize that the gaze of anyone working in the rice field below me would be level with my feet. I turn and take one step toward the nearest butterfly lake and look up toward the vacancy at the top of the terraced hillside where the great house, burned by Union troops, once stood. Visitors arriving by boat, as most did, would have been positioned in just this way: above the enslaved, below the Middletons. What intoxicating blend of wealth, power, and greed concocted such a landscape? Here are gardens that map relationships of power on the land, positioning me in an eighteenth-century slaveholder's hierarchy of value. The impulse to dominate is Henry Middleton's signature on the land.

Somewhere on one of the Middleton plantations, Ralph Middleton's ancestors toiled and died. Something Ralph said as we walked slowly back from the marsh at the far edge of his family's land comes back to me: "Sometimes when I walk here, I think of the tears. I think of who was here, who walked this land, what it was like for them."

The butterfly lakes are separated from the rice fields by no more than the width of a slave-built earthen dike. They were carved from the same swamp as the rice fields, by the same hands, under the same brutal conditions. When we are asked to find this landscape beautiful, we are being invited to forget the violence of its making. The will to remember who made these gardens, and at what cost, may well be the more important act of historical restoration, more telling than filling in the holes the great earthquake of 1886 tore open in the terraced hillside as it brought down the charred remnant of the old north wing.

"The land is God," Ralph Middleton told me. "And the land is God's. We see God walking through it. We're just caretakers. You do your part. Then, when you go back to God, you can say, 'I did what I could. I left it in good shape.'

"We'll hold this land for our children. I believe some of them will come back. Even if they don't come but once a year till they retire. That's what I did. All I do is keep the tree going. Someone else planted it. It's there to share. I'm just keeping it alive for the next generation."

3

PLACE

A Polish American Vintner and a Japanese American Berry Farmer

BAINBRIDGE ISLAND, WASHINGTON

"First you lose your costume. Then you lose your language. The last thing you lose is your food." After *hello,* these are the first words Gerard Bentryn speaks to me once I find my way to Day Road Farm and then, through the crowd at the harvest supper, to him.

In these three phrases, Gerard sums up the shock, the intense pressure to conform, and the losses that have shaped the lives of generations of immigrants to America. The story of how Gerard Bentryn, a Polish American, came to plant a vineyard here, on land he has shared for over twenty years with Akio Suyematsu, a Japanese American berry farmer, sheds light on one of the most precious legacies immigrants bring to America—an abiding love for the land. And the story of how hard they have had to fight to keep from losing the farm says a great deal about what America has so often sacrificed to fear of the stranger and too narrow an idea of what constitutes true wealth.

Though Gerard is well known in the Puget Sound region as

a passionate advocate for the environment—and, with his wife, Jo Ann, his son, Ian, and a young farmer named Betsey Wittick, for the wine they produce at Bainbridge Island Winery—he is little known for the immigrant heritage that has shaped him.

I have come a long way to meet Gerard Bentryn and Akio Suyematsu. Akio is a Nisei, or second-generation Japanese American. Since his father, Yasiji Suyematsu, came to the United States in 1904, the Suyematsus have been known as berry farmers. Except for the two years when his family was interned during World War II, Akio has worked this land for his entire life.

For these two friends, the experience of being displaced within their native country has been answered by a commitment to this place. Day Road Farm is the oldest and largest working farm on Bainbridge Island. It was nearly lost twice, first when the Suyematsus were taken away in a military truck and sent to Manzanar, the first of America's ten "relocation centers," in March 1942, and again in the past five years, as the development spawned by an influx of new wealth created by Microsoft and other high-tech industries in Seattle drove property values so high so fast that it has become nearly impossible to live off the land.

I reach Bainbridge Island late one night on the last ferry out of Seattle. When I awake in the morning, it feels as if the world has shrunk. Even the trees seem pressed to the ground by the heavy shroud of sodden grayness. But by noon the sun has burned through the fog, and a vault of deep blue has opened above. Thin ribbons of white hover above the ridgeline of the Olympic Mountains on the horizon. The world has grown huge again.

Following the directions Gerard gave me, I drive past the gates that say BAINBRIDGE ISLAND VINEYARDS AND WINERY, *The wine you drink is the landscape you create,* and see, just behind them, a green wooden farmstand with a large red-on-white sign that reads SUYEMATSU FARMS. A little farther up Day Road, I turn through a wide opening in the fence onto a dirt road with an old brown farmhouse on one side and a new shed on the other. A man is crouched on the roof, hammering. I drive past the pickups and cars parked along the dirt road until I can hear laughter and conversation, then park. Following the voices, I come around a set of small farm buildings to see a table that stretches the length of the barn, set out under the shelter of its roof, covered with bowls and platters of food and jugs of flowers. People are moving down the length of it, filling their plates and chatting.

There are great wooden bowls of green salad and ceramic bowls filled with red, white, gold, blue, and purple roasted potatoes. There is fresh bread—baguettes, rounds, and loaves—and white goat cheese, bowls of beans and plates of sliced tomatoes, a platter mounded with steaming corn. There are berry pies, bowls of fresh berries, cakes, and cookies. And at the far end, a smiling woman with straw-colored hair and bright hazel eyes is pouring wine. Her apron says *Bainbridge Island Winery.* This is Jo Ann Bentryn, Gerard's wife.

Nearby, tables and chairs are set out on the grass around a beehive oven shaped like a great frog with its mouth open wide. Betsey Wittick and a friend have stoked the wood fire and are making fresh pizza with tomatoes and basil grown in the field just yards from here, where homemade signs posted on metal stakes run along the top of the rows stretching into the distance. WELCOME TO LAUGHING CROW FARM—COME ENJOY THIS GREAT EVENING WITH US! the first sign announces, with Betsey's signature beneath.

TAKE A HORSE-DRAWN WAGON RIDE PULLED BY OUR BELGIAN DRAFT HORSE, SAMANTHA, TO SEE THE FARM. WALK ALONG THE TOP OF THE ROWS AND READ ABOUT THOSE OF US FARMING HERE. A little way down the path I see the blue wagon and Samantha, the draft horse, quietly waiting. Betsey has stopped taking people for rides long enough to get some supper.

WHAT WILL HAPPEN TO THIS FARM IN THE FUTURE? the next sign asks.

OPPORTUNITIES TO VISIT LARGE, OPEN WORKING LANDSCAPES LIKE THIS FARM ARE QUICKLY DISAPPEARING. THIS IS THE ONLY LARGE WORKING FARM LEFT ON BAINBRIDGE AND PROBABLY THE BIGGEST OF ITS KIND LEFT IN KITSAP COUNTY.

PRESSURES TO DEVELOP FARMLAND LIKE THIS ARE GREAT. NEW FARMERS CAN'T AFFORD TO BUY LAND AT DEVELOPMENT PRICES TO GROW VEGETABLES, YET OLDER FARMERS HAVE NO RETIREMENT INCOME OTHER THAN THEIR LAND, AND THEY CAN'T AFFORD TO SELL IT AT A PRICE THE YOUNG FARMERS CAN PAY.

SO HOW CAN WE, AS MEMBERS OF A COMMUNITY, KEEP FARMS LIKE THIS ALIVE, PROVIDING US WITH FOOD FOR BOTH BODY AND SOUL?

MAYBE YOU HAVE AN IDEA THAT WILL WORK!

All the way down the edge of the field, Betsey's signs introduce me to a new way to read a landscape. I read the biography of a working farm while eating food and drinking wine produced from the landscape before me. Betsey's signs invite me to know the people who have planted the rows I see. There are Betsey's heirloom varieties of potatoes and garlic, Akio's nursery trees, Ian Bentryn's statice. But then there are long, wide rows of vegetables, herbs, and flowers grown by people who have no land of their own—Gerard has invited them all to use the land for free.

IN THE DISTANCE YOU CAN SEE ONE OF THE VINEYARDS OF BAINBRIDGE ISLAND VINEYARDS & WINERY, the next sign says. I have only to look up to see the broad aisles of grapes following the contours of the land, like green rivers. Betsey works in one of these vineyards or at the winery most of the time. Gerard and Jo Ann gave her the opportunity to farm on the island and made it possible for her to start Laughing Crow Farm. All of the winery's grapes are grown on Bainbridge Island, in the six and a half acres of vineyards here and the one acre at the winery in town.

The last of Betsey's signs shifts the focus from what I can see to what I can't discern with my senses—the origin of this humanly shaped landscape and its place in American history. THE FORTY-ACRE FARM YOU ARE STANDING ON, Betsey's neat handwriting begins, WAS STARTED BY THE SUYEMATSU FAMILY IN 1928. They cleared the land with horses and dynamite, then grew strawberries, raspberries, Olympic blackberries, peas, beans, and corn. During World War II, when they and other Japanese Americans were put in internment camps, the family was fortunate not to lose its farm, as many others did. They came back to find the land covered in weeds and brush, but they worked tirelessly to bring it back into production. Akio Suyematsu was the only son who wanted to keep farming on Bainbridge. He has spent most of his life here, and at seventy-nine years old, he can outwork people half his age.

Akio had no children and none of his relatives were interested in farming here, so in 1986 he sold just over half the farm to Gerard and Jo Ann so they could grow grapes for the Bainbridge Island Winery. Gerard made an agreement with Akio that Akio could still farm any land not planted in grapes. Today Akio continues to grow raspberries, pumpkins, and Christmas trees on land he sold to the winery years ago.

IN 1990, Betsey's last sign says, AKIO SOLD ME A TWO-AND-A-HALF-ACRE PIECE BECAUSE I WAS INTERESTED IN FARMING. I GOT TO KNOW AKIO THROUGH WORKING AT THE WINERY. UNKNOWN TO ME AT THE TIME, HE WAS KEEPING AN EYE ON HOW GOOD A WORKER I WAS, AND FROM THAT MADE HIS DETERMINATION ON HOW SERIOUS I WAS ABOUT FARMING. (HE TELLS ME I WAS PRETTY SLOW AT FIRST!)

Everyone in Betsey's story is here at the harvest feast but Akio. He is the man I saw working on the roof as I drove in, Gerard tells me, which is where he will remain, the sound of his hammer echoing across the field, until the light leaves the sky and all the visitors have gone home.

When Betsey stands up and calls out to all takers that the last horse-drawn cart ride of the evening is about to leave, I ask if

I can come too. "Sure," she says, "climb right up," and she grabs my hand and pulls me onto the bench beside her. "How about if you hand out those songbooks?" She gives the reins a light shake, and Samantha lowers her head and pulls.

I reach into Betsey's canvas bag and grab the books. Eager hands reach to take them. In a minute everyone is singing. "Swing Low, Sweet Chariot" rises into the gauzy air of late afternoon in September as Samantha takes us up the broad dirt path into the fields. Drawing her right hand back, Betsey guides Samantha into the turn that takes us through a field of soft brown grass, eventually heading back toward the barn and the people now gathered around a fire. A man behind me with a firm, clear voice begins to sing the opening bars of "Amazing Grace," and by the second long note people begin to join him. Softly, everyone sings, stretching the hymn out beyond the first familiar verse. They split into four-part harmony. Betsey is singing beside me. With every footfall, Samantha pulls the wagon back toward the place we left from. As night falls, the air grows chilly and damp and the cedars at the rim of the land become sharp black points against the sky.

"I came here because I wanted to have a way to live in beauty," Gerard says to me the next day. He has invited me down to the winery, where we sit at a picnic table in the fragrance garden, just beyond the blue barn, as Jo Ann greets visitors in the tasting room. "I learned in Germany that a family could own a small vineyard, make wine, and make a living on five acres of land. I saw the same thing when I went to Burgundy and the Loire. Relatively small amounts of land could be farmed and a family could make a living from it. Here at the winery we have one acre of grapes on three acres of land."

At the head of each aisle of grapes Gerard has planted roses. A wide swath of grass divides the acre of vine rows in two, inviting visitors to walk straight out the winery door into the vineyard, where they are welcome to stroll and sip wine, enjoy a picnic, or simply be still. Not far from where we sit at the picnic table, birds swoop low to catch bugs on the surface of a small pond. Enclosed as I am in this intimate, complex landscape, I can't tell that we're in the heart of Winslow, the urban part of the island. The winery is less than a mile from the ferry dock, from which many of the newest residents commute to jobs on the mainland.

"When we started here," Gerard explains, "wine was seven dollars a bottle and a house on an acre of land cost $62,000. Now wine still sells for between seven and ten dollars a bottle, but a house on the required two-and-a-half-acre lot costs $475,000. The issue here on the island is what's happened to us since we got all these new high-income people moving here. Jo Ann and I are probably worth something like one and a half or two million dollars in land, but our income each year is about $22,000 a person. We can't compete for goods and services on the island. We can't pay the taxes. We don't want to get bigger, so our income isn't going to go up, which means we probably have to sell this. Intellectually, it's clear that we should just sell it and take the most money we can get so we can insure our success up at Day Road. Emotionally, after twenty-four years, I don't really want to leave. And the thought of condemning the whole thing to bulldozers... Well, I'd have real problems sleeping at night doing that.

"It would be much cheaper for us to buy grapes. We could sell all the land—it's worth a fortune—and just keep the little place here and bring the grapes in and make wine, like everybody else does around Seattle, and nobody would seem to care. And that's what really bothers us."

When Gerard and Jo Ann came here, there were between twenty and thirty active wineries in western Washington; now there are three hundred and forty. Largely through Gerard's efforts, the region has a certified appellation. Its boundaries follow the rainfall line of sixty inches or less. Starting at the Canadian border in the north, it reaches to the foothills of the Olympic

Mountains to the west, to the foothills of the Cascades to the east, and down to Olympia, Washington, in the south. Of the forty wineries in the appellation, the Bentryns, with Betsey Wittick, are the only ones who grow all their own grapes and produce a truly local and sustainable wine.

"Have you offered this lady some wine?" Jo Ann asks, suddenly appearing from behind the hedge to stand beside me in her apron. "Would you like to taste some wine?" she says, turning to me. "We have a Madeleine Angevine, which is like a sauvignon blanc, or a dry Müller-Thurgau, which is like a chardonnay because it's oaked."

"It's not buttery like a chardonnay," Gerard says, "because it is oak and floral characters together, which is very unusual. Why don't you try that? They're all unusual—we don't make anything the way anybody else does."

Jo Ann brings me three white wines, the Madeleine Angevine and two wines made from the same grape, the dry Müller-Thurgau and a traditional.

"What you're going to get," Gerard explains as I lift the first glass, "is fragrance as opposed to body in our wines. The Madeleine is floral, very delicate."

It's like sipping a garden, this dry, light, crisp wine.

"You can see the difference in color," Jo Ann explains, so that I can distinguish between the two Müllers. "The dry is the darker."

The traditional is light and fruity, and the dry, with its light oak to balance its fragrance, is more substantial.

The last wine Jo Ann brings me, a siegerrebe, startles me as soon as I detect its fragrance. Their wine list describes it as "spicy like Gewürztraminer, but not too sweet." It's simply a knockout.

"In the United States, we've industrialized," Gerard says as he and Jo Ann register my pleasure. "The fake in wine has supplanted the real. Right now I can order color, flavor, and texture and make wine out of things that come in little bottles. Much of the wine people are drinking today is entirely made that way.

Ninety percent of the wine produced in Washington State is made by three transnationals. Mexicans grow their grapes and they irrigate from the Columbia River Basin. Native salmon die so they can mass-produce grapes in a climate unsuited to them. They're on corporate welfare. So how do you educate people to look for reality—to be willing to pay a premium for the real and pay less for industrial wine?

"I remember when we got interested in organic viticulture and we wanted to know how you did it. We went down to California to a place that was doing it. Weed control was Mexicans. It was a hundred degrees, and they were pickaxing weeds out of the vineyards. I said to the guy, 'God, that looks terrible.' And he said, 'Yeah, I don't know how those people do it...' So I said, 'Well, is this the ethic that we're trying to teach? That we trade herbicides for slavery?' He didn't have an answer. It just didn't bother him." What mattered was being able to market the wine as organic.

"Growing organic produce is an ethic, not a marketing tool. What we need to emphasize is the local. We need to emphasize what Betsey calls the least impact. That's the issue. And if the impact also involves fish and fieldworkers, we need to weigh and balance all those things. If we don't tie together what we do with what we believe, we're all going to fail."

A group has arrived for a tour, so Gerard excuses himself, inviting me to go into the winemaking area to talk with Betsey.

"People think winemaking is very glamorous," she says right off. "But for me, the whole romance of the winery is out in the vineyard. That's the exciting part. Here, you're standing around while the pump's doing work, making sure that something doesn't break. It's boring. It just takes time. And then you're cleaning. You're wearing boots all the time, year round, and you have a hose in your hand, walking around in raingear. That's what you do in a winery. It's like large-scale dishwashing with some chemistry thrown in. The real work of making wine is growing the grapes. Though we use a tractor for weeding and rototilling, we do a lot of handwork. In the field, it's me, Gerard, and Gerard's son, Ian. Sometimes people help us with things like leaf pulling—jobs that need to be done at a certain time and quickly.

"See how there are no leaves by the fruit?" Betsey says, walking me across the driveway and up an aisle of grapes. The vines have been plucked clean of leaves to a uniform height, around knee level. "We pull them off so we get air circulation around the fruit. It's getting close to harvest. It opens them up, so they're less likely to get disease. They ripen a bit better."

Three people tend a total of eight acres of grapes. At roughly 1800 vines per acre, that's 14,000 vines.

"When we get to harvest, we need other people out there. We have to pick between twenty-five and thirty tons over the course of maybe six or seven days. Not consecutive. We'll pick some on Friday, then we'll wait another week or so before we pick the next variety," Betsey explains.

Gerard and Betsey watch through the long, slow seasons of new growth, maturation, and ripening and then rush to harvest at just the right moment to capture the flavor. One of their specialty wines is the late-harvest siegerrebe. The grapes are allowed to hang on the vine longer than usual, until they are affected by a botrytis virus that softens their skins and renders them spicy and sweet and fragrant.

The winery produces about 2200 cases of wine per year and sells out at the end of every season. Betsey's commitment to the farm is total. "Sharing the farm works mainly because of Akio," she says. "He's great. He lets me borrow things I could never afford to buy. That's one of the advantages of being near other farmers, besides the emotional support and getting ideas from them.

"Akio is very quiet and very shy. He just keeps working. He was working last night. Did you see him up on his roof, hammering away? He gets to know you through what you do, not what you say. I could see that he was eyeing how I worked for a few years before he would even talk to me. Once he saw that I was serious about farming, he was willing to sell me the two and a half acres where I built my house."

At one point Betsey decided to go off to Montana to work with an older farmer who had experience farming with draft horses. "Gerard always wanted a draft horse, but he had never really worked with horses before, and neither had I, but I took it on," she explains. Now she wants another horse. She wants to start raising hay. Among the most toxic chemicals released in fields cultivated with a tractor are the residues from diesel fuel. It's hard to find the equipment to farm with horses, though Betsey salvaged an old cultivator recently, and built another from recycled parts she found on the farm. "I'd like to be able to farm only with horsepower," she says.

Samantha completes the farm for Betsey in another way. "I put aside a portion of my time every week for slowing things down," she says. "That's why I take Samantha and my wagon out on the road. I like to go with people, though it's hard to find anyone who will take the time. We'll go to breakfast. It can take an hour to get someplace you could get to in five minutes in a car. But I get people to slow down. I get them singing. I have my little songbooks, now, you know, that I pass out, because nobody remembers the words. It's all about time. It's the most valuable thing we have, and we don't appreciate it."

"Wine is a time and a place in a bottle," Gerard had said to me the night before. Time and place, a fully integrated life—that's what Day Road Farm is about. None of this would have been possible without the years of struggle of Japanese immigrants, people denied the right to own the land they devoted their lives to, denied the right to become citizens of the country they chose, clearing their land with horses like Samantha, blasting out trees, dragging the stumps away, so the entire family could plant and harvest labor-intensive strawberries.

Akio stopped growing strawberries a while ago. Now he cultivates eight acres of raspberries, from which he harvests twenty-five tons of fruit a season, doing all the work himself until the harvest. "Akio lives by deeds, not by words," Gerard explained.

It will take Gerard and Betsey days to persuade Akio to talk to me. In the meantime, I am invited to wander around the farm, which is alternately veiled in mist and bathed in dazzling sunlight. I am moved by the beautiful order of Akio's short rows of raspberries and Gerard's long rows of grapes. Akio's pumpkin vines spread sweeping curves out over the rich, dark soil. I sit in the lean-to where Akio's father once checked boxes of strawberries that Native Canadians had helped to pick, resting in the cool and quiet place that smells of straw and fruit. From that high point on the farm, the land falls away in two long waves. Someone has piled burned twigs, the leavings after pruning, in a field of soft golden hay. The low rectangle of one pile speaks of the degree of thought and care that goes into every gesture on this place; the tall, tapering mound of another suggests an ancient forest dwelling. On one acre of pinot noir—the only pinot noir grown locally—I find myself transfixed by the deep purple of the grapes, hanging from leaves that have turned a flaming orange.

I can see what Gerard meant about living in beauty. These fields, with their wild edges full of flowers, with a hundred species of birds and a ring of tall, dark cedars surrounding them on three sides, are achingly lovely, a harmony of wild and cultivated, a thoughtful composition of human dwellings, artful plantings, and the fallow areas of softness. To what Akio's family created, Gerard brought his own vision. What inspired it? Gerard answers with stories of the people and the places that shaped him. At the center is an experience of loss and cultural displacement so painful that the metaphor he reaches for is the classic one—the immigrant as plant: "You tear a plant from the soil, and the first thing it does is try to put down roots. It's a matter of survival."

But the immigrant is never simply uprooted or transplanted. The immigrant is not a plant but a gardener—shaping the world, not simply being shaped by it.

"I grew up in Green Brook, next to the town of Middlesex in New Jersey," Gerard begins. "In those days, Green Brook was still pretty wild. We had one bear that used to come down into the water recharge area, and a lot of deer and pheasants. We lived at the end of the school bus run. The bus would drop me off and go one way, and I'd head in the other. I had about a half-mile walk to get home.

"In summers I lived in the woods. And I became really shy. I couldn't talk to people. Barefoot, in just a pair of shorts, with my dog, I wandered around collecting birds' eggs, climbing trees, identifying plants, and things like that. And then one day I rode my bicycle across the county line into the next town, where there were scattered old houses. And there was an old man selling vegetables, so I stopped to talk to him. His name was Web Townsend. He had been born in the 1860s and lived in an 1840s house. I was eleven years old when I met him, and I knew him until, oh, I think I was about eighteen or nineteen when he died. I spent a lot of time sitting around listening to him.

"When I first met him, it was all farms, dairy farms, and they were growing silage corn for the cows all around there. And then gradually the farms all around him disappeared. It was the big wave right after World War II when suburbanization was coming in. The first real housing developments. You know, on Long Island and in New Jersey. And I watched him. I watched his heart break as he saw it all go. He died on his tractor. They found him slumped over the steering wheel, with the engine idling.

"I didn't see him," Gerard says with sadness. "One of the other children told me, 'Oh, Web's dead.' One of the great regrets of my life is that I never went back. I didn't go to his funeral, I didn't talk to his wife. I was just so heartbroken. I couldn't handle the idea that he was dead. I still feel guilty. This was very, very formative for me, because it made very clear to me that there was this incredible beauty in the world, intricate systems of nature, but then, when people came in, ugliness came, and destruction. It seemed as though people equaled ugliness.

"My father was born in Poland. In 1914 my grandfather was sent to the United States to buy machinery for a little factory. The machinery was still on the dock at Danzig, or Gdansk, in Polish, when the war broke out, so he ran and got his family—my father was the oldest child—and put them on a boat and brought them to the United States, and that was it. His name was Kazmiercz Leszczynski, and that should be my family name. It's a fairly common name in Poland. A *leszczyna* is a hazel tree.

"In America, my grandfather went on to be head of a machine shop that built some of the first submarines the United States used to fight against the Germans. Because they had no money, my father had to go to work. When he was twelve, he got a job on the Jersey Central Railroad, which was entirely run by Irish unions. He was beaten up regularly. There was a tremendous anti-Slavic feeling among the Irish. They had made it; we were the next rung down, the newcomers.

"It was my father's mother whose name was Bentryn. We traced that back to the Germans coming into Poland in the 1600s with the name Bindren. Then, when the Russians took over, it was changed into Cyrillic, and then later back into the Roman spelling, and apparently that's when it became Bentryn. Since nobody else could figure out what Bentryn was, my father took his mother's maiden name. To the Irish union members, it seemed to be Welsh, and that was all right—you know, with the *y* ending. He began to get better and better work. All he had to do was to deny who and what he was. So that's where my name comes from."

So to Gerard's list of losses, we have to add his name, which carries not only the history of Poland's suffering as a country annexed and occupied repeatedly but an accounting of the price immigrants pay to become Americans.

"For years I didn't understand why my last name was different from my grandfather's and my cousins'," Gerard says. "When I came to understand the truth, I had already come to think of myself as a Bentryn. Later, I could see the pain in my grandfather's eyes when he asked me if I ever wanted to be a Leszczynski like him. But I believe that I knew inside that it was safer being what I was—passing for white in a land that feared the strange or unusual."

In the early years of the twentieth century, when Gerard's family arrived, southern and eastern Europeans were not counted as white people in the American census. The virulence of American nativism during World War I, when even the long-established German immigrant community found that their adopted land could turn on them in an instant, intensified in the early 1920s. The Bolshevik Revolution that brought Lenin to power in 1917 ended three hundred years of rule by the czars. The murder of Czar Nicholas II, his wife, Alexandra, and their children, the last of the Romanov dynasty, launched the Red Scare, which swept across Europe and the United States. For immigrants to retain their foreignness, even in spirit, was considered an act of "moral treason" by the right-wing "America is for Americans" movement, led by Senator Henry Cabot Lodge of Massachusetts.

"It was my grandfather who gave me a sense of the land," Gerard says. "My father was too busy just surviving. My grandfather would tell me stories about what it was like in Poland. And when I go back to Poland—I've been back twice now—the beauty of it just grabs me. I tell my son that I feel that we're just as much a part of our environment as the jays and the juncos and the hummingbirds. You can't live in the same place for a thousand years and not have it profoundly influence you.

"My grandfather would talk about collecting mushrooms in the forest. When I was little, he still went mushroom hunting. He'd take me into the woods and show me which things you could eat. He'd take me into the Pine Barrens and teach me to identify things. He always had a big garden, with whitewashed trees. In Europe, if you grow fruit trees, you always whitewash the bottom to keep the bark from splitting. He grew a lot of vegetables and lots of flowers that aren't in fashion, or are just coming back, like hollyhocks and cannas. He wrapped his fig trees so they could survive the Jersey winters, as the Italians did too in that area.

"You know, back then people didn't have garbage pickup as we do now. Everything went back into the ground. When we would go fishing, anything we didn't eat would go into the ground. They didn't throw away anything organic. I mean, they absolutely didn't waste anything.

"In Poland, the garden was where you entertained people. I remember how my grandfather would sit there twirling his mustache while everyone served him. He was the real boss, that was clear. The garden must have covered at least three or four acres of ground. And there was a little pond in the back. I would help him in the garden as much as I could at the time, though I was pretty little. But then my parents moved away from my father's parents, and all that ended. They decided they didn't want to work for other people anymore. They wanted to go somewhere where they could start their own business. So we weren't around family any longer.

"So we had this complete break, and then I ran into this farmer and he took me under his wing. I think that's why Web Townsend meant so much to me. My grandfather never really told me what he felt about it all. The problem was language. It was just a terrible loss of something . . ."

Here is the loss Gerard spoke of in the first moment I met him—the beloved man who introduced him to nature and instilled pride in his ancestry was separated from him as much by the loss of a shared language as by the physical distance his parents, driven to assimilate, put between themselves and their origins.

"My first words were in Polish," Gerard explains. "But my mother wanted me to learn English. I think the idea was to get ahead, and you didn't get ahead by speaking Polish. And I was very small, too. One of the things that profoundly shaped my life was that I wasn't good at sports. I mean, I could shoot an arrow and I could catch a fish and I could shoot a gun, but I couldn't catch a ball. If you threw a ball at me, I didn't know where to hold my hands. It was funny for everybody else, so kids mocked me. But I read constantly, everything I could get my hands on. I started to read early, before I went to school. My mother taught me. I began to realize that whatever I was, it was a product of my mind, not my body. But then all through school people would say, 'Dumb Polack.' And I didn't understand—it so confused me—because if I was anything, it was the way I thought. And if I was purportedly unable to think because of who I was, then who was I?

"When I got into high school, I got into the intellectual crowd —the boys that didn't like sports, that were afraid of girls, that sat around and played chess all night, things like that. And they made fun of me. Even those. It was constant. All of the friends I grew up with, their parents were lawyers and architects, and my father had a truck stop. We were killing chickens because we couldn't afford to buy them. I remember my mother sewing underwear back together again. My friends weren't wealthy, but they were upper-middle-class. They were white Anglo-Saxons and I wasn't. I think because of that I was not coopted into American culture so easily."

One can be set apart first by ignorance and prejudice, then through conscious choice. The trick is to remember what being on the margins makes possible, so that one is not driven by a hunger to conform just to ease the pain.

After high school and Web Townsend's death, Gerard got a job at Bell Labs. He was placed in an apprenticeship program and sent to engineering school, where he was trained to create things from start to finish—to initiate an idea, create a design, determine the materials, and then fashion it—an experience he has translated into the making of wine, from planting the first vines by hand to selling fine wine directly from the vineyards. Within a few years he and Jo Ann married, and then he was drafted and sent to Germany.

"I hungered for cultural wealth, and then I found it in Germany, which I should have hated, but I couldn't—it was too beautiful.

"I got off the train after taking a boat to Germany in 1963 and signed into my unit, a guided missile repair unit. We were housed near the Reichsparteitage. I don't know if you've ever seen *Judgment at Nuremburg,* but at the beginning they show this big marble edifice with a swastika, and then they dynamite it. That was part of the complex we were in. And the U.S. Army had turned what looked like a big stone parade ground in front of it into an airfield," he says.

Assigned to a former SS barracks in Nuremberg, where the walls were full of bullet holes, Gerard had been sent to what had once been the epicenter of Nazi Germany. The Reichsparteitage, the Nazi Party rally grounds, was a four-square-mile complex designed for Hitler in 1933 by Albert Speer. The edifice Gerard remembers from the famous movie about the war crime trials was the Zeppelin Tribune, a colossal structure designed to accommodate 60,000 people. A famous *Life* magazine cover from 1945 shows a jubilant American soldier waving from his perch just in front of the enormous swastika before it was blown up. The airfield that looked like a parade ground where Gerard learned to drive a truck was part of the Great Road that Speer had designed to connect the old city of Nuremberg with the rally grounds. Completed in 1939, it was sixty yards wide, more than a mile long, and paved with 60,000 slabs of granite put in place by enslaved Jewish prisoners.

Less than two years after the trial of Adolf Eichmann in Jerusalem introduced Americans to the details of Nazi atrocities, Gerard was transferred to one of the former death camps. "From Nuremberg we were moved to an SS barracks at Dachau, where one of the field units we were assigned to service was located. I remember wandering around the facilities at night, by myself. I was just twenty-five, and it was soaking into me."

Haunted by all that he saw and alienated by the younger soldiers' apparent detachment from the history of what had happened there, Gerard decided to go out to meet local people. "I had been in cave-exploring clubs in New Jersey and Alabama, so I went to the local library and I said, 'Is there a cave-exploring club here?' And they said, 'Yes, there's a meeting tonight.' I went to the meeting, and a few of the people spoke some English. At that point I didn't speak any German at all, so I had instant friends. I spent all my free time until Jo Ann got there with Germans, not Americans.

"North of Nuremburg was Würzburg, the Franken wine area, where some of the families of the people in the cave-exploring club had inherited little strips of land. You could walk through a vineyard and there'd be stakes with markers on them. There'd be one here, one there—that was Harry's, Bill's, Bob's. I started looking around the countryside, and I suddenly realized it was incredibly beautiful. And I didn't understand why, because there were so many people. Statistically, I think there were ten times the number of people per square mile as in New Jersey. And so I began to ask the Germans I'd meet this question again and again. Why? Why is there beauty here? It was against everything I'd learned in my life. And one of the most frequent answers was, 'Well, why would you want to live where it's ugly?'

"Then one of my German friends who knew the brewmaster at the local brewery said, 'Would you like to work in the brewery for three days?' I said, 'Sure.' He said, 'Okay, well, he can't pay you.' I said, 'No, I don't expect to be paid, I don't know anything.' So for three days I worked in a brewery in the town of Fürth, north of Nuremburg, for a guy named Johann. I'd build a big wood fire, then work this big bellows with a crank. It heated tubes in the floor to toast the grain. The floor was so hot we had to walk around in rubber boots as we raked the grain with wooden rakes.

"And I would hear Johann rant—as I now rant about industrial wine—about keg-mixed beer. The real making of beer, he'd say, is selecting the grain in the field and then malting it. The last part is to take the malt, add water and yeast, and make beer. Almost all microbreweries in the United States buy the grain pre-malted from a few major factories in the world and then add water and yeast, and that's called local beer. To Johann, that was evil.

"So I decided to ask him the question. 'Why is there beauty here?' And he said, 'I have the answer, and I want you to come home with me.' He lived in what's called the Strassendorf by geographers. All the farmers live along the road, with houses on each side, and the fields lay out behind them. Very different from the North American idea of every farmer living out in the middle of nowhere on his own field. So we're sitting there behind his house and he puts out our plates. And we're eating, and he's looking at me quizzically, and I'm wondering what's going through this guy's head. He wasn't that good in English, and I certainly wasn't very good in German yet.

"Then he says, 'Taste this. Do you understand?'

"And I said no. I didn't understand. So he pointed at each item on my plate and then to the field that it had grown in—the poles on the horizon with the hops, and the fields of barley for the beer, the fields of rye for the bread and the potatoes, the cabbage for the sauerkraut. And then he said—and it haunts me to this day—'If you cannot see where your food comes from, you are doomed to live in ugliness.'"

What a sentence to pronounce. The force of it feels inescapable. The truth it discloses—a relationship between culture and nature, between people and the land—feels piercing for all it implies about our situation in America.

Did Gerard understand immediately?

"It changed my life," he says, and then adds, with characteristic modesty, "But it took time to unfold. The ugliness part of it answered my questions. And being of a place, that came pretty quickly to me. It wasn't just the landscape that he was emphasizing, but cultural integrity. And none of that really registered."

An encounter with a Native Canadian not long afterward, when Gerard had finished a degree in geography on the GI Bill and had gone to the Pacific Northwest to do fieldwork, helped him finally grasp the idea of cultural integrity.

"When I worked in British Columbia," he explains, "we were doing surveys on wilderness perception in Strathcona Provincial Park. I spent days alone in the woods watching people through binoculars. When I would come down out of the woods, I'd eat at a logging camp. One of the guys who worked in the mess hall and would sometimes be having coffee while I was eating there was a Native Canadian. One day he says to me, 'Oh, so you're out in the woods, and you're learning about this valley.' He said, 'I've never left this valley. Everything that I eat comes out of this valley. Everybody that I'm related to, all of my family, is buried in this valley. When I eat, I eat the people and the place. I'm made out of Vancouver Island. But look at what you're eating.' I said, 'Yeah?' and he said, 'You're made out of tin cans. Because that's what you eat out of.'

"He was teasing me in a good-natured way, but I thought about it and he was right. We use the phrase 'We are what we eat,' but I also think we are *where* we eat. That's the thing that people miss. This need to be of a place, to be of a community. So to have someone say that to you—and to be of a place—was very powerful."

Soon after this, Gerard and Jo Ann chose to begin a life where they could support themselves by working with their hands. Gerard says, "I began to take my vacations in other countries where I'd work for people. I was really lucky to run into a guy named Reiner Eschenbruch, a German who was the head of wine research in New Zealand. I sent my son down to work with him. And then he came up here to work with us. We've been back and forth many times. He made connections for me in Germany and in New Zealand, in Australia and California. And I worked for two little wineries in southern England he led me to and learned that way.

"I decided that I wanted to grow grapes in the coolest possible place where grapes would ripen, because I wanted wine that was fragrant and delicate and intricate. That meant either western Oregon or western Washington. So I came here in 1977 and bought land and started planting grapes. This was the first vineyard. Then about sixteen, seventeen years ago, Akio sold me the twenty acres up at Day Road."

"How do you plant a vineyard?" I ask.

The land Gerard and Jo Ann bought in Winslow was a former strawberry field grown over with alders. "You come home from your day job," Gerard says, "climb a tree, attach a rope, winch it to the ground, then dig around the roots to unearth it. When the land has been cleared, you plant the slips." They had six slips, to be exact, which they got from an experimental vineyard in British Columbia. "Then you propagate from those."

We have sat for so long, talking, that we are both startled to realize we are late meeting Akio up at the farm. When we arrive, Akio is not there. A light rain begins to fall, and we take shelter under the overhang of Akio's new shed just as he drives through the gate. It takes several minutes to persuade him to move inside rather than get wet, and I realize that he is hoping that if we stay outside, the rain will make me go away. But Gerard prevails on him to go inside, and we do.

"I've got raspberries, pumpkins, and Christmas trees," Akio begins. "It's his raspberries," he adds, laughing, passing the conversation off to Gerard. "They're on his land."

"So Gerard's grapes grow on your land, and your raspberries grow on Gerard's land?" I ask.

"It's the closest thing to communism we've got around here," Gerard says. "And Akio's the closest thing to a relative I've got here."

"This was our original homestead," Akio says, beginning to

tell the story. "We cleared this. It was forty acres of forest." His family hired loggers to cut the trees, expecting to sell the wood, which belonged to them, to help start the farm. "They logged the whole place here and my dad never got one red penny. Not one red penny!" It's the only time Akio raises his voice. "My father never went to collect what they owed us. Who went there? I went there. A young guy, only fifteen years old. 'You going to pay your logging money?' No way. You know what I mean?" The wrong is still vivid, and with it the frustration of being the firstborn son, the first to learn English, and his parents' representative.

Akio and his brothers helped his father dynamite the stumps. "There were six of us. Strawberries, that's all we had. When I was small, we all worked on the farm. But when we left here, you know, just one brother came back." After the war, Akio's brother went to work for the post office. "Then I was the only one here," he says.

As the oldest, Akio was the first to go to an American school. "It was hard," he says. "Nobody taught me English. It was all Japanese at home. I did two years in the first grade, how do you like that? So I got a better education than anybody!"

"That must have been hard," I say. "You just had to sit there, not knowing what was going on."

"Well, that's just the way it was. It's not just me. How about you?" he says, turning to Gerard.

"Polish was my first language. My father came from Poland, and he had to learn English. But my mother was born here. So my mother made sure that I knew English by the time I went to school," Gerard replies.

Akio nods. "Sure, but my mother couldn't, she just knew Japanese. My folks, they raise six kids. You know what that cost? We didn't have any money. I lost my youngest brother. Nine years old. We never did find out what was wrong with him. There weren't any doctors who spoke Japanese on the island. There was no English in my house. It was really tough. You didn't have money, you didn't have enough food, you didn't have nothing. You know, you have no money, you couldn't do hardly anything. You know what I mean? What could you do? We couldn't buy anything. We just had to . . ." Akio stops, looks down, then finishes quietly. "We had some tough times."

The history of a friendship emerges as Gerard adds what Akio would never say. "I remember looking in some of the old sheds around here and seeing shovels worn completely down. And you know that you don't dig with a shovel when it's worn down to nothing unless you don't have any money. Because you can't dig with a shovel like that. You don't see people wear a shovel down anymore—it breaks before it wears out. So that's the kind of thing I think he means, that you couldn't even replace things you needed on a day-to-day basis, things that you needed to make a living. Like your brother being so sick that he couldn't go to the doctor," he adds. "That's a real story."

"Well, they should have taken him to the doctor, but they didn't," Akio says. "My mother took care of him. He went to school. He was in the third grade, I think. And my mother thought he was getting better. He wasn't getting better, he was getting quieter, and then he just died. You know what I mean. He didn't throw up or nothing, and she thought he was getting better, but he was getting worse."

He died in the house. Akio was with him. The Japanese community helped his family pay for the burial. "At that time, that was in the early thirties, everybody would donate. Port Blakely Cemetery is mostly Japanese. That's where he's buried."

How did they get by in the hard times?

"We went fishing a lot. We hunted, shot deer. My mother made bread." They kept a vegetable garden. "We would grow beans and corn. Mostly American stuff." No matter how poor they were, they kept the traditional feast days. "New Year's, that was the biggest. My mother would cook all that special Japanese food. Everybody did it." They built a *furo*, a wooden tub heated with a wood fire. It was not a luxury, like our hot tubs, but a traditional Japanese bath. "They all had it," Akio explains.

How were they treated when they took their berries to market, when they went to public school?

"We were looked down upon, that's for sure," Akio says. "You know what I mean. You know how they are in school. They'd bring your whole family in. 'Don't talk to Japs.' Behind your back. You don't have to tell me who said it, I knew them all."

His parents never spoke of the constant discrimination—the ethnic slurs, being cheated when they took their harvest to market.

As Akio speaks, his arms crossed, Betsey slips in and stands beside Gerard, facing Akio. I thank her inwardly for this show of solidarity—Akio might talk to me longer if another woman, a trusted friend, is here too.

"When the war started," Gerard explains, "certain families on the island said the Japanese couldn't be trusted. You know, till she died this one woman said, 'We had to put them in camps. It was for their own good.' That's why when we tried to get the grange going again, Akio said he knew he wouldn't join—he felt he wasn't welcome."

"It was Filipinos too, not just Japanese," Betsey adds. "Filipinos were discriminated against because they talked to Japanese. When the Japanese were interned, a lot of the Filipinos helped to maintain some of the farms. And they were shot at by white people. They were considered conspirators."

"Were you allowed to keep anything?" I ask.

"Keep?" Akio offers in reply.

"What became of everything you left behind?"

"You know what happened. You don't have to ask that one." But I didn't know. "A lot of people lost the land. I mean, you had to give it away."

Though many Japanese families put their belongings in storage and had money in the bank, neither the government nor the Federal Reserve Bank guaranteed the safety or return of their property or their money. The Japanese community suffered unrecoverable losses of millions of dollars in homes, businesses, and life savings.

"There were one hundred thousand Japanese, wasn't it? There were at least ten thousand in the one I went to in California. And then I went to Idaho, and that was bigger yet. Then they had how many more beside that?"

Akio never uses the word *internment.* He never uses the name of the camps where 110,000 Americans of Japanese descent were held behind barbed wire for most of the war years. He just says "California" for Manzanar. After that, he adds simply, "We went to Idaho," meaning Minidoka.

Akio's cousins, B. D. Mukai and his family on Vashon Island, the biggest and wealthiest berry growers in the Puget Sound region, were warned ahead of time and relocated until the war was over and they could return.

"They had enough money, right? So you can go where you want to," Akio explains. He turns to Gerard. "Would you take a chance if you had no money, and go down to Moses Lake and try to farm, if you didn't have a penny?"

"No," Gerard answers. "Tell her about the radio," he adds. "The radio and the guns. The stories you told me. How they broke the radio..."

He has struck a nerve. They take turns speaking to me, piecing together the story.

In March 1942, a curfew and other restrictions were imposed on all Japanese Americans before they were removed from the restricted area, which included the western half of Washington, Oregon, and California. All Japanese Americans were forbidden to have in their possession firearms, war materials, and shortwave radio receivers or transmitters. The Suyematsus' hunting rifles, the dynamite they used to clear stumps from the fields, and their one luxury—a radio in a wooden cabinet—were all construed as violations of the new rules.

"People were angry," Gerard says. They knew the radio

couldn't be used to communicate with the enemy. "They wanted to break the radio up just to get even."

"They put it in the woodshed and took an ax to it," Akio says. "It was a real fancy wood radio."

Akio's family had had two guns, shotguns they used for hunting. "I had one real nice one," Akio says. "I never did get that one back."

"And one real junky one," Gerard breaks in. "He got the junky one back after the war, which he gave me. The nice one disappeared."

"What are you going to do?" Akio shrugs, looking at Gerard and then at me. "That's already bygones.

"I went to the camp," he says flatly of what happened next. "I didn't stay in camp that long. Then I went to Montana. I worked on a farm. Harvested that. Came home. Then I went to my cousin's. Worked for my cousin. And then they drafted me. You either volunteered or they were going to draft you. What are you going to do? I took the training for, you know, the 442."

The 442 was the all-Japanese-American regiment, the most decorated regiment in the history of the armed forces. When the ban on Nisei joining the American military was lifted during the war, many enlisted to demonstrate their loyalty. Some helped liberate Nazi death camps. Dorothea Lange and Ansel Adams recorded the scenes of Issei parents saying goodbye to their American-born sons in uniform or numbly receiving a folded flag when a son who'd left a camp to go to war was killed in action.

"I was on my furlough when we found out the war in Germany was over. And when I went to get on a boat, they put me on MP duty. So I ended up in the military police for two years in Germany. I got back in 1947. My dad came back here first. In '46. The place was a mess. And my brother, he couldn't be drafted, he had a heart problem. So they fixed it up pretty good.

"Actually, I'm not even supposed to be here. You know, a North Coast Electric man owned this. He said, 'If you still want to pay the interest, you can have the land.' I said, 'Sure, why not?'

I paid no interest, no principal, for how many years—two, four?" He turns to Gerard, who turns to me.

"This is why Akio's nice to other people, because here was a guy who was a millionaire who was a real gentleman. He could have taken the land back, but he chose not to. So when I bought land up here, Akio said to me, 'If you miss any payments because of you, I'm going to take it back, but if there's a depression or a recession and you can't make the payments, then I'm going to let you stay.' That's his way of paying back something that was done for him."

"He was a millionaire for sure, for sure," Akio adds. "But most rich people, you know how they are. They say, 'Get out!' He was a good guy."

Until ten years ago, when Akio had a massive heart attack, he lived on the land in complete independence. He recovered well, but he won't take his medicine. It's too expensive.

"He told me if I find him out in the field, I better not call the rescue squad," Gerard says, looking at Akio, challenging him. "He doesn't want anybody saving him."

"Well, what use is saving somebody for a zombie or something? You crazy?"

Dying on the land, dropping in his own field—that's part of Akio's independence. He knows Gerard will honor his request.

Though Akio wants this land to remain a farm, no matter what happens to him, the pressure of development and the tax burden it has brought to him pose a constant threat. "If you were in my shoes, would you want homes here?" he asks me.

Of course not, I say.

"Sure, I want open space," Akio says heatedly. "But you got no choice at the end. He's not going to have no choice either."

"Not unless the town does something," Gerard agrees. "I told them that if you drop dead out in the field, we're all out of here." Akio laughs. Gerard doesn't. "I mean, seriously, if he dies, unless a miracle happens, they're going to have to cut this place up to satisfy all of his heirs. And once there are houses here . . ."

He pauses, shaking his head, looking down. I look down too. In the silence, I can hear the rain on the metal roof as I study their feet, the worn workboots of three farmers whose lives depend on this land—Akio at seventy-nine, Gerard at sixty, Betsey at thirty-five.

"We're down to forty acres," Gerard says. "Once twenty of that's developed, then it doesn't make sense to keep the other twenty open anymore."

"Does it make you angry?" I ask. Akio answers first.

"Angry? Why? Well, what do you get out of it, huh? You don't get angry, do you?" he says, turning to Gerard.

Their gazes meet. "Sometimes," Gerard says, "but I try not to." Betsey and I are watching them, listening as they say aloud what goes unspoken most of the time.

"I get angry too, but you don't let it get you." There's a slight shift in Akio's tone as he responds both to his friend and to me. "I mean, don't let it get you. Sure, it's bygones, bygones. I been through this all my life, ever since I was a kid. You know, you've been stepped on all your life—what are you going to do?" Now Akio uncrosses his arms. He reaches out with both hands. "Are you going to stay on this side, where they step on you?" Akio gestures to his right, pushing down with the flat of both hands, as if shoving someone under water. Three of us grow still and listen carefully, our eyes following his hands as he speaks. "Or are you going to go over here?" he says. "You're gonna get on this side, aren't you?" He moves his open hands to the left, palms up. "I mean, over here you're farming, and nobody's stepping on you."

Gerard, moved, says quietly to me, "He's just staying away from the bad and going to the good."

"Everybody else just wants to make money. They want a big job and they don't want to work in the dirt," Akio says.

"Akio is happiest when he's driving a tractor," Betsey says, and the mood shifts.

"Yeah," Akio says. "I'd start at five o'clock. It was so peaceful, quiet. You know what I mean?"

"No one else is up," Betsey adds, "and you're alone, you have the quiet time. And the birds are out, and that's about it."

"It's all your own accomplishment," Akio says. "When you go out there and work, you accomplish something. When you work for a company, it's altogether different. You're just getting money."

Gerard and Betsey agree, warming to the subject.

"When you go to work in Seattle," Gerard says, "you work by a schedule. When you work here, you work by a task."

"You do what needs to be done," Betsey says.

"It's so different!" Gerard says. "Some days when you're picking berries, you're up at four, getting ready, because it's light by four-thirty, and you start picking. Sometimes I'm out pruning in the winter and it's raining and thirty-five degrees and I should be miserable. But I'm out there by myself, and I'm listening to Mozart on my Walkman, and all of a sudden the sun comes through and the Olympics come out for a moment. Or an eagle flies by. You don't get that when you work in an office in Seattle."

"I like pruning at the end of the day," Betsey says, "when the sun is setting and five hundred widgeons come in, sweep real low, and I hear the sound of their wings. You can't hear that when you're sitting in an office."

"But they're taking it away from us," Gerard says. They all nod. "You have to defend everything you do."

"You can't go out and start a tractor at five o'clock in the morning anymore," Akio says. "The neighbors would be bitching." He shakes his head, looks at the floor. Betsey and Gerard murmur agreement.

"It used to be enjoyable, farming. Now it isn't. Too many complaints. Everything you do, you get complaints. You pump the water, the guy is six hundred feet away and he's complaining. About little things. It's not enjoyable to farm anymore.

"That's enough!" he says, and it's final. "You should talk to my sister, she knows more, for sure. You can call her. She lives over there on Mercer Island, she'll talk to you."

Akio's sister, Eiko Shibayama, is so amazed that Akio has spoken with me and urged me to call her that she can't help exclaiming, "My closed-mouth brother spoke to you?" Then she laughs with amusement. She is the carrier of family history. She has even traveled to Japan to visit the towns her parents came from.

Yasuji Suyematsu came to America in 1904, when the big logging companies of the Pacific Northwest were recruiting cheap foreign labor. First he worked as a cook in a logging camp in Anchorage. When work brought him down to western Washington, he visited Bainbridge Island, where a Japanese community of berry farmers had established themselves beginning in the 1880s, and he decided to stay. Several years later he returned to Japan, where he married Mitsuo Tsuchida. Mitsuo was from the village of Kumamoto, on Kyushu, the southernmost and third largest island of Japan. In 1920 they sailed back to America, where they became strawberry growers. In 1928 they bought the forty acres at Day Road in Akio's name. They were not allowed to own land, so they put it in Akio's name when he was still a boy, since he was born in the United States.

Akio's sister remembers when her father and brothers cleared the land. They would make her go inside before they blasted, and she would crouch by the window, watching. Four Japanese families helped each other plant and harvest their fields. "The older ones would make the hole, and then we younger ones would drop the strawberry plant in and the parent would come behind us to fill in," she says.

She stopped eating the berries early on, and to this day does not enjoy them. There were just too many of them. When they harvested, they carried wooden trays divided into six compartments, and when they were full, they carried them up to the lean-to at the top of the fields, where her father inspected them. They had a truck for hauling the berries to town. All the berry growers were paid by the grade of their fruit. Often, Eiko says, the dealer would choose the worst flat and offer them a price on the entire harvest based on that one box. Farmers would complain to each other, but there wasn't much they could do—he was the only dealer on the island.

Every third year they had to put in new plants. "You only get three crops per planting," she says, and she laughs to remember how much she loved school because it meant not working in the fields. On weekends and during the summer, they all worked on the farm. Every summer, Native Canadians would come down to help with the harvest. They lived in cabins on the farm for six weeks every year. "We would have been lost without them," she says.

When Franklin Delano Roosevelt signed Executive Order 9066 in February 1942, authorizing the forced removal of all aliens to the internment camps, the first people forcibly removed from their homes were the Japanese Americans of Bainbridge Island. On March 23, notices with the heading "Instructions to All Japanese Living on Bainbridge Island" were posted. More than 70 percent of Japanese residents sent to the camps were American citizens whose constitutional rights were annulled with the first sentence of the instructions: "All Japanese persons, both alien and nonalien, will be evacuated from this area by twelve noon, Monday, March 30, 1942."

With the second sentence, the Nikkei who had lived on Bainbridge Island for three generations became virtual prisoners there: "No Japanese person will be permitted to leave or enter Bainbridge Island after 9:00 A.M., March 24, 1942, without obtaining special permission from the Civil Control Office established on this island near the ferryboat landing at the Anderson Dock Store in Winslow." They were given one business day, from 8 A.M. to 5 P.M. on Wednesday, March 25, to send a responsible family member for further instructions.

Eiko remembers that her parents remained calm. "That's the way the Issei were raised. It was a high priority to remain calm and keep things to themselves. I don't remember being very frightened until the fathers were being taken away." It's a chilling phrase, and she utters it calmly.

"I never saw my parents get excited, not even when my dad was taken away. Somebody came and got him—it had to be the FBI—because he had the dynamite"—for blasting stumps, Eiko reminds me, for clearing the land so they could plant the berries. "Then, when we got to the camp, he was returned to us. I remember the truck ride, but I don't remember walking down the ramp to the ferry. I remember being in Seattle and getting on the train. All the soldiers stood watching us. I noticed that all the shades on the train were pulled. It was getting toward evening. We were traveling at night." She pauses. "They were nice to us, the soldiers."

In photographs of the ferry ramps and train stations, the soldiers are dressed in battle gear, their rifles fitted with bayonets. The shades in the trains were drawn so that white people would not see the Japanese Americans inside and throw rocks at the windows.

Eiko remembers that they were allowed to take one suitcase—per person, she thinks—but she does not remember carrying anything herself. In photographs of the forced evacuation, huge piles of luggage, each with a ticket, are piled in great mounds, waiting to be loaded onto the trains.

Eiko remembers being taken from the train to Manzanar by truck. "I remember thinking, 'What kind of place is this?' There was hardly anything there. They were just building the barracks." The barracks were built of quarter-inch boards on a wooden frame covered with tarpaper. "We had only one big room with the cots. It wasn't quite ready, because I remember there was no insulation. When we had a sandstorm, it could come in. We had only blankets separating our beds. I remember the living quarters and the mess hall where we had to go eat." Each person had to carry his or her own plate and eating utensils, which they would clean at the communal sinks. For every 250 people there was a common mess hall, shower, and laundry.

There was no privacy. There was no running water in any of the barracks.

The Suyematsus were at Manzanar from April 1942 until February 1943, when they were transferred to Minidoka Relocation Center in Hunt, Idaho, joining other Nikkei from the Pacific Northwest.

Eiko's mother worked in the mess hall, and she can't remember what her father did. She remembers that they were calm through it all. "It seems like our parents just accepted it. But they were very happy that we could finally get out."

Unlike many, who never returned to their homes, Eiko's family went straight back to Bainbridge Island. "We had to start over," she says. "We had to cultivate the fields and plant again. We were having a hard time and we weren't able to pay the rent, but the owner said we could stay." His name was Harry Burns. "He was a true gentleman," Eiko says. "My parents hadn't been able to pay the mortgage or even the interest for years, with six hungry children to feed."

Harold Ickes, the secretary of the interior under FDR, referred to the evacuation as "the great uprooting." Ansel Adams wrote that "the human challenge of Manzanar will rise insistently over all America—and America cannot deny its tremendous implications."

Milton Eisenhower, Dwight's brother, resigned after serving for three months as director of the War Relocation Authority. In a letter to the man who replaced him, he wrote that he could not sleep and do the job. "How can such a tragedy have occurred in a democratic society that prides itself on individual rights and freedoms?" Eisenhower later wrote in his memoir. "... I have brooded about this whole episode on and off for the past three decades."

"It's bygones," Akio said.

"You know, it's odd what I don't remember," Eiko said.

One true gentleman, a millionaire, made it possible for the

family to stay on the land. He recognized the dignity of their labor and seems to have been moved to generosity by the injustice they had endured.

Last year Akio sold his portion of the farm to the city of Winslow, after securing an agreement that it would be preserved in perpetuity as open space. He will live on it until he dies, secure at last.

This year, when the property taxes came to twice Jo Ann and Gerard's annual income, the winery and the vineyard near the ferry were sold.

Up at Day Road, a new winery has been built. Gerard and Jo Ann are renovating the simple house where Gerard's mother still lives. Day Road Farm is now home to Akio, Betsey, the Bentryn family, and the winery. The blue barn that was the original winery is going to be moved to a new location, for use as a 4H center.

Once they'd emptied the barn and removed the winemaking equipment, Gerard went back to dig up the fragrance garden. He moved as many of the roses, trees, and shrubs as he could up to the new place. On one of the last days, working alone in the original vineyard, he found himself undoing the work he'd begun twenty-five years earlier, pulling out grapevines in order to recycle the posts. The vines could not be moved, he said, because they don't transplant well. "Like people, I guess, or people who are well rooted."

After some time, looking up from his work, Gerard told me, he saw that deer had come into the vineyard. He watched as they browsed nearby, eating the vines. They didn't even notice that he was there.

That was not the hardest moment.

Up at Day Road, Jo Ann and Gerard had a new winery built in accord with local ordinances. "They say that if you grow it, you can process and sell it from the same property," Gerard explained. But the new all-island government required them to make the agricultural building already under construction conform to requirements for a commercial building, which nearly doubled construction costs. Then, when the building was complete in time for the summer season, the city wouldn't let them open. They were told they couldn't sell retail on the property after all.

"That's when my heart stopped," Gerard said. He dropped to the cement floor in the barreling room. For a long moment, he had no pulse. Then his heart began to beat again. He very nearly died just as Web Townsend had.

A local newspaper reporter outlined the Bentryns' struggle with the city. Then a Seattle paper picked up the story. Next a local radio station, and soon after that a regional one, aired the story. People became indignant. The city, flooded with letters and phone calls, hired an attorney who specializes in land-use issues. He reviewed the case and informed city officials that they were wrong on several counts.

By the time the city gave the Bentryns permission to reopen the winery, they had been forced to remain closed for four months, missing Akio's raspberry harvest and so the chance to produce their elegant raspberry wine, a specialty that is an homage both to an enduring friendship and to the land these friends share.

Now Gerard and Jo Ann are working to develop a plan that will protect their portion of the farm as well so that it cannot be divided and sold to developers. Gerard has a vision of using the farm to teach people the deep meaning of what it means to be of a place.

He says, "Food, because it's the last thing we lose, because it's the thing that controls our lives—though we like to think it doesn't in modern life—is a key to finding the place we live in and finding the people around us. If we all eat from a place, if we all live in love with that place, then we all live in love with each other. What I'd like to do with the final part of my life is to figure out a way to bring people out to farms, give them a place to stay, go out and harvest the crops with them. Not a giant farm, but like what we have up at Day Road. Drive around with a horse-drawn wagon, give them a sense of the spirit of the thing. Pick some of the food, bring it back, prepare it together, eat it together, and then talk about it together. And talk about other cultures.

"I feel that the landscape of food, culture, and community are completely tied together, but in our society we've completely separated them. That's the issue I feel most strongly about—more than about being Polish, more than about being American, more than about wine. I just feel that we have to somehow get people to treasure that which is real, particularly in food, and I think a lot of other things will flow from that. When you really want to communicate, you sit down and have a meal, you eat together. It's spiritual.

"People know that what Betsey's doing, what I'm doing, what Akio's doing, what the young people who don't own land are doing, is somehow important to them, but they don't seem to understand how important until it's gone. They see it going, and they remember it—they grew up with it, and when it goes, they feel empty. They're not sure they're willing to pay for it, but they don't want it to go away. So that's what the meeting was about the night you first arrived. People will pay for schools, they'll pay for police, they'll pay for roads," Gerard says, "but *farms*? 'Maybe we should,' people say to themselves, 'but I don't know that I really want to do it.'

"My dream is not to just save Bainbridge Island but to save the beauty in the world by getting people to eat from where they live. That's my last mission in life."

4

REFUGE

The Khmer Growers

AMHERST, MASSACHUSETTS

"We came in 1982, early spring, still cold. And the trees—no leaves. We thought all the trees were dead. Then everything started to grow. It's like my life started when the trees, the leaves, and the flowers came out. And here I am, living and getting along with everything, growing with the flowers and the trees."

Sokhen Mao opens his arms wide, lifts his face to the sun, and laughs, a sweet and happy sound. He had seen so much death by the time he was eighteen that it's no wonder he thought it was possible that all the trees in America had died too.

Translator, teacher, and community organizer, Sokhen Mao is a bridge between Cambodian and American cultures. He spent the first eighteen years of his life in Cambodia. Since coming to America, he has lived near Amherst, Massachusetts, where his family has created the garden I have come to see.

Five minutes' drive from the Emily Dickinson homestead and the Lord Jeffery Inn, a group of rice farmers from Kampong Chhnang province in central Cambodia, refugees from a decade of civil war, genocide, and invasion, have translated a three-thousand-year-old farming tradition into the local idiom of a New England field. Two of Sokhen's aunts created the gardens, and they remain the backbone of the small group of gardeners known as the Khmer Growers of Western Massachusetts. In creating a garden for their community in exile, using public land they can never own, they give new meaning to the idea of the garden as refuge.

"This is Wentworth Conservation land," Sokhen says as he guides me up the path toward the garden. "Dog trails, people trails. A beautiful place."

It is cool under the leafy canopy of New England trees—oak, maple, hemlock, and pine. We've stopped halfway down a wide dirt track that passes through a late-summer tangle of wildflowers and bramble. Sokhen picks wild blackberries, then reaches toward me, palm up, offering me some. They're dark and sweet.

"The first Khmer family arrived in November 1981," he says. "Then, one by one, the local churches sponsored Cambodian families. Most of the families that came to Amherst were converted to Christian and are former farmers, rice farmers, as I am myself."

"You converted?" I ask him, not sure I understand.

"When we left Cambodia, which we call Kampuchea," he says, "we went to the refugee camps in Thailand controlled by the UN. There's a lot of missionaries. In order to come to the United States, you had to be sponsored by the churches. All of a sudden, as soon as you left your country, you become the Christian. You sort of go along with that, because you want to come to America." Sokhen has been baptized three times. "We don't care what we become. In the Thai border camps," he says, "we'd go to the Buddhist temple in the morning, offering the monks breakfast, then lunch, their last meal of the day, then we'd go to church. We did that here too, for a few years. Now we just go to Buddhist temple."

They did whatever it took to keep the family together, to get out alive.

"So, my whole life in the rice field. I work side by side with my aunts, my uncles, my cousins. In Cambodia, as soon as you big enough to pick up a hoe, a rake, you go along with the parents. If you cannot do the rice field, you take care of the oxen and water buffalo."

Was Sokhen's father was a farmer too?

"Well, he used to farm," he says, "but when the French came, they harass him so much he became a Buddhist monk. Then the French wanted to disrobe him, so he just became a soldier. In Cambodian culture, every family travel with the soldier. So when they fight, the children are in the foxhole while the husbands are loading up their gun and shooting. I live through wars all my life. I see death and skeletons. There were so many massacres. I'm in my foxhole, watching. Flares everywhere, shooting everywhere, the whole forest turn to gunfire, bombshell. We don't carry bodies. We use a tractor to bury them, because so many die. So it's a sad history for Cambodia," Sokhen says, slowing his walk, his voice slowing too.

"But the riches . . ." He begins again, brightening after a long pause. "Everything is so mountainous. You walk to the woods, all you could hear, just animal cry. You could hear monkeys, you could hear deer chasing each other. You could see elephants grazing tall grass. In the countryside, there's plenty to eat. You don't need to go to the market. You feed yourself. Lots of edible herbs and fruits and spices all over the forest. And I used to know them all, because I used to go there with my grandparents, my uncle, and my father too. And each house has mango trees all around the house, and jackfruit, at least five kinds, and papaya trees, banana trees, everywhere. Sometimes you just sit on the porch and use a hook on a long stick to pull on the fruit and just pick it right there, or you climb the tree. So that's why there was no starving in Cambodia before the wars."

Before the wars, rice and water shaped the land and the lives of the rural people of Cambodia, where *Khmer* (pronounced "k-my") signifies both the people of the majority ethnic group and their language. The Khmer have more than a hundred words for rice. In Khmer, *si bay,* "to eat," translated literally, means "to eat rice." For millennia before Pol Pot's Khmer Rouge seized control of the government in the 1970s, the cycles of daily life revolved around the growing seasons. In April, during the brief period between the late winter harvest and the seeding of nursery beds for replanting the fields, the Khmer traditionally celebrated their New Year. It was a time of feasting and celebration, when the world, and each individual, was washed clean. Having performed the rites of cleansing and renewing themselves, each household then carried the statue of the Buddha from its family altar down to the water and washed it too.

In addition to the rites each family observed, the whole nation awaited the traditional opening of the planting season. Every spring the king would come out into his garden and make a ceremonial pass over the land with a plow. Then everyone could begin planting. In Sokhen's time, it was Prince Sihanouk who performed the ritual opening of the land.

Even though there is no one in America to plow the "sacred furrow," it would not occur to the Khmer Growers to begin their planting season without performing the ancient rites of blessing the land. Before the growers planted for the first time, Sokhen explains, a holy man offered prayers and blessings. He asked the spirits from the past who dwelled there if they would please leave so the Khmer could carry the spirits of their own ancestors into the fields they were about to sow.

As we emerge from the woods, I catch my first glimpse of the garden—a huge, intricately patterned field, lush and exploding with life. Yellow and rust-colored heirloom sunflowers sway in the light breeze at the near corner of the field, and just beyond them sodden sneakers, shirts, and pants hang upside down on stakes to dry. Farther down the path that runs along the bottom of the garden, I see a field hut constructed from large branches, its roof a large blue tarp. "All this," Sokhen explains, "is done by two ladies."

We stand before hundred-foot rows of yellow, red, green, and orange chili peppers. Beyond these, trellises support what appear to be cucumbers and ripening melons unlike any I've ever seen. Long rows run east to west, short rows north to south, a mosaic of green. Here and there, swaths of white cloth—remay—cover long beds. An air of peace and plenty rises from the warm, wet earth.

As Sokhen leads me toward the field hut, I turn and see a figure in dark, loose clothes wetting down one of the long beds covered in white cloth. She wears a conical straw hat and stands quite still as she directs the spray from a garden hose over the thin white veil. All around her the beds of vegetables and herbs whose names I do not know, some lifting sprays of small white flowers above ruffled, deep green leaves, spread to the distant edge of the great field rimmed with trees. Above the trees, a raft of soft white cumulous clouds floats in a turquoise sky. Where am I?

The motionless figure in the distance summons countless images of the war in Southeast Asia. At Christmas 1972, midway through my last year of college just down the road from here, Richard Nixon, advised by Henry Kissinger, ordered the United States military to blanket the Cambodian countryside with bombs. The assault focused on villages, markets, and temples—on civilians—not just on the jungle at the border with Vietnam. A visceral memory of the fear and dread and sorrow of that time takes hold of me. Here in a town I once knew well, I find myself face-to-face with the survivors of the television war of my coming of age, the war that split apart the generations and racked our nation. I am shaken to realize that I feel as if I am in a foreign country, unable to speak the language and suddenly afraid.

Raucous teasing, abrupt calls in syllables I cannot understand, come to us on the wind. I see a thin woman dressed in a dark, long-sleeved shirt and baggy pants, her head wrapped in a dark red woolen scarf, move out of the hut toward the row she had evidently been weeding. A sturdy woman dressed in a black hooded L.A. Raiders sweatshirt and blue nylon pants calls after her. Then she turns and bends from the waist, as if still in the rice fields of home, and lifts two handfuls of freshly rinsed greens from a blue plastic kiddy pool at her feet. When they see us walking toward them, both women rise from their stooped postures and stare, impassive as we approach.

"Remember, we bow to show the elders respect when we meet them," Sokhen reminds me. As soon as we exchange bows and smiles, I begin to feel more at ease.

The two ladies, elders referred to as *Yeh,* are Sokhen's aunts, Prak Ky, the woman in the L.A. Raiders sweatshirt, and Prak Kom, who wears the red scarf. Their family name, Prak, precedes their first names. As Sokhen's mother's name is Prak Kann and his brothers, sisters-in-law, and cousin all use a variation on the name Mao, it takes me some time to learn who is who. They are all sweetly patient with my mistakes.

Sokhen introduces me, then speaks in Khmer with his aunts for a few minutes. He will show me the garden, he says, and then, when Prak Ky's daughter, Mao Danh, arrives from her job at the University of Massachusetts, he will leave me to visit with the women for a few hours.

Every available space inside the hut is crammed with burlap bags and brightly colored plastic tubs of purple, red, green, orange, and yellow chilies. Bunches of herbs lie nestled in boxes. I look up and see that the growers have tucked lengths of cord, plastic bags, clothespins, and feathers under the ropes that lash the blue plastic tarp to the limbs supporting it.

"This shed here?" Sokhen says, following my gaze. "Every child, man or woman, boy or girl, they have to learn to make this in the rice field. So you make this under a palm tree, and then you attach strings to the tree and tie cans to the string and then just sit under the shade when the sun becomes too hot at noontime. Then you can just pull the string and scare all the animals, elephants and things like that, away from the field." He leads me out of the shade into the heat as we talk.

"Elephants?"

"Oh, yes," he says, laughing. "Plenty of elephants. My uncle had two."

"What did he use them for?"

"My grandfather was an herbalist. We used a lot of elephants for hunting and at the same time for collecting herbs and spices from the forest. This is sweet basil," he adds as we pause by a plant, thrusting the leaves he has plucked toward my nose. "Smell it?"

Fresh lemon, without the bite. I pause to taste it while he keeps going.

One by one, Sokhen introduces me to every plant in the four-acre garden by name, scent, taste, folklore, and use. For him, the story of this garden is also the story of the beauty, and destruction, of Cambodia.

"In Cambodia, the countryside is so beautiful," he says wistfully. "Everything I do or walk or sing or dance, Cambodia is always in my mind. I look at the trees here, not my trees. I drive on the road, and it's not the road that I used to be on. I look at the sky, sometimes it's too gray. Cambodia, the sky is just white and blue. It's almost like you're looking at a canvas, a painting of a deep blue sky, it's so beautiful."

In moments here in the garden, Sokhen remembers the Cambodian landscape as if that lost world of peace and plenty might still exist somewhere. He slips easily from the past into the present tense, touching each plant tenderly as we pass. It is as if the middle period, the time of terror and suffering between his early childhood and the present, never occurred. In the garden, it is possible to make this return.

Sokhen pauses before a long, raised tier of trellises woven

from slender branches. It looks ceremonial. "These are yard-long beans," he says, once again an energetic and cheerful guide. "We usually grow at least ten beds, and each bed has two rows." Prak Ky and Prak Kom cut and wove all the branches to make the trellis.

"This is spiceall. It's ugly and disgusting. But what you do is cut it and dry it. Smell," he says, breaking a leaf and handing it to me. Gasoline. My head jerks back. Sokhen laughs.

"You only be able to eat it when it's dry and you pickle it. After you boil rice, you pour the hot rice water over the spiceall, then you put hot peppers and other ingredients, and you make into pickle. Then you eat it with smoked fish. The elders, the men, they love to sit under the tree drinking plum wine, eating smoked fish made with this." He tosses the spiceall leaf away.

"This is Thai basil," he says when we reach the next plant. It is his favorite among the five basil varieties they grow here. *Gee krahom* is dark green with an inverted purple V on each leaf. Beside it grows purple Vietnamese basil, and beside that fish-cheek basil, which tastes like a delicious blend of citrus and salt. Next come two rows of farm-crab basil. Its yellow-green leaves resemble oregano but give off a delicate scent and taste light and fresh. This is the basil in greatest demand in Asian markets, used for seasoning soup or fish. "You put that and Thai basil in your chicken soup and you're in heaven, baby," Sokhen says.

He sweeps by the large beds of frilled lettuce and past the small patches of pigweed and cilantro the gardeners grow just for themselves, then stops to pick a leaf of frog's-leg basil and hold it out for me to smell. "This garden is not only for Cambodians," he says, "but for Vietnamese, for Laos, and now the Americans start to be interested.

"These are sweet sticky pumpkins," he explains as we move on. "This has a harder shell. We'll let it stay like that until the plant dies. The longer it stay in the field, exposed to the sun, the harder and thicker the shell, so the longer we can preserve them, because in Cambodia there's no refrigerator, no freezer. We use the inside mixed with coconuts and sticky rice to make a nice dessert. Have you ever heard of Hippie Delight? In Cambodia, you mix everything in with this, you in heaven again."

Sokhen peels the outer stem off a section of pumpkin vine to show me how Cambodians prepare it for cooking. "If it gets too old, we do this," he says, pinching out a blossom's pistil and stamens. "The flower you put in at the end for color and smell." He holds it before me.

I lean into it, startled by its delicate fragrance. "Why don't we make perfume out of this?" I ask, holding the fleshy yellow flower to my nose.

Sokhen finds this wonderfully amusing, and I can hear him laughing as he sweeps me past three kinds of pumpkins that send their vines in profusion down the aisles of rich, dark mud. We step over them and come to the wax melons. The bean trellises are dwarfed by these sapling trunks and the intricate thatch the women have woven across the top to support the weight of the ripening fruit. The height and heft of the trellises will give the melons room to grow to their full length—three feet—and to curl in a wide graceful arc at the bottom. In Cambodia, these melons would be harvested three or four times a year. In New England, they can be harvested only once.

Winter melons share the trellises. They're fatter and shorter, fuzzy and deep green. In the next aisle Sokhen reaches out for something that looks like a warty, crenellated cucumber. Bitter melon, he says. "I hated these when I was a child. I'd cry when my mother sent me out to harvest them."

We keep moving, sweat glistening on our skin. Here and there in the garden we pass the women at work, weeding, watering, harvesting.

Sokhen tells me about the hard times in the first two years of the growers' use of the fields. Birdwatchers complained that the noise of the pump, which draws water from the adjacent pond for one hour in the morning and one in the late afternoon, frightened away all the birds. "They used to hear animals singing and talking, but now they hear water pumps, and they say it scare all the animals away and they cannot hear the animals anymore," he says.

Someone cut the growers' irrigation hoses, and then their pump was stolen. All the proceeds of the year's labor, four thousand dollars, went to replace it. It was stolen again. Sometimes local residents out walking on the conservation trails, angry over the growers' use of a few acres of conservation land for the gardens, let their dogs chase birds through the newly sown fields. In one season the growers had to replant their garden three times.

Gradually, they have been accepted. Within a few years of planting their first seeds, the growers easily produce enough to feed the 150 Khmer people in the area. They sell some of their organic produce to a local upscale grocery store and to Asian restaurants in town, but they take most of it to farmers' markets in Lowell and Springfield. With the money they raise from the sale of their produce, the growers have helped fund the two temples, or *wats,* for Khmer families in the area, Wat Kiry in Leverett and Wat Santivara in Pelham. They send money back to their native village, where five hundred American dollars will build a school and one hundred will pay for a clean well. Most precious of all, they have been able to help restore the village's Buddhist temple. As word of their generosity spread, the growers began to receive letters from eleven other villages. They try to help as many as they can. Their nonprofit organization also sends donations to Amherst's sister city in Nicaragua.

Walking slowly back toward the hut as we speak, we come upon a row of magnificent three-foot-tall plants with huge translucent leaves, each shaped like a heart and veined like a great river delta. "*Kbat,*" Sokhen says. "Arum. A cousin of the taro. You eat the stems, and then the root is for dessert. It's beautiful. In Cambodia we don't have plastic or paper bag to go shopping, so we use arum leaf. When you go to the store, if you buy rice, they just put it right in the center and wrap around. It's very flexible. Or sometime you want to cook fish, you roll it up in three layers, you bury it underground, make fire on top, and an hour later, there come the fish, and the skin just come off with it."

The taro does not flower. When a plant no longer reproduces in the wild, that is usually interpreted as a sign that it was domesticated long ago. The tie between this plant—now known as elephant ears—and Sokhen's ancestors probably reaches back thousands of years.

We have been making a wide loop back to the hut. Thirsty and hot, my shoes caked with mud, I am grateful when Sokhen reaches down, parts thick green leaves to pick what looks like a fine green apple growing from a knee-high leafy plant, and hands it to me. Its crown mottled as if a thin white glaze of sugar has been poured over it, the Asian cherry eggplant is a gorgeous, glistening orb on his open palm. Just as he moves to throw it away, I take it from him and bite into it. Its flesh is soft and pulpy. It tastes nothing like eggplant but is as sweet and refreshing as an actual apple.

Trailing just behind Sokhen, listening, thinking, I eat as he talks. "And here is the famous water grass," he says. Long, wide rows of bright green leaves. "It's like asparagus," he explains. "You cut it and it grow right back." Water grass is the growers' main crop; it sells fast, in great quantities, at Asian markets. The growers have timed the planting of each hundred-foot bed to provide them with a continual supply. In Cambodia, it would be grown in water, but because it would be invasive if grown in the pond beside the garden, they have learned to grow it in raised beds covered with remay to hold moisture and protect it from pests and the harsh sun.

We have stopped before Prak Kom, the woman whose head is wrapped in a dark red scarf. She works doubled over at the waist, pulling the long blade of her knife through the stalks with little rasping sounds, as if shaving a man's stiff beard, stopping just short of her bare toes. She appears agile and light as she takes hold of the stems and tosses them onto a neat pile beside her. She must stand, bend, and lift hundreds of times a day. When she first glances up at me, she looks forbiddingly stern. Then she smiles, squatting low to rest for a moment, her long knife loose in one hand. She looks young and confident, serene and at ease. I notice that there are deep scars at her wrists. Her hands are gnarled, the knuckles enlarged. There are livid scars around her ankles as well.

As a car rounds the corner of the field and stops beside the field hut, Sokhen looks up to greet his cousin. Mao Danh's arrival marks the end of our garden walk. Sokhen introduces us in English. We bow shyly to each other. Then Sokhen turns to say that in a few hours he will come back to take me up into the hills of Leverett to see the temple.

It's quiet in the cool of the hut, where I take a place on a plank inches above steaming July mud and learn to shuck water grass from the Khmer women working beside me. Mao Danh tells me how she and her family escaped from Cambodia in 1979.

"I left over from the dead," she begins. "We walk through the jungle. We almost to the Thai border. Everywhere people dead—children, man, woman, all dead. Then we see a line of Vietnamese soldier come out of the trees. I think, 'Oh, no, we going to die again.' My mother say, 'At least we die together.'"

What does it mean to be left over from the dead—"to die again"? Mao is as sure that her English is inadequate as I am that she is speaking in spontaneous poetry, language of such elastic inventiveness and compression that it startles me time and again. Hers is a consciousness that has registered the threat of random annihilation not once but many times. It is as if she is her own ghost and visits herself, full of disbelief for the life, or lives, she has passed through.

From 1970 until 1979, from the time she was eight until she was eighteen, Mao witnessed unspeakable atrocity and was threatened with death over and over again. For four years, from 1975, when Pol Pot came to power, until 1979, when the Vietnamese invaded, she lived outside, in a work camp, sleeping under a palm or a mango tree. "Never had a house to sleep," she says.

In their rural village of Trophong Chhnang, the five Prak sisters worked the family's farm, using oxen and water buffalo to tend the rice. "We use bamboo pole with two buckets to carry water," Mao explains. Their father had died young; their brothers had become Buddhist monks. They worked hard and lived simply, their lives revolving around the two centers of Cambodian culture, the extended family and the Buddhist temple. Then the wars began.

The family was driven from its village repeatedly, as it was captured, then liberated by warring factions. By the time Pol Pot and the Khmer Rouge seized control of Cambodia during the New Year's celebrations in April 1975, declaring "Year Zero," many in the Prak extended family had relocated to Phnom Penh. The Prak family was among the millions who were forcibly evacuated from the capital city in a matter of days—the largest mass exodus of an urban center in modern history. Many of their kin, most of them men, were executed. Those who survived were separated from one another, segregated by age and gender, and sent to work camps, where they endured years of forced labor, starvation, and terror. Many were tortured.

This was the era of the "killing fields," the reign of terror when the Khmer Rouge waged war on their own people. Anyone who had served in the military, as Sokhen's father had, or who was educated—and wearing glasses was enough to mark you as one of the educated—was captured, killed, and buried in shallow mass graves just outside each village.

Of Cambodia's fifty thousand Buddhist monks, only three thousand survived. Village temples that were not destroyed—their stones used to build roads—were systematically desecrated, used to store weapons or manure. Some were transformed into places of torture and death. A policy of enforced agrarian reform uprooted millions, both urban and rural, and within a few years devastated land that had been kept fertile for centuries. The population was pushed to the edge of starvation. Skilled rice farmers were forced to adopt disastrous irrigation policies. "With water we can have rice, with rice we can have everything," a slogan of the Khmer Rouge, accompanied the violent imposition of collectivized, intensive agriculture on people who had traditionally practiced small-scale, sustainable rice farming and fruit and vegetable gardening. Starving in fields of rice they cultivated at gunpoint, the Khmer were forbidden to eat anything they grew.

In 1979, the Vietnamese invaded. "I'm eighteen year old," Mao says. "Sokhen's younger than me. We run together through Thailand."

Thousands of Cambodians fled through the jungle. Many were forced back across the border, walking on paths sown with land mines. For every hundred who attempted to cross the Thai border, ten survived.

"We stay in Thailand for a year," Mao continues. She shows me how Thai villagers drew their fingers across their throats as the Khmer refugees passed by on the trucks that picked them up as they emerged from the jungle. As she makes this gesture, Prak Ky and Prak Kom, who have been chattering and laughing while clipping and bundling water grass, fall silent. Then only the sounds of birdsong and the humming of insects punctuate Mao's story.

For years each of the sisters thought the others were dead. Now they work side by side in the garden, except for Sokhen's mother, Prak Kann, who is partially paralyzed from the aftereffects of torture. It was she who reached America first. She worked as a chambermaid at the Lord Jeffery Inn for seven years, earning the money to pay someone to find news of her sisters. One by one, as they were located, Prak Kann used her savings to bring them to America to join her.

As Mao tells me her family's story, we sit before a mountain of bright green, working steadily. The slender and flexible stems of water grass branch into beautiful spearlike leaves four or five inches long. Mao shows me how to strip the lower leaves from a fat handful of the stems, separating out those that are too small or have yellowed. The Khmer women are dexterous; they work quickly, gracefully, every movement efficient and smooth.

First we sort the water grass into healthy bundles, then fasten them with rubber bands. Prak Ky takes the bundles I have lined up on the plank beside me and evens up the stems with a knife she sharpens on a rock beside her bare feet. I watch, amazed, as she holds the water grass on her thigh and slices through it. These women handle their field knives with unblinking confidence. When Prak Ky, Mao's mother, has a big enough pile ready, she stands, bends from the waist, and rinses bundle after bundle in the blue plastic kiddy pool beside her. Bunched, clipped, and washed, the beautiful greens are packed lightly into boxes and covered with damp cloths until they are taken to market.

A pot of soup simmers on a fire built among rocks just outside the hut. The smoke helps a little against the mosquitoes. I am in shorts and a sleeveless shirt, my braid pinned up, my skin slathered with bug repellent. Prak Ky and Prak Kom, who have been working in the fields since dawn and will work here until dark, are dressed in long-sleeved tops and long pants. Each has wrapped her head in an improvised version of the traditional *kroma*, the Khmer scarf that serves as baby sling, shawl, or grocery bag, as need arises. They work the fields in these heavy clothes, barefoot, using their sharp serrated knives for harvesting. They take turns picking the produce, then washing, sorting, trimming, and packing it for the market.

Every now and again Davi, a twelve-year-old girl whose black hair is pulled up in pigtails, rolls a wheelbarrow mounded high with freshly harvested grass to the edge of the hut. She unties her load, and we add it to our pile. She is the youngest of Mao's children, the first generation born in America, and she comes to work in the fields with her mother, her grandmother, and her great-aunts.

"My mom's mouth is sharp as a gun," Mao says. "Sharp as a power, you know? She gave me double life."

Mao calls me back to her story. Since I am not sure just what she is telling me, I simply listen.

"I forget nothing yet," she says next. Her narrative moves forward with what sounds like a memory—"Always hungry, always hungry"—but then it becomes the story of a dream. "Sometimes I dream of going to a rice field and stealing rice. I get caught. I wake up and I'm shaking. Sometimes it takes me a minute to know where I am." She pauses, then adds in a hushed voice, "Sometimes I dream I have to go back to my country and wait till my name come up again."

The story that frames these fragments suggests the powerful logic of traumatic memory, its creative force—a collage, associative, cumulative, full of fragments and elisions. This one ends in surprise.

Once a year the Khmer Rouge allowed family members to see one another, always under the fanatical guard of Angka, or CPK, the Communist party of Kampuchea. Mao Danh tells me a story from one year when she was reunited with her mother. "One time I go to steal the rice to feed the family. It was not ripe, so we put it on the fire. One girl got caught and they beat her. I heard the screaming." Prak Ky had made a fire between three stones to cook the rice. They heard the screaming of the girl who'd been caught nearby, but they could not see her. Then suddenly the screaming stopped. Prak Ky told Mao to hide the rice, so they stuffed it into the mosquito netting where they slept. In a moment the Khmer Rouge soldiers came to them where they sat on the ground. One asked Prak Ky at gunpoint if they had any rice, threatening to kill her if they did. "She invite them to go in," Mao says. Then, quoting her mother, she adds, "'If you find one grain, you kill me, no question.'" The soldiers left.

I can see it: a woman staring down a soldier, perhaps no older than one of her own sons, daring him to search them, knowing they would be killed if he did. Prak Ky's voice triumphs. They are saved. But Mao cannot forget the girl who got caught with rice they stole together; she was probably beaten to death. Though

Mao is safe in America and has been for twenty years now, she returns to this moment in her dreams over and over again, hearing the cries of the girl whose death she cannot forget. Random cruelty, arbitrary survival. It will not come to rest.

Mao's memory of the girl who died while she was spared finds a counterweight in the story of Prak Kom, the aunt, as Mao says, who came back from the dead—the slender woman whose ankles and wrists bear thick scars. She was captured with her husband, a soldier, in 1970. The family assumed she was dead, executed by the Khmer Rouge. Then one day in 1980, in the hospital tent in the UN border camp, they heard a woman call out Prak Kom's name to a skeletal patient curled up in the fetal position. When Prak Ky heard her sister's name, she drew near to study the emaciated face. Mao remembers the moment when her mother and the sister she hadn't seen for ten years recognized each other. How they wept. Then they made a plan.

"I steal her from the doctor," Mao says. Late one night they put Prak Kom in a borrowed baby stroller and snuck her into their tent. Mao became her nurse. "I remember changing her. My aunt smell. Ooh! Diarrhea, look like mucus coming out." Mao ate less so she could give her ration of food to her aunt. "I feed her, I give her a bath, I wash her clothes. She stink. It so hard to take care of her. If she die in the house, what are we gonna tell the Thai soldier?"

Mao remembers the night they had last seen her, when she was taken away. "They take her because her husband was a soldier—they lived at the base. The Khmer Rouge, they shoot that night. Look like I gonna die that night. Oh my God. A lot of people die that night."

Mao cannot tell me when or exactly where this was. Her memory and the story Prak Kom told her when they were reunited ten years later seem to have fused, forming a seamless present tense.

"They tie her, like a dog, you can see her hands—they used a chain. She got an infection. They tie her to a pole. They want to kill her. They killed her husband right away. The Khmer Rouge broke in. She saw him killed, ten feet from her. Couple months she kept prisoner. They ask her, 'Are you a farmer? Are you rich? Are you Vietnamese?' Anybody related to the Vietnamese they kill. My aunt and my mother look like Vietnamese. She say, 'I'm a farmer. I'm Cambodian. If you don't believe me, give me a rope and I'll make a cow leash.' And my aunt do everything real good and real fast. 'Okay, you're free,' they say, 'but don't go far. We watch over you.' They thought she was going to fight back. They pushed her to work hard, harder than other people. They treat her like a criminal. 'We don't have to torture you,' they say, 'you'll die anyway.'"

A trick with a rope woven by damaged and swollen hands, and a woman is unchained. At least in the fields she would not be alone. Prak Kom could do the work she knew, touching the earth, feeling the way it remembered her.

Prak Kom was lost to her family more than once. Before she could recover enough to travel, the family was offered the chance to come to the United States. They had to leave the Thai border camp without her, so they bribed someone to go to her later, giving them money to feed her and nurse her back to health so she could get her papers to leave. A year later they brought her to America to join them. "When she get off the plane to come here, and my mom, she see her all these years later, oh, how she cry. They just cry and cry and cry, they so happy," Mao says. "We eight people in my family," she adds, her head bent over her work. "We all get out alive."

In a book of maps showing genocide sites documented by the Cambodian Genocide Program at Yale, I find the Prak family's province. The legend reads: "Burials: 28. Mass Graves: 1,943. Prisons: 10. Memorials: 2."

Davi has begun to linger near the hut, so I ask Mao if it is all right if I go for a walk with her through the gardens. "Sure," she says.

As we both stand so that I can be properly introduced to Davi, Mao adds under her breath, "She born in America, she don't know nothing." I must look confused, because she clarifies. "My children grow up safe here. I work to send them to college. I no want them to clean toilets like me for the rest of their lives." She turns from me as she says it, her voice expressing bitterness for the first time. I hardly know what to say.

"Your work has dignity," I offer. There are so many others, so many immigrant and refugee gardeners I have met, who also clean our toilets and wash our dirty laundry, sweep our houses, clean our offices, mow our lawns. In their gardens, they work for pleasure. They are knowledgeable and skilled. In what they create, they see a reflection of their true worth, which may rarely be glimpsed by the uncomprehending.

Inside the hut, the others fall silent, sensing something in the air.

Davi is ready for our walk, so I thank Mao and follow her daughter out into the fields. She takes me to her favorite part of the garden, the rows of ripening baby corn.

"Do you think of yourself as Cambodian or American?" I ask her.

"Both," she says. "It depends." It depends on where she is, who she is with.

We are far from the hut now. Davi walks along the irrigation pipes, one bare foot before the other, using her outstretched arms to keep her balance.

I ask her if she has ever been to her family's village in Cambodia. No, she tells me, she doesn't want to go to Cambodia. First she says it's because they have snakes there and she hates snakes. But then she adds that the first time she tried to watch *The Killing Fields* she couldn't sit all the way through it. It made her cry, and she couldn't sleep for days. Then, when she realized that she needed to know how it had been for her family, she made herself watch it straight through to the end.

"That part where the guy sucks the animal's blood right

through its skin because he was so hungry?" Yes, I say, I remember that. "I realized how horrible it must have been for them then. I was afraid to ask them if they were ever so hungry that they had to do anything like that."

We're both quiet for a moment. All around us, food. The sound of birds. Peace.

When I ask Davi what she thinks of the garden her family has created here, she does not hesitate. "I think: they have done well. I think: they are very strong and brave. I am proud of them."

As we pick our way back through the rich mud of the fields, past rows of water grass ripening under the white remay held down by clumps of mud, we see Sokhen talking to two men sprawled under a white van just outside the hut. Davi's uncles are making some last-minute repairs so they can help load up tonight. At 4 A.M., Prak Ky and Davi will rise, eat, and drive east to sell their produce at the Lowell Asian market.

It is blessedly cool in the car as Sokhen takes me up into the hills of Leverett to see Wat Kiry, the Cambodian Buddhist temple the community has built. We park along a rutted dirt road and walk up a hill toward the temple. Along the way I notice piles of stones, some taller than others, some made with large stones, some with small, at the edge of the road. "Each stone is a prayer," Sokhen says, not pausing to look.

A path of wide, flat fieldstones with pine needles, princess pine, and ferns showing between them curves ahead and disappears into the trees.

"Where does that path go?" I ask.

"Nowhere. That's where the Buddhist nuns do walking meditation."

I feel as if they're here but I just can't see them—there is such lightness to the air, a sense of serene presence.

Inside Wat Kiry, Sokhen and I stand alone before the main altar, surrounded by a riot of color and the random collection of offerings, from grandfather clocks to vases of plastic flowers. Sokhen attempts to teach me how to distinguish among the many statues of the Buddha, each representing a distinct branch of Asian Buddhism. One small Buddha sits isolated on its own step.

"Is that one special?" I ask.

"That one is made from the ashes of a holy man."

As I stand before the altar, transfixed by the Buddha made of plaster mixed with human ashes, Sokhen walks out the back door and calls for me to follow him up a path through the woods. As he rushes ahead, I walk with my head down, as much to shield my face from twigs and branches as to try to absorb what I have seen. Just as I realize that I have lost track of Sokhen, light spills onto the path, which has ended at the verge of a green meadow. I look up and am blinded by the light of the midday sun reflected by a great white dome looming several stories above me, no more than twenty yards away. An enormous golden Buddha sits in serene meditation in a shallow niche set into the dome's outer wall. I am so stunned that I do not hear Sokhen calling to me until he has turned and come halfway back, gesturing wildly for me to follow him.

The Japanese Peace Pagoda stands by itself in a great clearing with a sweeping view across the valley. It was built, Sokhen tells me, by Japanese monks promoting the practice of nonviolence. We sit on a bench beside a small pond in a clearing below the vast white dome with its four golden Buddhas, each facing one of the cardinal directions. Behind us are the ruins of a burned-out Japanese temple. Wildflowers bloom from cracks in the crumbling steps. At the far edge of the woods opposite the pagoda I can see the arched frame of a new temple.

"People come with hammers, and skills, some days," Sokhen says. "Anyone who feels spiritual, wants to use their time to earn merits, they come."

Wind stirs the Tibetan prayer flags—yellow, green, red, white, and blue—strung between the trees around us. We can see fat golden carp in the pond. Frogs sun themselves on slabs of rock arranged to form widely spaced steps that appear to float on the surface of the water. We step from one to another to cross from the grassy meadow beneath the Peace Pagoda into the temple garden. Eight-foot-tall Tibetan marigolds sway in the breeze. Behind me is a cairn, stacks of white prayer leaves held down by rocks.

"At the rice fields, in the evening, or here," Sokhen muses, "it's really beautiful. The crickets, the frogs. In the evening, so quiet. The frog came out. The snake chasing the frog around the pond. Crickets came out. The birds. Everything. It's so beautiful. It's like you listen to music." He comes by himself often in the evenings.

As he turns to look at the water, sorrow draws near. Sokhen, who touches each green thing in the garden with knowing tenderness and can recount its names and uses, its place in his people's culture, chooses this serene place to tell me how beautiful Cambodia was in his childhood, how rich and full a life his family and his village once lived. "Let me start at the beginning," he says. "Cambodia would be compared to South America, or the Amazon, tropical. Beautiful. Rain, cold, and then hot. Three seasons. Rice growing three seasons, along with the weather. We grow with the monsoon season, so the rice taller. And the dry season, tends to be shorter. And then the cold, which is another shorter rice. When the leaves start to fall off, the evening cold. Late in the evening before they go home, they build fire, put rock inside the fire, then wrap towel around it, and you take it to your bed with you, to warm you up. Or if a house not too tall, like an elephant height, ten or fifteen feet, then you make a fire under the house and then you spread charcoal. There's no insulation, so in winter it's really difficult, but also enjoyable, because family members, friends, all sit around the fire telling ghost stories until midnight, when you go to sleep.

"Rice farming is really hard work in Cambodia. You get up at five o'clock in the morning. You had to work before the sun hit you. By eleven it is so hot that you have to put everything away and take a long rest for a couple of hours, then you go back again until seven o'clock in the evening. So by seven o'clock we round up all the animals, pack up, and leave the fields, back to the village. Then we make a fire for the animals, to keep the mosquitoes away, and all the animals that attack the livestock. And then we'd go back again after late dinner or supper, eight o'clock at least. You work again till eleven or twelve. So it's hard labor, rice farming, but these people feel connected. It doesn't matter how hard you work, because the thing that they used to touch, and the thing that they used to taste, and the thing that they walked through, then cooked by their own hand and sweat, they love it."

Quiet for a moment, Sokhen watches a frog leap from a rock into the water. When he turns back to face me, his narrative makes an abrupt leap. "Nineteen seventy-five," he says, "this is the last day. The Khmer Rouge turned Cambodia to communism, and then turned Cambodia to slavery. Culture stop," he says, slicing the air with one hand. "No more Buddhist, no more childhood, no more school. Everyone had to live under one roof, so that the leaders can watch you all the time. That's when the educated people, the soldier, and anyone who resist their movement were killed."

Dappled light spills through the trees, lighting his face as Sokhen recalls a night of chaos. "My whole family were about to be executed. They came to the house. They spare the young people. They know we educated. These people have to be destroyed because they city people, they have been corrupted, they been spoiled by the Western ideology. So that's when they took all of us and kill one by one. My family were in jail, and my mom was being tortured and my father was executed, and no one know what is happening."

The fragments do not cohere. Sokhen's narrative veers forward and back in time. They did not kill "all of us . . . one by one," because Sokhen is here now. As for Mao, so for Sokhen, it seems nearly impossible to sort *I* from *we* when speaking of the collective unit—"the fabric of this closeness," as Sokhen puts it —torn by the violence.

Above him, the prayer flags stir in the wind. I hear the plash and clunk of frogs disappearing into water. Then Sokhen says something about his brother's bones. Which brother? Surely not the two I have met, each with a lovely Cambodian wife and healthy children, each with a lovely garden around his American house. What bones? Until now Sokhen has never said he had a brother who died.

This brother was a doctor, so beloved by the whole village that they dared to send representatives to the executioners to beg for his body so they could give it a proper funeral. Sokhen describes the outpouring of grief, the chanting, weeping, and singing, as they burned his flower-laden body. It seems incredible, but somehow Sokhen and others found a way to perform this Buddhist ceremony. Later the family sifted the brother's bones from the ashes, divided them up, hid them in their clothes, and carried them out of the country when they fled through the jungle to Thailand. When they were finally able to leave the UN border camp for a relocation center in the Philippines, they had to figure out how to get the bones out of the country with them. One of Sokhen's brothers had married while in the camp and his wife had given birth to a child, so they hid their brother's ashes in a container of baby powder and carried them safely to America.

"After you cross the war-torn country," Sokhen says, his eyes meeting mine again, "and all the trouble, then you face a new war—is America, the new culture, the culture shock. The most culture shock is not the eating or behaving but is the language. A lot of the Cambodian elders cannot speak the language, and they feel depressed. Their skills, they had learned from their parents for years, those skills have been in Cambodia for thousands of years. Now they feel very paralyzed. They feel useless. The language that they use to speak with is no longer useful to them. The skills that they have learned from their parents, the things that they used to do, is no longer exist in America. And nothing else for them to do in America. In Cambodia they would be venerated for their wisdom."

The sorrow in Sokhen's voice reminds me that for every gain these immigrants make in America, there has been an attendant loss—of language, landscape, kin, and culture, the deepest meanings of home. You can be free and marooned at the same time.

"What they give up in Cambodia," Sokhen says, "it's a tragedy. Because now they have to give up even their own identity. They want to do something, to be creative or to be useful, maybe not to Americans but to themselves, while they have a few life left in America. So they start to grow their garden. And a lot of the Cambodians have their kitchen gardens. You can see at the different apartment complexes, each family has a few feet or so. These are the skills that they came with—their hands, their knees, their legs, this knowledge. So as soon as they put the seed on the ground and it grow, they feel special. Maybe they're not good at raising their children in America, but this is thing they wanted to show America and their children—this is the thing that they're good at. In Cambodia, they're good at building their own house, they're good at raising their children, they're good at farming, they're good at everything. But now, since they're no good, they feel so useless. This is the best skill that they will contribute to the society.

"The garden is their spiritual place. As soon as they start to see the thing grow, they feel so connected. They can be here all day long. They even ask people if they can build a house here, because they don't want to go to town, they don't want to see anyone, they just want to talk to their own garden. And that's how they want to do, these growers. I mean, they're not crazy. This is the thing that's so kind to them. It doesn't speak a foreign language. It speak their own language. Whatever they touch, it grows right out."

It is not only words that have the power to bind and connect, to shape the anarchic flow of human experience into a continuous narrative that begins to heal what has been torn apart by violence. There is also the silent and mysterious transaction of a hand burying a seed in the darkness of the earth.

It is the Year of the Iron Snake, and Sokhen has invited me to come to the Khmer New Year celebration in mid-April, the festival celebrating the time of rest after the rice harvest.

The first time I saw Wat Kiry, it was empty but for Sokhen and me as we stood before the altar while he explained the origin of each of the statues of the Buddha. Now not an inch of floor space is showing. Rugs have been spread for us all to sit around the altar. Cambodians from all over western Massachusetts have crowded into the room, many in fine clothes and jewelry. Squeezed in beside Sokhen, I can see whole families, young couples with small children held close. To the right of the main altar, a man speaking in Khmer is shouting into a microphone. A huge floodlight towers over him. Behind me, a Buddhist nun, all in white, leans forward, smiling, greeting friends. All around us everyone is talking. On the altar, the main Buddha has been draped in a glittering length of cloth. In addition to the array of large Buddhas that Sokhen showed me months ago stand countless little Buddhas, including one with an electric Day-Glo whirligig attached to its back, a psychedelic halo turning in dizzying spirals back and forth, back and forth.

Behind us the doors open. I feel a hand touch my leg. A woman to my right gestures that we must make room—the monks are coming. As I squeeze myself into an even smaller space, bare brown feet appear beneath the hems of saffron robes. I look up to see a monk reach back to take the hand of the monk behind him. Like schoolchildren asked to link up on a class trip, a string of grown men holding hands pick their way carefully through the parting crowd. Feet, robes, hands, the din, the lights—in a moment they have somehow reached the raised platform. Each monk sits beneath his own portrait. Some wear orange, some brown, some saffron. The monk whose robes brushed by me, the one led by the hand of a younger man in front of him, was, I now realize, the Venerable Maha Ghosananda, the father of Cambodian Buddhism. He sits quietly at one end of the dais, waiting patiently for the moment when they will all begin to eat.

I remember the story the abbot of the New Haven Zen Center told me about Samdech, as he is known. In the early 1980s, Maha Ghosananda came down from his temple in the mountains of Thailand to begin his peace walks. He stopped to plant a tree in every village of his homeland that had been deforested during the war, wrapping a swatch cut from a monk's robe around its slender trunk. Then, bowing with respect, he taught those who had survived the genocide and religious repression to revere the tree as they would a monk, for both were now quite scarce in their land, once richly fertile, where all the temples lay in ruins.

Today the men and women of the Khmer community lay a feast before their venerated monks, climbing the steps from the kitchen below with huge round trays bearing bowls of rice, soups, vegetable curries, noodles. They make their way without spilling anything, bending to rest their trays on the edge of the dais while they place the great array of dishes before each of the waiting monks.

In Cambodia, for these people to fill a monk's simple bowl with food harvested from their rice fields and vegetable gardens was to participate in an ancient tradition. Here in this modest temple tucked into the hills of Leverett, the ancient connection between food and the sacred is restored.

"Chaos!" Sokhen shouts in my ear, laughing. As I turn to face him, I see a young father dressed in a dark suit praying, his head bowed over his folded hands, his tiny boy in his lap. The boy catches one strand of the man's prayer beads with a small finger as he too, guided by his father's whispers, bows his head to pray.

Fragments of memory like bright fish rise from the depths of memory. I can see my Italian immigrant kin crowding into our house after a family baptism, first communion, or wedding, feel the emotional pitch, the din, the blend of sacred ritual and earthy irreverence. Hardworking people who kept their faces impassive, their inner lives veiled in the world of white people, they crowded together in church, dressed in their finest clothes, then afterward pulled their chairs in close around the family table, drinking coffee and eating pastry, the men in fine suits and fedoras with colorful feathers tucked into their satin hatbands, my great-aunt Mary in her finery, a cloud of perfume following her everywhere, together with the jangle of her big silver bracelets and the glitter of her earrings, necklaces, and rings. An ethnic enclave, a minority people at ease among their own, easing into their native dialect, gesturing with their hands, throwing their heads back to laugh. We too had once been part of a network of kin whose lives revolved around a sacred calendar. We celebrated every sacrament and feast day with a meal that recalled the old country, with recipes passed down through generations.

From feeling overwhelmed and outside, I have passed into a state of longing for my own people, and find myself comforted by this glimpse into another ethnic community's rituals of adaptation and self-preservation.

Once all the food has been laid out before the monks, they begin to eat. It seems impossible that anyone could consume such an enormous meal. The growers, I know, are happy to work in the kitchens and have been preparing traditional Khmer food for days. The years of starvation and forced labor under the brutal Khmer Rouge, the time of terror and torture and death, when it seemed their entire culture would be annihilated, find an answer here in the spectacle of plenty, the obvious joy in the faces of those who serve the food, the gathering of the remnant people, who will spend hours in the temple today, to cleanse themselves for a new year.

When the din has numbed our senses, Sokhen takes us out into the woods beyond the temple to show us where Maha Ghosananda and the other monks slept before the temple was built.

It is a long dank shed, with light showing between the boards, primitive kitchens, a bare earth floor. It seems impossible that the monks lived here through a New England winter.

Later, in a friend's backyard in rural Leverett, the assembled generations of Khmer friends bring food for a picnic. A successful son arrives from Lowell in his flashy car and is solicitous to his mother, Prak Ky, who is dressed in a stylish pale peach suit. Prak Kom sits down beside her, her thin frame enveloped in a clean white shirt and pants. I show them photos of the summer days I spent with them in the gardens, and they sit and pass them around, pointing and laughing at each other.

By late October, when I visit again, there have been several hard frosts in Amherst. The last of the melons, wax and winter, have been harvested. The sweet sticky pumpkins have been picked up. The withered vines and brown cornstalks have been pulled for composting. The beds are being prepared for winter.

The trellises have been dismantled and the hut is being taken down bit by bit. Winter is coming, and with it the sadness of having to move back inside. Then Prak Ky and Prak Kom feel their old hurts again: the diabetes that follows years of starvation; aching joints and racing heartbeats and headaches, the physical aftereffects of torture, starvation, and forced labor. Soon there will be long dark months when nightmares and flashbacks, the psychic legacy of extreme prolonged trauma, return to haunt them. With the move back indoors, away from the garden, the wide blue sky, the blooming flowers and singing birds, the long hours of hard but satisfying work in the sun, depression and a profound sense of uselessness threaten to return. Winter is when they feel most like refugees.

"What was it like to come to America?" I ask Mao.

She thinks for a long moment before she answers. "It's happy and sad together. Culture shock, like you come from nothing and you see more and more. I don't believe myself what I'm seeing.

I don't have much to bring—one pot, clothes. We hungry a lot, we don't have money. It's so easy here. If we stay here, we'd be strong as buffalo. I can't believe it, you know? I still can't believe it. What push me here? I never think, I never dream of a life here. I have electricity, lights, refrigerators, but I still crazy about language. At my age I don't want to go frontward anymore. It's okay if I just speak a little now. I don't want to put any more in my mind."

When I ask her what it's like to work in the garden with her family, she bows her head and says something so softly that I almost do not hear her.

"Heaven," she says. "We calls this place heaven."

5

MEMORY

Two Italian Gardeners from Mussolini's Italy

REDWOOD CITY, CALIFORNIA, AND LEVERETT, MASSACHUSETTS

Maska Pellegrini stands holding open the kitchen door. "Come in, come in," she says. "You must be tired. Are you hungry? Would you like some coffee and cookies? Sit down, please."

She is eighty-five, firm of step, with a wide, beautiful smile, clear blue eyes, and a quick, dry wit. Her white hair frames her face in soft waves as she looks me straight in the eye. Her handshake is warm and strong when I introduce myself.

I'd called to say I would be late. Though I lived only two towns away during the 1980s, I got lost in familiar territory, searching for Maska's street in Redwood City, a dense suburb twenty-five miles south of San Francisco on the peninsula between the Pacific Ocean and the bay. I was distracted, having driven up Route 280 from San Jose, where I'd visited my mother for her birthday. She had just turned eighty-six. She lived in a group home now, having succumbed to severe dementia. Though I would not know it for three months, the day I went to meet Maska would be the last day I ever saw my mother alive.

Each time I flew back to California in the aftermath of my mother's death, I would visit Maska and Mario Pellegrini. Maska is from the Veneto and Mario from Tuscany. Back east, between visits with the Pellegrinis, I began to meet with Tullio Inglese, an ecoarchitect in Leverett, Massachusetts, who had been raised as a shepherd in a remote village that faced one of the most imposing mountain ranges of the Apennines east of Rome, La Maiella. Meeting these Italian immigrants just as I was losing my mother, hearing stories of traditional rural life in Italy, of lives irrevocably changed by the politics and poverty that compelled them to leave, and hearing what it was like to come to America and become Americans was like encountering the ghost of my family's past. It gave the writing of these two stories an inescapable elegiac quality. My conversations with Maska, Mario, and Tullio became a kind of ritual of exchange. I would ask questions and listen; they would answer both my questions and my unspoken need to hear anything that might help me imagine my family's origins.

Maska Pellegrini is from the north; Tullio Inglese is from the south. Maska left Italy as Mussolini was consolidating his power, Tullio in the wake of his bloody and ignominious defeat. Maska's mother took the family to join her husband in California; Tullio and his father came to join his mother just outside Boston. Tullio's family, like mine, knew only their local dialect; Maska's family learned to speak high Italian. Both remember coming through Ellis Island.

To arrive in the United States was to become a stranger, to America and to themselves as people moving between nations and cultures. To garden was to become American on their own terms, a symbolic as well as a practical gesture. To garden was to keep alive parts of themselves that could not be known here, could not be experienced as present here in any other way. Their gardens represent distinct ways of embodying the memory of the Italian landscapes that shaped them.

Maska and Mario Pellegrini

As I close the gate behind me and walk toward Maska and Mario Pellegrini's house, the line of fat, blooming roses down one side of the driveway feels comforting and familiar. I grew up in a house surrounded by roses. On summer mornings when I was a girl, my mother would go out the back door in her nightgown, an old Easter basket on one arm, and walk the perimeter of our yard, cutting roses with her long-handled shears. Fat bouquets spilled petals of pink, white, lavender, yellow, flaming orange, or dark red onto the dining room tablecloth, filling the air around them with clouds of sweetness. On Friday nights she would send me outside with a dinner plate piled with fishbones to bury under the bushes, which were taller than I was. We inherited our roses when we bought the house, several miles inland from the old beach town where I'd grown up within walking distance of my Italian grandfather's house, and we let them go wild, sprawling over the fence, their canes growing fat, their bark thickening, and their thorns growing long and fierce.

Here at the Pellegrinis', the bushes have been pruned to hold their graceful vaselike shapes. Their green leaves shine, and the soil beneath them is dark and crumbly.

"Please, sit," Maska says as I enter her kitchen. "Then we will look at the garden."

You can't see the complex world that is Maska and Mario Pellegrini's garden from the road. Out front, a single redwood towers over the yard, where one mature orange tree and a crepe myrtle grow in a small area surrounded by hedges.

Maska puts a plate of homemade almond biscotti before me. The little metal percolator on the gas stove soon begins to pulse as the jet of water in the glass knob on top turns a dark, rich brown and the air fills with the aroma of freshly brewing coffee.

The smell of coffee stirs memories of other visits, other plates of sweets. On sunlit days when he came down to the shore in his three-piece suit to play the horses at Monmouth Park Race Track, my great-uncle, Giro Iannaconi the casket maker, would arrive from Jersey City, a feather in the satin band of his fedora, with a square white box of Italian pastry tied up in red and white string—canoli, pasticiotti, sfogliatelli. It was my job to put the coffee on and run to the door to greet him. My mother always put out her finest china—fragile cups with delicately curved handles, fine wide saucers, and cake plates, each with a single red rose at the center.

When Maska sits down across from me, she smiles then says my last name aloud softly. "What is that?" she asks.

"It's German," I say, explaining that my father was half German and half Welsh. His mother, Gwladys Thomas, came here from Wales as a girl in 1907. It was my mother's parents who came from Italy—from Caserta, near Naples.

"Ah, Caserta," Maska says, nodding as she puts a folded napkin beside my plate. Then she asks me mother's maiden name.

"Natale," I say.

"Natale. Oh, Christmas. Third generation, you are. Well, I'm glad that you feel the way you do, because it's quite important. Yes, it is. I know my daughter feels so much like that too—she's proud of being Italian. When I came over here, I was ashamed to be Italian," she says, pausing, "because . . . just being Italian, we weren't welcomed." How carefully she phrases it, like a guest who remembers being treated rudely. "It was the same way Mexicans are treated right now. That's the way we were treated. Everybody goes through the same feeling. It's the same struggle for all of us."

When Maska came to the United States, she was part of the largest migration from a single nation in modern history. To nativists eager to defend America's mythic Anglo-Saxon origins, the millions of southern and eastern European immigrants who arrived between the 1880s and the 1920s represented the threat of cultural dilution by "darker races."

"What was it like to come to America?" I ask.

"It's a sad thing...," Maska says, then pauses, unsure whether to begin with the moment of departure and loss or the moment of arrival and reunion. She draws a breath and starts again. "It's a great thing to come to America. But then to leave everybody behind..." She shakes her head, her voice dropping. "It was sad, very, very sad.

"We were brought in by my father. He came over in 1921 and settled in Los Gatos. My aunt was there, and his cousin. That's the way it was at that time—one called the other. He worked and worked and became a citizen. You had to be here five years to be able to call the family. We came in '27, all except my brother and my oldest sister. He had to serve in the military before he could come. My sister was in love and got married the day after we left. But she met us in Genoa, and we said goodbye there. It was a real sad parting. Real, real sad. Especially to leave my grandparents, because we knew we probably wouldn't see them again. And we never did.

"We came from Veneto," Maska says, "from Tolmezzo, about twenty miles from Austria and Yugoslavia, maybe a little bit more. We are on the triangle. It's a beautiful area, but at that time it was very poor. My father had to go abroad to work because there was no work in Italy at all. I think I saw my dad three times before I was seven." And then not again for six years. Coming to America meant the family could live together for the first time. "My mother had to work in the fields all the time, so it was my grandmother, Angela, my father's mother, who took care of us. She was Contardo, her maiden name. My grandfather was Valentino Pillinini. Those were the two who lived with us, so when we left them I felt that the whole world would just end."

Here is the immigrant's sorrowful knowledge—that worlds end, relationships cultivated over generations can be severed in a moment, and the place you know yourself by can vanish, as if it is leaving you, though you are the one who is going away. Does Maska remember leaving Italy?

"Just like now," Maska says with energy. "We took the train

to Genoa. We had never been to a city. Then we went to a hotel. It was right above the statue of Columbus. So we took the ship. It was in December. We had such bad weather. It was stormy, stormy, all the way through. We landed in New York, then came across with the train. In those days they had some kind of a... Oh, I'm sorry. What are they called—the people that ring the bells around Christmas?" she asks. "What are those?"

"The Salvation Army?" I offer.

"Yes, something like that. And then we got off in Chicago. Took another train. And there were all these Salvation Army people in their uniforms. Oh, they were great. They knew we were coming and they would wait for us every time the train stopped. They would pick us up and bring us to another train. We couldn't have done anything else without them. We would have probably gone to South America or something." We laugh together, Maska's laughter a trill of three sweet, high notes.

"I don't know if they still do it—do you think they still do that for immigrants?"

Her question fills me with sadness. "I don't think so, no."

"Anyway, we got here. The train came to Oakland."

"And was your dad there to meet you?"

"Oh, yes. I can still see my dad with his overcoat. I could see him in the corner, waiting for us. And it was just the most wonderful thing that I can ever remember, seeing him there. He still had the coat that he had taken from Italy. And he had a car, mind you, a Ford. And for us, you know, it was never mind—a wheelbarrow, fine—but not a car, okay? He took us all the way from Oakland to San Jose to Los Gatos.

"Papa had everything ready," Maska continues, seeing it all still with the eyes of a young girl. "He had rented a nice home for us. It was very comfortable, all furnished, with all the food ready, so we arrived and we ate. He even had friends there ready for us. We thought, 'My gosh, this is heaven!'" she says, opening her hands wide. America, the Promised Land.

"Yes," she says, sighing, "I think that was the best moment of my life, actually, yes. I was thirteen. It was the best birthday present I ever had. Thanks to my father. That he sacrificed six years, seven years, here by himself. Yes. Strong. Like all immigrants, you know?

"In Los Gatos we had a nice piece of land and we grew everything. We had a windmill too, for water. They even delayed the beginning of the school year so that children could go pick food in the farms. To help their families, you know. And now you don't see a farm anywhere in the Santa Clara Valley. It's terrible. It was so beautiful then. In the spring, when the fruit trees were in bloom, there would be so many blossoms, it looked like snow. There was no place like Los Gatos. It was America for us. You know, the real meaning of America. You go to America, you'll just be the happiest person. You'll have everything you want. And like they say, you just shake the dollars from the trees."

Maska laughs her beautiful high laugh and then says seriously, "But it's not true. No. My father was a *worker*. A mason. He was just so proud to have us here. He wanted us to speak Italian and also try to speak the English. In Italy we just spoke the dialect, which is like another language. It's got a little bit of everything in it. Mario used to get so angry when I'd speak it, because he couldn't understand. Wanting to be really American, my father wanted us to learn quick. We'd all sit at the table every night. They would make us study, my parents. He tried to teach my mother. He wanted her to be modern. But she couldn't at first, because she was shy. Up north, in the Veneto, we are very shy. Not like the Tuscani—they're quick. It was so hard for her. She didn't know the language, and she wore different clothes. You know, over there she used to wear these long skirts with the blouse tucked in at the waist. She'd worked hard in the fields. She got up to milk the cows at five, five-thirty, and then cleaned the stalls, brought up the manure in the wheelbarrow."

In six years Maska's father had adjusted to America. He had

become fluent in English and learned to drive a car. He dressed like an American and was used to handling American money. He had earned his citizenship. Now Maska's parents inhabited two different worlds. Her mother was still a rural peasant while her father had become a modern American. Hers was the old world and his the new.

"My mom was Maria Picottini. My dad was Pillinini—Giuseppe, of course," Maska says, laughing. "And now I'm Pellegrini—not too far," she adds, as if names are like countries and can share borders. "Almost the same, except with the *g* there."

"Your first name sounds Russian," I say.

"Yes, it is," she says. "My dad was quite a reader. And he picked it up from a book. *Across Siberia* was the title. Actually, maybe it was Masha, and he made it Italian, Masca. But I changed it with a *k*. To give it a little more zip," she says, laughing. Her son and daughter have Russian names, as well—Ivano and Sonia—chosen from the work of her favorite Russian writer, Tolstoy.

"You came in 1927." I've been waiting for the moment to ask. "Were you aware of the Sacco and Vanzetti case?"

"Yes," she says with great feeling. "From my father. Because he was so very much against them being executed."

As I tell Maska the story of Vanzetti's garden and how I came to it through a photograph of my mother taken on the last day of Sacco and Vanzetti's lives, August 22, 1927, she listens gravely.

"I'll show you a picture," she says, rising from the table to lead me into a study off the kitchen. A charcoal drawing several feet wide and high hangs on the wall, three vignettes drawn from photographs. One of her nephews drew it as a gift for her father. "This is my dad, all these three," she says. On the left a distinguished-looking man in shirtsleeves leans over a desk, wearing wire-rimmed spectacles, a book open before him. "He was quite an intellectual," Maska explains. "Up to third grade, that's all they went. The rest was just self-taught." Giuseppe Pillinini read everything—history, literature, politics, philosophy.

He read in Italian and in English. In the long years he spent working in Germany and Austria, he had learned about other cultures, had begun to pick up other languages. He knew what was happening in the larger world.

In the middle, he wears a topcoat and hat. A woman in a long coat, a soft hat, and good shoes stands close beside him, her arm drawn through his. "This is my mom. This was the day they left to go to Italy in 1949. They went back to see my sister. I made her the coat." They are prosperous Italian Americans now.

To the right her father appears again, this time in work clothes, leaning over a board spread across two sawhorses, a hammer in his hand. "These are his tools," Maska says, pointing to his workbelt and the bag near his feet. Work and the dignity of work define this family's heritage—and the belief that there is no necessary conflict between the life of the mind and working with one's hands.

At the center of the huge drawing, above the image of her parents preparing for their first return to Italy, loom the faces of two Italian immigrants who fought for the right to a just wage and decent working conditions for the working class—in America, the class that has always included millions of new immigrants—Nicolo Sacco, his gaze full of sorrow, and Bartolomeo Vanzetti, with his drooping mustache and eyes that blaze with defiance. The drawing captures one of the most famous photographs of the two condemned Italian anarchists: they are handcuffed together, dressed formally in dark suits, and seated on straight-backed wooden chairs. Just below their likenesses Maska's nephew has drawn another famous image from the summer of 1927, a group of protestors carrying placards that read SACCO AND VANZETTI MUST NOT DIE!

"That was a terrible time for immigrants," I say.

"Oh yes, it was," Maska agrees. "It showed right there," she says, pointing to the two prisoners staring back at us. "That didn't soften their hearts, didn't soften their minds, nothing."

Mario Pellegrini has come in the back door. He stands at the threshold of the kitchen and calls out teasingly, "Is this the lost lady?"

"Yes, this is the lost lady," Maska says in a tone meant to quiet him.

He comes to the doorway to the den. "What are you looking for?" he asks me gruffly, his eyes twinkling. He is a compact man with a shock of white hair. His baggy jeans are held up by wide suspenders.

"She remembers Sacco Vanzetti," Maska says quietly, their iconic names bound together as one, in the manner most Italian immigrants still speak of them.

Mario nods and says nothing, his face serious. In a moment we hear the kitchen door open and close as he goes back outside.

"You know, my father was an anarchist," Maska says. "Not a communist, because anarchists and communists didn't get along, you know. There was quite a group in Los Gatos. What was that paper that Papa used to get? *L'Adunata*—that's it. He read it every day. I remember one of the gentlemen and his wife, Aurora, who were the editors. I used to go to the opera with their daughter."

L'Adunata dei Refrattari, "Gathering of the Recalcitrants," was the longest-running newspaper of the Italian anarchist movement in America. It was published in New York from 1922 until 1971. *L'Adunata* published essays Vanzetti wrote in the Massachusetts jail where he learned English and kept up a voluminous correspondence with supporters from all over the world.

Maska's father had left Italy just as Mussolini was coming to power and arrived in America at the height of the Red Scare, in 1920, the year Sacco and Vanzetti were arrested and put on trial for murder. What must he have thought, reading the news from home, as Fascist Italy became a prison, watching as his adopted country offered up two Italian anarchists to the irrational fear that marks this period as a historic low point in the history of civil liberties in America.

Giuseppe Pillanini's years of working and waiting to bring his family over were the same years that Sacco and Vanzetti spent confined in separate prisons, when *L'Adunata* kept every detail of the case before its readers. Though America had not yet grown into its democratic ideals, there could be no going back to Italy, where by 1927 Mussolini had used every violent means necessary to become dictator. The family's only chance was in America, where Giuseppe encouraged them to learn high Italian, so they could read their country's great literature and pass on their culture, while they strove to become American by learning English as quickly as possible.

Very gently, Maska asks, turning to face me after a long moment of silence, "Would you like to see the garden now?"

Passing through the little wooden gate, I brush against a waist-high shrub covered with tiny blue flowers, forgetting the symbolic importance of thresholds until the pungent scent of the fine green needles makes me stop and turn. Can this be rosemary? I've never seen it grow so large. I pinch a sprig and sniff to be sure. The herb of memory and fidelity, rosemary has been prized for centuries for its power to heal and cleanse. Its presence reminds me that to be invited into a garden is to be ushered into a private world. It is best done quietly, with humility, and with all one's senses alert.

A long path three feet wide divides the garden in two lengthwise. Side paths separate the front from the back, with a grape arbor on the left and a toolshed midway down to the right. All the paths are lined with large, square stepping stones that Mario has made. He built the wooden forms and poured the cement, dying some the color of terra cotta, leaving others a soft grayish white. A neat square of dark earth alternates with each bright stone, the perfect balance drawing the eye through the garden.

With Maska leading, we walk the paths slowly, the only sounds our footsteps rustling the dry leaves, the birds calling, the light wind moving the tops of the redwoods and eucalyptus trees at the edges of the property. Rectangular beds for the annuals, all densely interplanted, are separated by the paths, so the space feels like many small gardens. "Mario gets my ground ready," Maska says. "And I seed." This is a collaborative garden, reflecting both Mario's tradition as a Tuscan and Maska's as a Venetian.

The first bed to the left of the path is for the herbs and greens and, just beyond them, the tomatoes. Beyond that, near the fence, the Pellegrinis have planted three kinds of figs. A tall ladder stands beside a tree hung with ripe fruit. At ninety-three, Mario still prunes, though they both do grafting. To the right of the central path, Mario has created a small grove of trees—a plum, a grafted apple tree full of green, red, and golden fruit, and a persimmon. Small bushes line the fence, sagging under the weight of cranberry beans. We pass a row of bright green Italian flat-leaf parsley beside a row of dark green Genovese basil, its sharply defined leaves contrasting with the ferny tops of carrots and *chioggia,* white radishes from Italy, and the upright stems of green onions.

"Swiss chard," Maska says, pointing. "Radicchio," she continues, stopping.

Radicchio? But this is a row of loose heads of green leaves that look like a hardy form of lettuce, perhaps romaine. Where is the tight little bundle of dark red leaves that resembles a small cabbage?

"We don't like the red one," Maska says with great firmness. "We are green radicchio people."

So few words to sum up a cultural heritage. She tears off a leaf and hands it to me. It's crisp, moist, and bitter. "Would you like some?" she asks. And she leans down to cut, then hands me the thick bunch of leaves.

Italian culture is defined by regions, each distinct for its dialect and cuisine. The Veneto is famous for its radicchio, a member of the chicory family, but for the red varieties, not the green ones that Maska loves. She grows two, with seeds brought from

Italy years ago—*Pan di Zucchero,* or 'Sugarloaf,' and *Zuccherina di Trieste,* 'Sugar of Trieste,' named for the cosmopolitan city on the eastern shore of the Adriatic, across from the Veneto. Trieste, as Maska calls it, pronouncing the soft final *e,* is her favorite. Its name suggests the mix of cultures that has influenced her native landscape, dialect, and foodways. Once food for poor folk, radicchio has become popular as an ingredient in fancy American salads only in the past few decades. In the Veneto it grows wild. Food is not about fashion for the Pellegrinis; it answers a hunger for continuity. Food is a form of deep memory. Through food they are linked to their native landscape, to its soil, its water, and its trees.

In the corner of a nearby bed, one radicchio plant has been allowed to bolt, and its white flowers are beginning to turn brown. Soon it will set seed. Here and there throughout the garden, a specimen of each herb and vegetable has been allowed to do the same. Ungainly, they tilt under the weight of ripening seeds, which Maska will not pick until they have dried in the pod. Which seeds, I ask, has she been saving longest?

"Oh, golly, let me see. It would be the bush beans. We just call them Italian beans, you know. I guess I've had those, let's see, sixty years, anyway."

Sixty years ago it was common to save seeds; they were a part of every harvest. Now people buy books to learn how—and why—it is crucial to preserve them. For Maska, it is a given, part of her culture. She thinks the first bush-bean seeds might have been her mother's, a gift when she married Mario nearly seventy years ago.

How many kinds of time are represented in this garden? There are fast greens that quickly replace leaves as they're cut, like radicchio and lettuce; then the indeterminate tomato plants, whose fruit ripens in succession; next, the slow root vegetables and legumes, which are harvested only once. Slower still are the vines—the kiwi, kumquat, and grape. And slowest of all are the fruit and nut trees, and then the redwoods, thriving in a crowded suburban neighborhood, reminders of California's vast natural abundance. All around us, the garden is filled with life in every stage of generation and decay—newly seeded beds, freshly sprouted seedlings, maturing tomatoes, peppers, and beans; the ripening fruit of apple and fig; the apricot and walnut trees picked bare; the browning pods of specimen plants chosen to bear a harvest for the longest stretch of time, seed time. How fixed in linear time the nongardener can feel! But here, as Maska and Mario work, the world is being born, ripening, and dying every day, and they are part of it.

We pause near a bed filled with rows of gorgeous peppers—green, yellow, and red—which glisten beside two rows of purple-black eggplants, one the slender Japanese variety, the other "just *round*," as Maska says. "You want to take some peppers?" she asks. "I should have brought a bag." As we stroll, she fills my arms with food.

Strawberries. Chinese onions and tarragon. Thyme. Chinese beans a foot long. Maska pauses to feel a drying pod, hoping for a good harvest of seed. Then cucumbers, for making sweet-and-sour pickles, which Maska will serve in winter with bolito, boiled chicken and beef. And of course "more radicchio," Maska says, "because we have radicchio almost every night."

Finocchio, green fennel, comes next. I pull the great feathery plume of its foliage through my hand, then press my open palm to my nose, savoring the sharp scent of licorice. Its fat white bulb shows just beneath the soil. "In my mother's dialect it's *fenuc,*" I say. "We ate it every Christmas."

"Oh, really?" Maska turns to me, looking pleased.

This garden, on this day, releases deeply buried memories in me. I think of my mother twenty miles down the road, parked in front of a television in her wheelchair. She would love it here. Just hearing Maska's voice as she speaks the names of things in Italian would give her pleasure. I remember how hungrily she listened when a new girl whose family had just arrived from Italy came to walk to school with me one morning. She greeted my mother with shy respect. When my mother heard the girl's accent, she said something to her in Neapolitan dialect and received an answer in Italian. "Oh!" my mother exclaimed. "You speak high Italian!" And then she begged the new girl to speak to her in *alto italiano*, literally "Italian of the north."

"These are the tools we've used all our lives," Maska says, drawing me back to the present as we pass the open door of the shed.

"This little hoe?" I ask. It leans against the wall, its wooden handle worn to a soft sheen.

"Oh, Mario made it." How casually she says it, as if there were nothing remarkable about this.

Behind the toolshed, a tall, slender-limbed kumquat bears its small, bright fruit, miniature oval oranges that glow against the cobalt sky. Beside it, a kiwi vine has woven itself through a trellis Mario attached to the back of the shed. In a long rectangular bed between the grove of fruit trees and the shed, pole beans have been trained up hand-cut branches that stand in four lines of twelve, long allées of bright green vines.

"And here, all volunteer tomatoes," Maska says. "Cherry tomatoes." They're growing around the bottom of a newly grafted tree—three kinds of peach on a plum scion. "Mario would say, 'Pull them up!'" she adds, pointing to the accidental tomatoes inside the hexagonal raised bed he has created for the young tree.

"But you can't bear to?" I ask.

"No." She shakes her head, smiling.

Maska grows at least nine kinds of tomatoes. Are any of them heirloom varieties? My question clangs like a cracked bell. This is no collector's garden, and even if her seeds are of a fine old pedigree, that's not what matters to her. To accommodate me, she muses her way through a list.

"Oh, let's see..." she begins. She knows two by their common names. There's *Cuor di Bue*,'Beef Heart,' as Maska calls it —her favorite. She likes it for its meatiness. It's a good tomato for sauce. Then there is the Roma, a full-sized red tomato for eating and also good for sauce. After these two come the rows of the anonymous: a large and a small variety of red cherry tomato and a sturdy plant whose beautiful yellow pear tomatoes hang like glowing lanterns. Next is one called simply "the Russian tomato," perhaps in honor of the family tradition of reading Russian novelists and giving children Russian names. The last three tomatoes are personal acquaintances: Dora, Joanna, and Harry, each named for the person who gave Maska the seeds.

When Maska and Mario have eaten as many tomatoes as they can and dispensed bags and baskets of them to kin, friends, and neighbors, the canning begins in the back room off the kitchen. Maska makes enough sauce to last all winter, of course, and more.

We are deep into the garden now. When I turn to look back over my shoulder through the leaf-dappled light, I can see tendrils of grapevines curled like fine wire around the slender trunks of trees Mario sank into the ground decades ago. The vines are festooned with clusters of pale green grapes, and further down, others that have turned a deep red.

"And these are boysenberries," Maska says, walking slowly on. "These I freeze. We don't make jam with the boysenberries. The children love them. We use them with crêpes." She means the great-grandchildren, the fourth generation to grow up in her garden.

Every fall Maska and Mario peel and slice apples and drizzle them with lemon juice before freezing them. They dry apricots and figs on screens, just the way they dry the mushrooms they bring back from Mount Shasta every autumn, a tradition of foraging that Maska brought from Italy. They cure forty to sixty quarts of olives a year. They make apricot jam and fig jam, and orange marmalade from the fruit of the tree out front.

We have reached the end of the path. On this end of the garden shed, Mario has placed an old sink under the downspout "to collect the rain," Maska explains. Nothing is wasted here—not light, not soil, not rain, food, time, or work.

Directly behind the shed are the compost bins. "Whatever I

have from the kitchen," Maska says, "I bring it down. We let it stay until the spring, and then we pass it through the screen and put it over there, so we'll have it ready." Composting is about patience; it's a way of participating in the earth's renewal of itself.

Across from the compost area is a stand of trees—an almond and several figs. This year the squirrels got most of the almonds. "But we don't mind," Maska says. "We share."

It's possible, standing here under a tall, widely branching fig tree laden with ripe fruit, to forget where I am. "Do you feel as if you're in Italy when you're back here?" I ask.

Maska's answer surprises me. It is neither yes nor no. "I am just in my own world," she says. "I love it. I'm happy. Out here, I'm in my glory. You know, sometimes I can't even sleep thinking of what I'm going to do the next day." She is radiant, speaking of her work. "I come down here, forget everything. Because everything seems great when you're touching the earth, you know. It's our life, you know. Do you want to see if we can find you a fig?" she asks, her voice soft and low. "There's one up there if you can reach. Pull the branch down. If it's soft, it's good."

The ripe fig comes away easily when I close my hand around it. I split it open and sink my teeth into its pink flesh.

Later, as Maska prepares dinner, I ask Mario to tell me his story of coming to America.

"My father came in 1904, by himself," he says. "He met my mother in Santa Cruz. She was from a village not too far from where my father was from, in Tuscany. Near Lucca. She was a waitress in an Italian restaurant over there at the port. They fell in love, they got married. They didn't speak any English at all. They were just off the boat. *Italiani.*"

Mario was born in Santa Cruz in 1908. "So we lived here until the First World War," he says. "Then right after the war, in 1920, we went back to Italy. Then when I was seventeen years old, I came back by myself. I came out here on account of Mussolini. Mussolini wanted to make a Fascist out of me, and I didn't want to become one. I'm saying, 'I'm going to America, what do I want to become a Fascist for?' So I got a beating. From one of my friends I went to school with. He was a blackshirt. So that put my arm in a sling for a couple of days.

"Before I left, I got him. I shouldn't have done it, but I did it. I was sitting on a chair in front of my father's house. We had a little place where people would all go out, sit at the bar, talk, you know, in the summertime. All at once come the same kid that helped knick my arm, and he tells my father, 'Why don't you go to America together?' And he knocked the hat off his head with a stick, you know, a baton? Jeez, my father never said nothing. I got up out of the chair I was sitting on and I went, *boom!* Like that." Mario makes a right hook in the air. "Right here, I cut him right through here," he says, stroking his jaw. "I was lucky, because the cousin of the leader of the Fascist group was right there with us and saw the whole thing, otherwise they would have burned my father's house and killed us all. Eight days later, I'm on the ship coming back to the United States. I said 'Goodbye! Now you can take Italy all for yourself!'

"I have a lot of stories about those Fascists, and I'm not even going to tell them to you, because I don't want to get you sick. Two brothers got killed because they were singing the communist anthem. They killed them right on the street."

"Italy went through a lot of dark times," Maska adds quietly. "It was like a religion," she says, remembering the schoolchildren in their little black uniforms. "They were indoctrinated very young, and once they were indoctrinated, well, that was it, that was the only way they would think. We never joined," she says, though she remembers how mesmerizing Mussolini's oratory could be, coming over the radio.

"I remember leaving very well," Mario says, finishing his story. "I can't forget it. Nineteen twenty-five, I left my town. I walked to Alto Pascio. My mother was the one who was hurt the most when I left. My brothers didn't give a hoot. They were just kids. My father took me to the train station. 'Good luck. Go shake the tree,' he said. You know, if you were leaving for America they used to say, 'Go shake the tree!'" Mario laughs hard, his eyes closing as he remembers the joke.

"So I came back to America by myself. I didn't have to stop at Ellis Island this time, because I was born a citizen. I had the citizen papers. I came right straight to California and I went to work. I went to school, night school, to learn English. Then I came down to Los Gatos, worked in the ranches. I did gardening, I did orchard work, I learned to prune trees. I would just go with somebody who would teach me what to do. I was a workman."

Work: the theme of their lives, the dignity of labor, the skill to fashion and use their own tools, the self-sufficiency of being able to provide for nearly all their own needs with their own hands.

As Mario and I set the table, he begins to recite aloud a little poem that begins "*La matina ascendo* . . ." His voice is soft now, musical. "In other words," he says, "when the sun comes up in the morning, it comes up to furnish us everything to eat." Homage to the sun—a poem to food. How Italian. Is this an old Tuscan saying, or did Mario write it himself?

"Sometimes when I'm sitting down, I think of something," he says. "I get up and write it out. I'm a crazy guy."

He hands me his notebook, and I read the next piece aloud. "'The clock of life is wound just once, and no man has the power to tell just when the hands will stop . . . on what day, or what hour. Now is the only time you have. So live it with a will. Don't wait until tomorrow, the hands may then be still.'"

"Crazy, isn't it? But that's the way I feel. When I want to express something, I just write the way I feel."

"Mario, are you getting ready to die?" I ask.

"He's been getting ready to die for twenty years," Maska puts in before he can answer. She's in high spirits.

"I got news for you, when you get to my age . . . I can't go fishing, I can't go hunting, I can't do this and I can't do that. What the hell am I doing here?"

"You're taking care of the garden," Maska says firmly. "That's the main thing."

"Yeah, that's what I'm doing."

Maska laughs at him, long and hard. "Oh, you're just too funny, Mario."

"Maybe we should just put you in the compost heap, Mario," I say. "What do you think?"

"That would be good too," Mario says, enjoying the tease.

"Forget it," Maska says, her voice now firm. "When it comes, it comes, that's all."

"Well, we got to talk about it before we go. We've got to say something," Mario says, an edge to his voice.

Maska gets up to finish cooking. The water has come to a rolling boil, and now she lowers into it the gnocchi she rolled and scored by hand in preparation for my visit, a traditional northern Italian dish. She will serve the gnocchi with fresh pesto, asparagus, home-cured olives, and a big salad from the garden. The only thing on the table the Pellegrinis haven't prepared themselves is the wine.

We take our places. "Okay, *buon appetito!*" Maska says, and we lift our glasses.

"She drinks plainly what comes out of the sky—water," Mario recites, inspired, nodding to Maska. "Patricia, my time is up! My lifeline is going now, so let's have a drink!" With great ceremony, he clinks his glass against mine. "*Salute!*"

"*Salute!*" Maska says, lifting her glass of water to ours filled with wine.

Tullio Inglese

Tullio Inglese and I stand on the roof of his newly built house looking down over the garden. Below us lies a landscape defined by rocks.

"Leverett is a very stony place," he explains, "so much so that we may have to import soil to fill the gardens. Every time I mention that to somebody in Italy, they can't believe it. They never moved, you know, from one village to the other. But when they did move, what did they take with them? They took the soil from their garden. They actually put the soil in baskets and carts and took it to the next place. Because soil, which most people think is this sort of neutral substance that's magically there, isn't, you know—you build it up over the years."

It's an arresting image, carrying the earth with you as you go. Tullio offers it casually, as if it didn't have the power to shift our understanding of what it means to live in relation to the land, to restore to the garden its primal place in human culture and to the gardener the role of culture-bearer.

This house in a clearing in the woods of western Massachusetts, Tullio tells me, was designed to harvest rain as well as sunlight. A water chain directs rainwater from the roof down through a narrow bed of rocks into a large oval garden pool surrounded by stones harvested from the site. As Tullio and his crew moved the earth to construct the house and as Tullio prepared the ground for the trees, the greenhouse, and the gardens, he kept finding what looked like river rocks. Those rocks now line the bed he has prepared for the rainwater flowing into the pond.

"This used to be part of the Connecticut River," he explains. Thousands of years ago, when Lake Hitchcock formed behind a glacier and then released its tremendous force as the glacier carved out the valley below, pieces of jagged ledge broke off and were polished by the rushing water. Here and there in the landscape, Tullio has placed one of the smooth oval rocks on or near a rough slab of ledge. The effect is subtle and pleasing, a mysterious source of tension in the fine balance struck between the cultivated portions of the landscape and the acres of undisturbed woodland just beyond it.

Below us, where Tullio has selectively thinned the trees, the terraced hillside draws the eye downward, toward a sweeping view of the Pioneer Valley. Two asymmetrical stone paths, one leading away from each of the glass doors that open onto a slatted wooden walkway, converge halfway across the grass of the first terrace, leading to the terrace below. Along the stone pathways and in the small triangular swaths of ground between them, Tullio's wife, Judith, an artist well known for her ceramic murals, has begun to put in a perennial garden filled with flowers and herbs. Just beyond her flower garden, Tullio has laid the foundation for a sunken greenhouse, which he has surrounded on its eastern and southern sides with a large vegetable garden already full of ripening tomatoes, eggplants, lettuce, basil, parsley, peppers, and onions.

"All the landscaping is edible," he says as he points out the pear, plum, and apple trees, slender saplings with delicate leaves. These small and hopeful presences will fill the courtyard with fragrance and the sound of bees when they flower next spring. Before the house was built, when the land had been cleared and the foundation poured, Tullio came up to the site and began planting fruit trees. "I would have kept planting," he says, "but the ground began to freeze."

At the far end of the main house, Tullio has built a trellis for a newly planted kiwi vine. He has put in long, straight rows of grapevines. There will be blueberries in the summer too, beyond the grapes, just below the first terrace, where Tullio has filled the spaces in the stone wall with soil so that ferns and wildflowers have begun to seed themselves. Growing among the sun-warmed rocks, they help prevent erosion by anchoring the wall to the hillside.

On the broad terrace below the house and its gardens, Tullio has created a fire pit. It was the first thing he built, he says, with great flat slabs of rock in a circle around it. I'm struck by Tullio's choice. When he began to alter the landscape for human use, it wasn't the framing of a dwelling that came first but the clearing of a place in the open for the primordial act of sitting together around a fire. Only later, when I learn about his boyhood as a shepherd in the mountains of Italy, will I understand what inspired this and so many other choices.

What kind of garden is this? What kind of house and landscape? What is remembered here, and what restored?

All his life, Tullio Inglese has carried with him, as if carrying the soil of his native ground, the story embodied in this landscape and this house.

"Remember," Tullio says, "I came to the U.S. from Italy when I was nine. I'm sixty-two now, so it was a while back."

We sit in the loft of the old Wesley Chapel, which he and Judith bought for $30,000 in 1977, when it was scheduled to be demolished to make room for a parking lot. Pools of green, yellow, and blue light form on the wooden floor while we talk, as sunlight passes through the beautiful old stained glass windows. Downstairs, outside the front door, hangs a flag bearing the image of the earth seen from space, a cloud-wrapped blue, green, and white sphere floating in inky darkness. This is where Tullio's ecologically oriented architectural firm, Nacul, its name drawn from the words *nature* and *culture,* has its offices. It was here, leaning over his parchment, drawing by hand in meditative silence, that Tullio conceived his new house and, stone by stone and tree by tree, articulated changes in the landscape surrounding it. Only as he remembers his childhood as a shepherd in Italy and the shock of returning decades later does the act of transmutation that his new house and garden represent become clear.

"The chance for my parents to come happened when I was only two months old," he says, speaking of the difficult decision his family made in the hope of establishing their right to emigrate to America. "My mother came by herself, without me. My father was in the army. That just devastated her. She obviously didn't want to leave, but she thought if she didn't come, then we would never be able to come. Remember, these people are not educated and don't know what's going on in the world. So she did come. And she lived here by herself. Imagine how close Italian families are. So here's my mother coming by herself, leaving her parents behind. It was very, very hard for her. I don't think she ever got over it. I was in Italy, raised by my aunt and my grandmother. My uncles and father were all in the army. I didn't see my father until I was about eight years old."

It was 1938 when Tullio's mother sailed to America. Mussolini had been in power for sixteen years. Fascist Italy was engaged in endless wars meant to restore the nation to the glory of imperial Rome. Though Tullio grew up in a remote village, there was no escaping military service for his father. All the young men—shepherds and farmers—were conscripted and sent abroad.

"They didn't have a choice. If you're not educated, you don't have a perspective on life. You're basically a farmer, and if some authority comes and says to you, 'You go in the army,' you go in the army, period. If you didn't go, you went to jail, or something bad happened to you.

"I still have vivid, absolutely vivid memories. We had sheep. The sheep were rather precious. They were meat, they were wool, and they were even milk, for the cheese. Even I, as a very young boy, five, six years old, would be out grazing sheep in the mountains. Roccacaramanico was a very, very mountainous place—a gorgeous, gorgeous place. The village faced La Maiella. And Morrone was the mountain just behind us. My dog was a big white Maremma—a protective dog bred only in Abruzzi. He had a spiked collar in case he got in a fight with other big dogs or with the wolves that used to try to get the sheep. Beautiful dog. I remember him extremely well—Leone, Lion," Tullio says, growing thoughtful, his gaze distant as he remembers.

"There were times when we were grazing sheep higher on the mountains. You didn't go home that night, you stayed out. You could get under rocks to stay warm. They had tents. Not fancy tents, cloth tents they would set up. On a few occasions I would be left there alone. I believe they did it as a rite of passage. It was a scary, lonely experience. If I didn't have that dog sitting there . . ."

He does not finish the sentence. Tullio was six years old the first night he was left to tend the flock of sheep alone. Everything he wore—his shirt, his trousers, his shoes, and the blankets that kept him warm—had been made by hand by people he knew.

"I remember seeing the women spin the yarn and do their own weaving. They made all their own clothes. They made their own shoes. Very fancy shoes. There was nothing we didn't make. Remember, the town had no money. So you basically did everything yourself. There was a communal bakery, a communal mill. And you brought the grain to the mill, and they would grind it for you and you'd bring it home in a sack, the flour. When you made your bread, if you didn't have a baking oven, a masonry one, outside or inside your house, you'd bring it to a communal bakery. There was one in town. That's where women used to go and bake bread and visit and talk.

"Usually every family had at least one pig, which they slaughtered in the winter, since they had no refrigeration. Keeping the animal alive was the way that the meat was preserved until you needed it. So in winter, you ate some meat, but that was it—not much meat at all. But then we'd have a big feast. They may have dried some meat, used the rest for sausages. We grew fruits, vegetables, everything. I grew up knowing how to keep the soil."

When all the able-bodied men were called up, the women held the village together, gardening and farming, taking care of the cows and sheep. Tullio's aunt Bambina carried him out to the fields in a basket, just as Maska's sister Angelina had carried her, so the family was always together.

"I was always outside. There were cousins working with us too. The village was one big family. It really was. People sang when they worked outside—I remember the women working, hearing them singing." *"Chiesa nelle Alpi,"* Tullio says, "Church in the Alps," or *"Un Mazzolin di Fiori,"* "A Bunch of Flowers" —songs of broken hearts and lost love. "And then the women would bring food out there. Some men who didn't go in the army, older men, they'd be working in the fields too. At lunchtime, someone would come out with food—bread and cheese—and they'd all sit down.

"The potato fields were on the slopes of the mountains because they didn't use the best land for potatoes—potatoes can grow anywhere—so they'd dig them up with this tool with two points on it. We called it a zap, short for *zappore,* 'to work.' I have one in the barn. I can show it to you later. I remember that sound echoing over the valley. We were surrounded by mountains, so any sound was very apparent, you know. The soil was so old and worn, there was nothing left there. They'd have to distinguish rocks from potatoes. There were hardly any trees left there for the fire.

"You couldn't drive there," he says. "You can imagine how beautiful and quiet it must be. So here's this rather idyllic place. But we had no conveniences—no bathroom, no running water, no stove, no electricity, nothing. Then suddenly, one time, up the road are coming tanks." They heard the sound of metal against metal—a strange and foreign noise, as if all the villagers were striking the stony mountainside with their zaps at the same time. It was a German panzer unit arriving to occupy the village. "They were in the process of retreating from southern Italy back to Germany," Tullio explains, "right at the end of the war—I was around six or seven. They occupied the village for six months, during one whole winter.

"They hardly had any food, so you can't blame them, but they took all the livestock, butchered all the livestock. My grandmother hid a pig behind the woodpile in the barn. You'd look at the wood and think it was against the wall, but actually there was a space behind it. She had the pig back there. She'd have to take the wood down to go feed it. One time the Germans found it—they were in the barn, the pig made a sound. They butchered the pig. They made a big demonstration of it—butchered it in front of our house, actually. They took our milking goat. They took everything. They didn't understand that they should leave some animals so we could live, or for the future. They were desperate, really desperate. I don't have any bad feelings about it. It was a condition of the war. That's what it does to you.

"During the winter people still had beans, dried beans they'd hidden away, stashed, and dried corn. So they still had a few things. They actually ate some of their pets. The Germans took over some houses and a municipal building—there was only one in town. They took over the church. The municipal building became their headquarters. They set up barracks in there, bunks. I remember them well, even though I was very young. They were okay to children. I've always been afraid to ask how they were to the women. I didn't want to ask my aunt. I just didn't want to know. But I think some bad things could have happened.

"In the spring the Germans left. And then we heard that the war was over, that there was a treaty signed, that Germany and Japan had surrendered. And of course Italy was surrendering. I remember there was a big party one night, because it kept me up —they were shooting guns outside our window, celebrating, firing up in the air."

Sometime in 1946, Achille Inglese made his way back to Roccacaramanico. "My father finally came home when I was eight," Tullio remembers. "I was sleeping in the same room with my grandmother, in the same bed, and then I just remember suddenly there was a man sleeping in there as well, and they said that he was my father. But it didn't mean something specific to me."

Tullio had always been told that one day he would make the journey to America, where the mother he could not remember was waiting for him. So one year after his father returned from the war, he left the grandmother and aunt who had raised him. "Leaving the village was devastating," he says. "I was told we were going to be leaving soon, but it's not the way we leave now. We leave now knowing we'll see that person again, because you can fly anyplace now. Leaving then was knowing you would never see each other again, absolutely never. My grandfather died just previous to our leaving. My grandmother didn't want to come. Leaving her there, and my Aunt Bambina, and all my friends, knowing that I'd never see any of them again—and I didn't—that was really hard.

"And leaving my donkey! Your donkey is not just your donkey, you know, it's your pet. Bruno, he was quite a character. Stubborn guy, but nevertheless . . . And a dog is not just a dog, it's an animal that has protected you. It's the watchdog, tough. One time my father left a piece of rope in the field by accident, and Leone didn't come home for two days. My father decided that he must be still out in the field, so he went there. And the dog was guarding the piece of rope, without eating or drinking. He figured my father would come back. Property was so precious. A piece of rope—you don't just go buy a piece of rope. Leone was a dedicated dog. He was willing to die for you. He never came into the house. Then, the night before we left, he picked himself up from the barn. Now, the barn was not near the house, it was on the other side of the village, on the outskirts. So Leone walked to the house and was sitting at the door and then came inside for the first time. And nobody knew how he figured out that we were leaving. When my father saw him there, he just started bawling.

"So it was just my father and me when we left. My father told me, 'We're going to take a truck, go to Naples, take a ship, and go see Mama in America.' We just walked a ways down the mountain till the truck could come for us, and then we got on the truck. There were no vehicles in the village. Not even a bicycle, nothing. We brought very few belongings. Just one bag, not much. We had some cheese. It was in pretty tough shape by the time we ate it. Stored in warm places—it was full of maggots. I remember my father eating the cheese anyway. I couldn't touch it, but he said, 'Oh, maggots, that's too bad.' The truck took us right to the docks, where there was a *pensione*. We stayed overnight. Naples was my first city. I'd never seen so many people in one place, never been in a place that had a bathroom with a flushing toilet and running water.

"We took a boat, a U.S. Marine transport ship called the *Marine Shark*. I still remember it—a small boat carrying a battalion of Marines going back to Texas. They were all very tall. Up to then, I'd never seen an American, never heard an English or

American word spoken. Of course, we didn't understand English anyway, but trying to understand them—forget it. I'd never seen the ocean, or any water. Never been on a boat before. It was pretty traumatic. Of course we got seasick. We went out on the Mediterranean. I remember passing the Rock of Gibraltar. It's a very narrow strait, and you know that once you get beyond that point, that's it, you're out on the ocean. It was scary. My dad was consoling. He had been home only about a year. I'd never really known him before that. Tata, that's what I called him. That's our dialect."

Days later, when the boat came within sight of the Statue of Liberty, Tullio's father called him to the railing to see. For years Tullio had imagined America, but not like this. "Americans were blond, blue-eyed people dressed in flowing robes, which might have been lavender and blue and white," he says. "America was heaven, the same as heaven. But then, coming into New York and seeing smoke and chimneys was not in keeping with my vision at all. I told my father, 'This can't be the right place. It's not white. This place is smoky and dirty and dark.' And my father said, 'What did you think—did you think you were going to paradise or something?' I still remember that," he says, laughing. "I said, 'Yeah, I thought I was.'

"My mother was there to meet us. I remember that clearly, seeing her there, in that place at Ellis Island where you wait to go and be greeted by your family, and my father saying as we approached her, 'Now make sure you hug and kiss her and say 'Mama,' because that's your mother.' He had to convince me that I'd better be friendly and loving and call her that, which I couldn't do. For close to a year I called my mother Zia, which means 'aunt.' I don't think she liked that very much. The only person in America I really knew was my father.

"We stayed in New York for a few weeks, to acclimate, you know—just kind of be here." Then they moved to a town just outside Boston, an Italian enclave within easy reach of the North End. "It was a rather urban place, Cottage Street, right on the

Watertown-Cambridge line. We lived in a basement, literally. Not a basement apartment but a basement, we were so poor. It meant sleeping next to the furnace. Just a couple of tiny windows —those high basement windows. The sink was a utility sink, and that was it. We lived in one room. There was a blanket between my bed and my parents' bed, just hanging on a pipe. That's where we lived. A couple of years of that. Possibly three.

"There was a parking area outside the basement that wasn't being used. One day my father ripped up the asphalt with a pick and shovel. There was pretty good soil underneath, it turned out. He dug it up, and before you know it he had this incredible garden. It wasn't a big garden. He planted intensively, so he'd have one thing growing into another. I used to carry the water out to the garden in old tin cans. He had zucchini, a lot of tomatoes. All the lettuces. Radicchio. Basil, a lot of other herbs. And Romano beans, which you couldn't buy anywhere then. They're big, but you eat the entire bean. They're wide and flat. You take off the string, cut the ends slightly, and boil them to tenderize them. Then you can cook them in olive oil and garlic. They're great.

"He got his seeds from friends. They would go to each other's gardens and investigate and talk. If somebody's crop—say, lettuce—didn't do well, they'd give them some. There was a lot of exchange. That was a gift they could give to their neighbors. They never bought seeds. They didn't spend money on the garden. Otherwise, they thought they were defeating the whole purpose of a garden. There was a fellow up the street who had a slightly bigger garden who used to give away tomato seeds. And then after that, once my father got it going, he propagated his own tomatoes.

"Then we moved to another house in the same area, which was only slightly bigger. But it had a piece of land next to it, so he put in a slightly more substantial garden. He had a fig tree that he covered in the winter, and grapevines on an arbor." Each time they moved, Tullio's father would walk the yard, choosing the best place for a garden.

"He always made his own wine. He got the grape slips from other Italians in the neighborhood. So when they visited someone, what did they bring? In the summer, you bring a bag of vegetables. Other times, you bring a gallon of wine. Not just a little bottle, a whole gallon. He made three or four barrels of wine a year. Each barrel was about forty gallons. Of course they drank wine on a regular basis, but he would give wine away. I'd always help him. We never bought wine, not until the last ten or twelve years. He made his own wine press, he and a friend, with recycled parts from the place where they worked. I still have it. I carried it with me every time I moved. When my father gave me that, it wasn't an easy thing, because it meant he wasn't going to make wine the next year, and I knew why. My mother was not doing well. That was 1987."

Tullio's parents both died in 1988, Virginia first, Achille soon after. "He gardened up until the very end," Tullio remembers. "He loved that garden."

In the summer of 1967, when Judith and Tullio were married, twenty years after he'd left Italy with his father, Tullio took Judith to see Roccacaramanico.

"I didn't realize it was going to be so traumatic to go back," he says. "My town was originally about eight hundred. When I went back, there were fourteen people, mostly older women who just didn't want to leave. Only a couple of the houses were left standing. My house was actually still there. And my aunt was still living there when I went back."

He remembers walking Judith through the town, up to the stone church, then through the cemetery, where he found the graves of his grandfather and grandmother. The graveyard was untended, full of weeds and wildflowers, the stones broken and falling over, the wall around it caving in. Tullio showed Judith what was left of his house, with its fine stone arches and the openings beside the front door where the baking ovens had been.

And then he tried to find the barn, but there was nothing left but a stone arch. "My barn was down, disappeared."

Tullio's eyes pool with tears, his voice breaks, and he cannot speak. "I don't want to remember," he says. "It's hard to say why, you know. It was such a horrible experience. You remember a place that was vital, alive with people, and then suddenly it isn't there anymore. The barn is where I used to play. It's where all the animals are. Our second barn was on the lower part of our house, which was on a hill. We brought the animals in there in the winter. You could just go down and take care of them, feed them. The village was at a high elevation, so there used to be several feet of snow. So it was hard to get around."

Between nature and culture, the barn is one of the few structures we as a species have ever created that acknowledges how dependent we are on other creatures. Maybe that's why the barn is so powerful, because finally it's not simply for our own use.

"I thought maybe I remembered the place as beautiful because I was a kid," Tullio says. "But going back when I was older, I was astounded by the beauty. La Maiella is a six-thousand-foot mountain with beautiful formations. And then there are other mountains around the village, and the fields, the vineyards and orchards. It's breathtaking. I've never seen anything as beautiful. The land is so old. And then, knowing what silence is. Do you know what silence is? No," Tullio says gently, answering for me. "They all did. And they knew what they were missing. You know, they would talk about the stars being so intense, as if there were more stars there than here, and why was that? Of course there weren't, but it seemed that way because we had darkness there."

No longer resisting the power of memory, Tullio slips from *they* to *we* as he remembers the silence. When he returns to using *they*, it allows him to honor his parents and to keep the hurt of his own loss at a distance.

"They knew they had left a very beautiful place, and they were hurt by it. At the same time, they knew they had to leave.

There was no way they could be there any longer... Most people in America don't understand what it means to endure such a loss," Tullio says after a moment, "because they've been so protected.

"Being in the U.S. was devastating for most of my parents' generation," he continues. "My father was a shepherd in the mountains and liked to be outside. He was uneducated, so he became a factory worker. He worked for Hood Rubber, which later became B. F. Goodrich. But making tires, working with rubber, was smelly, horrible. And he had another job doing masonry. He was a pretty good mason. He got out of his job in the evening and he'd go do somebody's porch steps or build a garage or a chimney or something. He worked weekends. He liked that work better. It was more gratifying, but it wasn't as secure. He dragged me along many times when I was a teenager. And that's how I got interested in building, actually, from him.

"What a life. He just worked all the time. They missed Italy. They were here, accepting America in terms of opportunities, but they also thought it was an intensely competitive place where it was very difficult to do anything of quality. You know, everything was quantity—working to make money to get a car. People got into this rat race that everybody else was in and they lost touch with nature and the beauty they had lived in.

"It's staggering, what that first generation did, the pioneers. I have great respect for them. All they gave up... they gave up their whole history. They disengaged one from the other, families, so my generation could be educated. What they did was very important, it was very good for us. And then what it makes possible for the generations of my children and grandchildren now. Had I stayed in our village in Italy, I would have been okay as a shepherd, but I wouldn't have known what I know now. I prize what I've gained in terms of my knowledge. My mother could just barely write, my father not at all. I used to educate my father, when I was going to school. I'd hold up a basketball and say, 'You know, the world looks like this, it's actually turning around, and every twenty-four hours is a day and then a night.' I would try to explain it all. He was totally skeptical. They just barely knew the world was round—barely. At the same time he really appreciated that I was enjoying the learning. He was very respectful. If anything, he would glorify my accomplishments to his friends. 'My son doesn't have to work anymore because he's an architect now,' he'd say."

Tullio laughs. "I didn't have to work, you know? My hands were clean. He'd tell people how I made drawings and carried them to the building site and watched while other people worked. But they were ambivalent, because they knew they would lose me to this culture, which they did. I pretty much disappeared from their lives. In a way, that liberation is what made me what I am today. Otherwise I would have been a mason or an auto mechanic, and I would have stayed in Watertown and been part of that culture. But instead I went to the University of Oklahoma, of all places, thousands of miles away. I went because some of Frank Lloyd Wright's disciples, people who worked with him, were teaching there. After that I just kept going, without coming home. I went to Arizona to work with Paolo Soleri. He was about twenty-five years older than me but came to this country from Italy the same year I did, right after the war."

Soleri became a mentor and friend. At Cosanti, Soleri's city in the desert, Tullio lived in Earth House, one of the dwellings called an arcology, a fusion of the aesthetic principles of modernist architecture and the science of ecology. "It was hard to leave," Tullio says, but the most important encounter of his life came soon after he came back east.

Hoping to earn a place at Louis Kahn's architecture firm, Tullio took a room in Philadelphia and volunteered in Kahn's office. As patient as he was persistent, he finally earned Kahn's attention. After studying the drawings Tullio had made during his apprenticeship with Soleri, Kahn said little. Then he surprised Tullio by asking him to look at his own new drawings. Even more astonishing, he asked Tullio what he thought of them. Afterward, Kahn took Tullio and Judith out for dinner. "You have some good drawings there," he said. There would be projects coming up that might include a place for Tullio, but not for two months.

Work with Kahn never materialized. Instead, Tullio began to shape an architecture informed by gardens and by the human scale of the handmade buildings of his native village. "Architecture must become an environmental science rooted in the fundamental principles of nature," he says. "Too many architects preach sustainability and can't grow vegetables or make a good soup or compost their kitchen waste." And they can't build what they design. "In all these years," he says, "I have never stopped being a decent carpenter. I think all architects should get away from their drafting boards and computers and become master builders again, as they were when the great cathedrals were built."

"What goes on inside of you when you're making a garden, Tullio?" I ask.

"I'm paying homage to my parents, very consciously, in the garden," he says without hesitation. "You know, our parents die, but they're always with us. They're in our consciousness. They come in a spooky way. I hear my father. Sometimes I sound just like him. Some of him is inside me. So I do it for that, of course. And it's therapeutic and meditative. I'm too restless to meditate. The closest I get is architecture. I will look at a drawing or a model for a long time, deciding whether or not to remove a wall. I'm not exactly without thought, but close. Gardening is like that. It can be meditative."

I think Tullio is going to talk about planting trees or growing tomatoes, harvesting his grapes, but no, it's weeds that come to mind.

"You know how it is to weed. When you're weeding, you're doing something for the benefit of the plant. It's a service, so it's going to be good for you. That's what I think.

"You know, for a long time I never realized it, but there are people who don't do gardening," Tullio says. "So what is it that makes us do it? Now there are fancy words for it. 'Sustainability,' being 'ecological,' recycling organic waste and having a compost pile. But you know, they just did it. It's important to know that. It's important to know how to cook, how to grow your own food. It's something I feel I have to do. I feel it's my destiny to do it. Maybe it comes from my roots, some instinct that I have. I've never analyzed it, and I've never discussed it as I'm doing now. I've just done it instinctively. It's always just been there. It was what you did."

In so many ways, the new place in Leverett is Tullio's homage to what has always just been there—Roccacaramanico. The flat roof celebrates height, the reward for climbing up being the contemplation of what lies below, a shift in perspective that restores a proper sense of scale, reminding us of our modest stature in a world that was not designed simply for our use. The house, like a mountain, lifts you up toward the night sky. And when you stand on the roof in the silence of the night, with the dark woods all around, the valley spread below, there is nothing to dim the light of the stars.

6

PEACE

A Punjabi Garden

FULLERTON, CALIFORNIA

"I told my father, 'I will be poorer in America, but my conscience will be free.'"

I write the words on a paper napkin and turn it to face her. "Is this right? Is this what you just said?"

"Yes. I did not come to America to trade my cultural heritage for money."

I take the napkin back and write the second sentence as well. Her words are so striking that I do not want to rely on memory alone to record them. Ruhan Kainth is telling me why she left Indira Gandhi's India in the late 1970s to come to the United States.

I first met Ruhan, a middle-school science teacher from Fullerton, California, and her husband, Atma, an engineer, in New Haven. They were visiting colleges on a crisp and shining day in early autumn, and they were looking for a place to take their youngest son, Hunar, to lunch. From Atma's turban and the steel bracelet on his right wrist, a *kara*, I knew that they were Sikhs. I tried to think where the nearest Indian restaurants were.

"My son would like some pizza," Ruhan said.

The handsome boy with dark, shining eyes, his thick black hair pulled up in a rishi knot, looked up and smiled.

I explained their options—Naples Pizza, just around the corner, or Pepe's or Sally's, across town in Wooster Square.

"We would prefer to walk," Ruhan said. "Would you join us?"

While Hunar enjoyed his pizza at Naples pizzeria, I asked Ruhan why she had come to America. She came for freedom of conscience, fleeing India during a period of intense political repression. And then I asked if she and Atma had a garden.

"Oh yes!" Ruhan said. "We have a beautiful garden. And I have a tree that is rarely grown outside of India. It is called the neem tree. In India, the neem is a sacred tree. There is a story to go with this tree," she added, leaning toward me. "The emperor Ashoka, whose name means 'without sorrow,' converted to Buddhism. He was India's first Buddhist emperor and led India on the path to nonviolence. He dedicated his life to promoting peace, prosperity, and health for all of his people. His edicts about how we should treat each other in every aspect of life were inscribed on stone pillars that were placed in every village. You can still see some of them in certain places. Among the things he recommended was that every village should have a neem tree, first for shade from the intense heat, then for all of its wonderful healing properties. You must come and be our guest, and I will show you the garden, and you will see our neem tree."

Late the following summer I fly to Los Angeles to see Ruhan's Punjabi garden. After a long, slow drive from the airport, the van drops me in front of the Kainths' house at the end of a cul-de-sac in the sprawling suburb of Fullerton. Ruhan, slim and striking, her long black hair coiled in a chignon, comes out to greet me and introduces me to her two older sons, Koijan, a senior at Berkeley, and Daraspreet, a junior at Stanford. Both are members of the U.S. national field hockey team. When I arrive, they are unpacking new gear in preparation for an international competition. They step over the open boxes in the driveway, each extending a hand in greeting, then carry my bags into the house, where Ruhan offers me a glass of juice made from passion fruit and strawberries freshly picked that morning.

When we go out the back door a few moments later, the first thing I see, standing just beyond the terrace, is a pomegranate tree laden with huge dark red orbs. Native to southwestern Asia, the pomegranate is as familiar to Ruhan as an apple is to a New Englander. However extravagant the tree is in its beauty, though, it is by no means the most extraordinary citizen of this garden.

On less than one-quarter of an acre, Ruhan Kainth cultivates fifty-odd varieties of fruits, vegetables, and herbs. The thick canopies of the trees and the densely planted beds of herbs and flowers dampen the drone of traffic and block the view of neighboring houses.

"For years, nothing would grow here," Ruhan says. "The soil was dead."

I turn to her in disbelief. Later, when I peer over the fences that divide one yard from another, I see why. On one side, a perfectly weedless lawn mowed to uniform height rolls from the house to a row of dark green shrubs lined up in strict symmetry against a stockade fence. Decades of use of lawn chemicals to maintain the iconic suburban American landscape have destroyed the structure of the soil here. What little grew when the Kainth family moved in relied entirely on chemical fertilizers and pesticides.

To bring the soil back to life, Ruhan began to plant tiny trees, which was all she could afford. As the trees' roots threaded their way downward, they loosened the soil and slowly began to add organic matter. "Then the earth around them would begin coming to life again," she explains.

Until she came to America, Ruhan had never been able to make her own garden. How, then, did she know to plant trees?

In India, her family, members of an educated and prosperous elite, lived in Delhi, where they had a beautiful formal garden. They also owned a farm in the country two hours' drive away, where sharecroppers worked the orchard and grew sugarcane. As a girl Ruhan would go to the village with her father, walking through the fields chewing cane, sucking out the sugar, then throwing the husks on the compost pile. She drank freshly made jaggery from the press worked by oxen; the juice was boiled in a great caldron to produce a crystallized brown sugar akin to maple sugar candy.

When Ruhan's father became the private physician of the prime minister of Nigeria, which took him abroad for long periods, he put her in charge of supervising the farm, an unusual role for a woman. Her brothers were at Eton and Harrow in England, so the task fell to her. "Once a month I'd go out to the farm," she says. "They all welcomed me, but they'd be very amused, because they were not used to seeing a woman coming to do that. But they were very respectful." Even the fact that she drove there by herself made her remarkable.

As she learned to manage the farm, Ruhan studied the methods of the peasants who worked there. From watching them she learned the principle of returning everything organic to the soil. "Nothing goes to waste in those Indian villages," she says. The lesson has stayed with her. As has something else. "Those were times of great peace," she says, her voice soft as she remembers. On the farm, Ruhan stepped beyond the constraints of her caste, class, and gender.

At home in Delhi, the family garden was full of roses, fruit trees, and flowers. Peacocks roamed the grounds freely. Though she longed to work in the garden, Ruhan was expected to do no more than stroll and admire. She was not supposed to work with the soil. "We had a full-time gardener who would come to work in the evening. During the day he worked as the supervisor of the

Rashtrapati Bhavan, which had once been the residence of the British viceroy Lord Mountbatten." He became Ruhan's mentor. "He would treat me like the little granddaughter. I would follow him around the garden, asking him how to do things. 'Could you show me how you graft the roses?' I would ask. 'Little baby,' he would say, 'do you want to see this?' And he would show me. I can still see myself standing there. He would say, 'See, baby? See how you do this?' I learned so much from him. He would say wise things. Once we saw a mother being very angry and harsh in her discipline. So he said, speaking very gently to me in Hindi, 'A child is just like a plant. Just as a gardener might tie the branches to make it lean a certain way, the mother is like the gardener, and the child the plant. She directs her child.'"

Ruhan knew this man only as Mali, which means "gardener" in Hindi. He and his wife, who worked with him, were elderly. While he clipped, pruned, weeded, and grafted, his wife would carry the waste to the compost heap. Each evening, when their work was finished, they would take home some of the branches for firewood.

"He was of a caste who did not have the opportunity to go to British schools," Ruhan explains. "He rarely came in the house. And when he did, he would not sit down."

If he remained conscious of the expectations of caste indoors, she felt the strict limits of her gender and class in the garden. "I would go pick up the spade and maybe plant a seed or something, but nobody would ever see me digging." Yet she longed to. It was not considered appropriate for her to mingle with gardeners. As a female, she was not supposed to do such dirty work.

"Was there any other way to learn what I wanted to know?" she asks. "No—only from gardeners, only from the laborers."

Sir Albert Howard, the most famous advocate of soil restoration in India, learned how to grow things in the same way, upsetting British imperial presumptions about what constitutes knowledge.

In two of his most famous works, *An Agricultural Testament* (1940) and *The Soil and Health* (1947), he describes his education on the land among the rural poor of colonial India. A contemporary of Aldo Leopold's, he published one of the twentieth century's most important books on the relationship between agriculture and human culture two years before Leopold's classic work, *A Sand County Almanac,* appeared in America.

Trained at the Royal College of Science in London and at St. John's College, Cambridge, Howard was appointed mycologist and agricultural lecturer in the Imperial Department of Agriculture for the West Indies in 1899. From 1899 to 1902 he worked on plantations in Barbados, a former center of the English slave trade, where he studied fungal diseases of plantation cash crops, including sugar. "In Barbados I was a laboratory hermit," he wrote in the introduction to *The Soil and Health,* "a specialist of specialists, intent on learning more and more about less and less." It was "contact with the land" and the people who worked the land that showed him the fundamental weakness in the hierarchical organization of academic agricultural studies. "I was an investigator of plant diseases, but I had myself no crops on which I could try out the remedies I advocated: I could not take my own advice before offering it to other people." When he was offered the post of economic botanist at the Agricultural Research Institute in Pusa, India, in May 1905, Howard readily accepted. Having worked in labs far too long, he was eager to have land of his own to experiment on.

The chasm between science in the lab and practice in the field led Howard out the door and into the fields of India's peasant farmers, whose crops, he observed, proved remarkably resistant to pests and disease. Yet the farmers were illiterate, had no access to advanced technology, had received no scientific training, and never used chemical fertilizers, pesticides, or fungicides. Though they were poor by every standard of modern industrialized cultures, their soil, their crops, and their animals enjoyed robust health. How was this possible? What were they doing that made their agriculture so productive?

"I found," Howard wrote, "I could do no better than watch the operations of the peasants . . . and regard them and the pests . . . as my best instructors."

Though he had grown up on a farm in England and had received the finest education Britain could offer, it took Howard years to become as proficient a farmer as the rural poor of India. "At the end of five years' tuition under my new professors," he wrote, ". . . the attacks of insects and fungi on all crops whose root systems suited the local soil conditions became negligible. By 1910 I had learnt how to grow healthy crops, practically free from disease, without the slightest help from mycologists, entomologists, bacteriologists, agricultural chemists, statisticians, clearing-houses of information, artificial manures, spraying machines, insecticides, fungicides, germicides, and all the other expensive paraphernalia of the modern experiment station."

It was coming to understand the way in which living fungus threads in the soil invade the cells of plant roots, where they are digested, that helped Howard understand why rural farmers' practice of returning the manure of their farm animals to the soil proved so effective. Mycorrhizal association, as it is called, is the process by which plants feed directly from the soil, deriving the protein necessary to support life. If we interrupt this symbiotic relationship or destroy it with chemicals that kill microorganisms like the healthy fungi responsible for the uptake of proteins, the soil dies and nothing will grow. "One simple principle," Howard wrote, underlies the "vast accumulation of disease which now afflicts the world." The "undernourishment of the soil is the root of all." By 1940 he had concluded that "the slow poisoning of the life of the soil by artificial manures is one of the great calamities of mankind."

Disease travels up through the food chain—the "biotic web," the "chain of energy," as Leopold described it—from soil to plants to animals to humans. So too does health. The power to resist disease, to confer health and contentment on humankind, Howard argued, lay in mimicking natural cycles of growth, decay, and regeneration by returning all organic matter to the soil. "The failure to maintain a healthy agriculture," he wrote during World War II, "has largely cancelled out all the advantages we have gained from our improvements in hygiene, housing, and our medical discoveries."

Our economy, in other words, was backward, because we did not understand that our life depends on the health of the soil beneath our feet. To the imperial mindset that dispensed Howard to teach the rural poor to garden, he replied with the news that the flow of wisdom traveled in the opposite direction—up from the poor to the rich, from the colonized to the colonizer.

Ruhan Kainth made the same discovery forty years later. When she found the dead soil that chemical fertilizers inevitably produce in her backyard in California, the wisdom of her humble teachers in India helped her to restore it to life.

Before leaving India, Ruhan had pursued two kinds of education—one through the generosity of rural farmers and the family gardener, another at the university. In 1972 she was studying for her master's degree in economics in Delhi. It was a period of severe political repression and fear in India. It was also the first year Ruhan was eligible to vote. When a woman professor asked her for whom she would be voting in the upcoming election, Ruhan said of course she would never vote for Indira Gandhi. "No one in Delhi would dare speak openly against her," she explains. "You couldn't trust anyone. You couldn't speak. I knew university professors who disappeared. They were never seen again.

"In 1972 I decided to leave. I couldn't live under those conditions. If you lived in a country where you had politicians like

Mrs. Gandhi, who ruled with dictatorial power, then you could not be free, your conscience could not be free."

It was then that Ruhan told her father that while she knew she would be poorer in America, she was determined to go. He had hoped she would become a government minister. "I told my father, 'You have told me all my life how you have never compromised. It was you who taught me all this.'" Six years later, in 1978, she left her homeland to come to the United States.

Ruhan and Atma Kainth are from the Punjab, the Land of the Five Rivers. "The land I come from is right below the foothills of the Himalayan Mountains. The Punjab has a very rich history, because it's the crossroads of all cultures. The Greeks, the Scythians, the Parthians, the Mongols, the Arabs—just about everybody came by that route, trying to enter India. And the Punjabis had to meet them, sometimes had to fight them. That's why most Punjabis are very open-minded, very liberal, very accepting of other cultures.

"It's still very accepting. We've had all kinds of trouble, of course. When India was divided up in 1947, half given to Pakistan, which became a Muslim nation, all non-Muslims had to leave—overnight. The British, in dividing India and Pakistan, drew the political line that led to the exodus. The moment the orders were given, people began to cross borders. As they began crossing, let's say a trainload is coming from Pakistan into India, full of Hindus and Sikhs. Along the way it would be stopped, and all of the people were butchered by the Muslims. Even though they were leaving, abandoning their homes and their lands, they were killed. And the trains going from India to Pakistan, likewise, full of Muslims, were killed. There was mutual slaughter. The rivers turned red." Half a million people died in two weeks. "The few who were able to escape with their lives were lucky.

"Most of our relatives were on the Pakistani side of Punjab, so they had to cross over. Some had to live in refugee camps in Delhi for a time. My parents were lucky—they were able to get out.

They came to India. My father's ancestral lands were left there in Pakistan, their house, everything. All of the Punjabis living on the Pakistan side were uprooted. It would be just like dividing California between north and south.

"My husband's family was on the Indian side of Punjab, so they did not see this. My husband, Atma, came to America with his twenty-five dollars in 1972. He still has five of those dollars. He kept them as a reminder. You see, in the seventies the Indian government only allowed us to take twenty-five dollars out of the country. Now they're liberalizing, but then you couldn't sell your property there and transfer your wealth here. We got married in 1978, so I came here as the spouse of a U.S. citizen.

"Now," Ruhan says with great ceremony, "you have to see this," and she leads me out across the garden to stand under the canopy of a great tree whose branches are hung with fruit unlike anything I've ever seen. They're the size and shape of kiwis, but the smooth skin is magenta when the fruit is young, turning a purple so dark it's nearly black when they're fully ripe.

"Not many people have this tree," Ruhan says, with marvelous understatement. "It's called a *jamun* in my language, which means 'purple,' but in the Fullerton botanical garden it is listed as a jambolan. I went seeking it. I finally found it with a Pakistani woman who had it as a two-year-old plant. This is the first time it has blossomed and made fruit. For me, it was like a baby being born when it bloomed."

Ruhan has nursed this tree along for eleven years. "There's a special story about this tree. In India, my father was given twenty acres of land in lieu of his ancestral lands lost to Pakistan. So he gathered the pits from all the jamuns we had eaten and planted them as a windbreak so that when the winds come at high speed —sometimes the wind blows at eighty kilometers an hour—it would not destroy what had been planted. So I grew up with these trees. I remember eating this fruit as a two-year-old. Oh, it just feels so wonderful to have it bearing." She strokes the branches, whose bark resembles the drooping, wrinkled skin of an elephant's legs. "All of my relatives who are in L.A. are so delighted. Now they wait for the fruit to ripen, and I will share it with them."

Hunar suddenly swoops down, hanging by his legs from an upper branch, and holds out his hands, which are filled with dark purple fruit. He grins with pleasure to have startled us.

Ruhan smiles at her youngest son with great affection as she chooses the darkest fruit for me. I bite into the gorgeous sea-green flesh inside the dusky purple skin. It's tart, with a hint of sweetness, surprising and delicious, unlike any fruit I've ever tasted.

A few yards from the jamun, Ruhan shows me the sugarcane she planted in the corner of her backyard—a tall, upright plant with strappy leaves, a link to the years she spent managing the farm. "This is not the same sugarcane that grows in the Punjab," she says, "but it's very similar. We cut the dried husks down to use as compost. Here is some of the sugarcane that we just harvested. See how it's looking very messy and junky there right now?"

She turns around and points to the cherimoyas growing in a small grove beside the house. "I've noticed that since I've been putting the sugarcane husks under my cherimoyas, I've never needed to feed them. They are creating a soil web which keeps the plants healthy without my having to fertilize them or use any pesticides."

From deep within the cherimoyas we hear a squawk. "Ah, my chickens!" Ruhan says.

Chickens roosting in the cherimoyas? In suburban Los Angeles?

"We eat their eggs," she explains, smiling. And they help fertilize the cherimoyas and, when she lets them out, the main garden too.

Hunar leaps over the low fence that keeps them within the cherimoya grove, sneaks up on two, nabs them, and carries them back to us, one under each arm.

"These are Silkies," Ruhan says, taking one into her arms and stroking it as it clucks. They're huge, colorful beasts, with fearsome-looking spurs on the backs of their legs. "Then I have two Auracanas. They lay green-and-blue eggs." She calls them the Mothers. "I love them," she says, and it's obvious. "I had a third one, a male, and he started crowing and the neighbors complained. He was a show chicken, so beautiful, but I had to give him away to a friend. Once, when the hens laid eggs, they sat there, and I knew nothing was going to happen, so I went to the Buena Park High School, and I got fertilized eggs and switched them. The hens hatched them and took care of them, so that's why I call them the Mothers.

"These cherimoyas are my special babies. I have planted some of them from seed. Last year I had over three hundred pounds of cherimoyas," she says, as if this were not at all unusual. "I ate them, I juiced them, I gave them away. We had lots of friends who wanted them."

"You grew these from seed?" I ask, incredulous. The trees are as tall as the house.

"Oh, yes. In India, when I was little, I used to eat custard apples. When I came here, I looked and looked for them. One of my gardening friends said, 'Well, we have something similar we call cherimoyas. They grow up in Santa Barbara. They can't grow here because we don't have the bug that pollinates them.' I said, 'Well, how are you going to have the fruit?' She said, 'I'm going to hand-pollinate them.' So I said, 'Show me how to do it.' She taught me how to do it, so I hand-pollinated for several years with a brush.

"The flower is female in the morning, and by evening it turns into a male flower. So the trick is to collect the pollen when it's a male flower and then look for the next flower in the female stage, and then you pollinate them. I did that for many years, and I got a good crop. Then last year—can you see up there?—I got fruit at the very top of the trees, and I certainly didn't go to pollinate those. So I said to myself, 'Wait a minute. Perhaps I don't even need to pollinate anymore, because somebody has arrived in my garden who's taking care of the job.

"The custard apple I grew up with as a child is a cousin, a relative of the cherimoya. But for me, these will do just fine. They're bigger than the ones that come from my country. I enjoy them, so I have adopted them."

Just as I'm thinking about this garden as a biology lab—in the small triangle of yard that fences in the chickens and the cherimoyas, Ruhan has created a biotic community of remarkable complexity—she turns it into a kinship system. Adoption, not assimilation, is her model, a relationship of choice, and once you choose, you love what you've chosen as your own.

How do people respond to the botanical wonders of her backyard? Newly Americanized Sikhs as well as her American neighbors, Ruhan says, have been scandalized by her choices, each for different reasons. "People from my own country who came by and saw me back here working in the garden said, 'Why are you digging?' Why wasn't I inside watching TV and doing American things?"

Speaking of her American neighbors, Ruhan says, "Tell me, is there some law that says I can only plant flowers in my front yard?" It takes me a minute to realize she's not joking. The neighbors objected when she planted fruit trees in front of the house and strawberries and vegetables in the ground beside the driveway. It startled her to encounter such active resistance to her wish to use every available inch of her land to grow food. "I'm trained as an economist. I'm limited in my ground. I can't afford more land, so why shouldn't I be able to use every bit of it?"

To her Punjabi friends who wanted her to be at once more Indian and more American, she answered with energy. "I realized that I was offending people. But here, I don't have my gardeners. I don't have crop-sharers. I have only myself. I want to have a garden, a beautiful garden. And I am my only resource. The pleasure of planting a seed and making my own garden is a pleasure that should not be denied me."

How complex, the negotiation of so many boundaries in the garden. Questions of who plants, what is planted, and where it is planted make plain a host of unspoken rules about the decorum of how one ought to present oneself in the garden. The landscape is such a powerful marker of nationality and class.

Ruhan is mixing it all up. An educated woman from a wealthy family in India, she cultivates a peasant's garden in America, down on her knees, digging in the dirt. What her neighbors and friends from India cannot see is the act of faith in her labor, the patient devotion of her commitment, a healing of the land that comforts her and keeps her family healthy and strong.

As we walk the dirt paths that meander through her unplanned garden, we are never very far from the house or the back fence, never more than thirty yards or so from her neighbors' property, but the thick planting, the ring of trees around the perimeter, the rhythm of the tall and rangy next to the squat and full, the beautiful happenstance of planting things as she found them, suggests an impulse so democratic that it borders on anarchy.

"These are my guavas," Ruhan says, introducing me to the peerless Allahabadis native to the Punjab. Nearly seedless, this variety has a unique flavor comparable to the rich taste that sets basmati apart from all other rice.

When Ruhan first arrived in the United States as a new bride, she lived with Atma in a small apartment. The first thing she planted in America was a pot of mint. Next she planted coriander. When they were able to move to a house, it was wonderful, she says, remembering. "It opened up possibilities for me. I started looking for trees from my country. I wanted to eat a fresh guava so badly, so that was the first tree I planted. A friend who owned a factory knew that one of her employees, a Mexican, was a gardener." Ruhan's first seedling was the gift of another immigrant, someone also hungry for the foods of home. "I was so happy!" she says. "I would just look at it—I would watch it grow. These are things I need so badly," she adds, her voice growing soft, remembering her early years of adjusting to America. "When I put each of these trees in place, I am being true to myself.

"Oh, Hunar, go get that," she says, suddenly pointing to a ripe fruit, which he plucks and places in her hand. "This is a white sapote. Now in India, the one that I have is a brown sapote called a *chikoo*. This is the closest I could come to the brown sapote. It's so good that now I have adopted this one."

Hunar has fetched my dessert. After the homemade dal and chapatis and fresh yogurt, I will, Ruhan says, taste the sapote.

"Ah, here is my okra," Ruhan says, and I am grateful to see something I can actually recognize and have eaten. "I was raised with it. We eat it all the time in Punjab. I wonder how it went around the world—do you know?"

"With the slave trade, most likely," I say.

"Oh, really?" Ruhan says with a blend of sadness and surprise as we continue past it.

"This part of the garden is for my bees," she explains, gesturing to the brightly colored annuals and perennials at our feet. "I'm trying to plant as many flowers as possible to invite them. The hummingbirds love this part too."

Along one stretch of the back fence are her hives, square white boxes that seem odd in their neat, angular whiteness among the wild growth, the textured bark, the many shapes of leaves. So Ruhan harvests honey as well. To the trees, shrubs, sugarcane, herbs, spices, and chickens, she invites the great pollinators and orange-throated Anna's hummingbirds.

We pause before a white mulberry from Pakistan, like the ones she grew up with in her garden in Delhi. Close by, the beige perforated shells of ripe almonds hang from the branches of a tree native to a region north of the Punjab, where the climate is colder. A bougainvillea has climbed through the almond tree, draping its slender branches with the vermilion paper lanterns of its flowers. Close to the almond, Ruhan has planted a plum and a peach tree, so that they might help each other attract pollinators.

Close by are her papayas, and below them edible cactus. A swarm of four o'clocks, lemon yellow, grows at our feet—more bee food.

Along the back fence Ruhan's loquats are in bloom beside a stand of tall Jerusalem artichokes lifting their bright yellow flowers to the sun. Beside them, hung with fruit, is another Allahabadi guava and jicamas, a root vegetable like the Jerusalem artichoke but sweeter. Her first jicama was a gift from a Colombian friend from the California Rare Fruit Growers Association.

"Here is a phalsa—it has a special berry," she says. Like the strangely beautiful fruit of the jamum, the phalsa berry looks more like a jewel than anything you would want to eat. Ruhan fills my hands with the oval jet beads, whose sharp, sweet taste wakes the senses. When in flower, one variety of phalsa makes a stunning vermilion flower, the other a bright yellow. The phalsa is another of India's medicinal trees. Ancient texts describe using its leaves, seeds, and flowers to treat a long list of ailments.

Hunar, who has come up behind us, surprises Ruhan with a passion fruit. She receives it gladly, then sends him off for more. "Find one that's purple," she calls to him, "and then I can make a drink with it."

What, I wonder, will Hunar's memories of this garden be? I think of this child of the twenty-first century foraging in his mother's garden, thinking it's normal to know the history of your food, to eat from the land you live on, to drink only fresh juices from exotic fruit you have watched ripen and learned to pick at just the right moment. He could not have this experience in Delhi any more than Ruhan could.

Our walk is nearly finished as we once again come up beside the pomegranate. Its huge dark fruits are awash in the honey-gold light of late afternoon, so that they glow against the dark green foliage of the tree's great crown.

"This is one of the biblical fruits, isn't it?" Ruhan asks. For her, every plant must have its story, its place in a culture. To eat is not simply to consume but to dwell in history. To garden is to cultivate a relationship of kinship—with the earth, with dead soil returned to life, with plants, bees, birds, and chickens. As tiny as this piece of land is, it is home to a vast and intricate world.

"Ah, and here at last," Ruhan says, "is the neem tree."

Ruhan found her tall, straight neem sapling at a festival for all the chapters of the California Rare Fruit Growers Association. A nursery from San Diego had one specimen. Thrilled to have found it, she bought it, and now it grows with the phalsa and jamum, as it would in the Punjab.

"Do you see that little dome-shaped net? And another over here? They are full of neem seeds I am propagating," she says.

It is rare indeed to find this tree, or its seeds, anywhere in the United States, and rarer still to encounter anyone here who knows the story of its place in the history of ancient India. A tall, straight tree with pinnate leaves, the neem, when it blossoms in early spring, bears white, honey-scented flowers. Its fruit, a one-seeded drupe, resembles a large olive when young, turning yellow as it ripens. The word *neem* comes from the Sanskrit *nimba,* a short form of the phrase *nimbati syasthyamdadati,* "to give good health." In ancient Indian texts, the tree is referred to as *Sarva Roga Nivarini,* "curer of all ailments." Its bark, twigs, leaves, flowers, fruit, and seeds all have healing properties, providing natural forms of antibiotics, anti-inflammatories, pesticides, wormicides, and fungicides. For centuries Indians have brushed their teeth with neem twigs; women have known how to treat menstrual disorders using its leaves. Parts of the tree have been used for millennia to heal skin wounds, including snake and spider bites; it is a powerful remedy for malaria, leprosy, and common fever. Postpartum mothers and their nursing infants are strengthened by the juice from its leaves.

The neem grows fast and huge. It repels most pests without killing them while providing nutrients to the soil, birds, insects, and bats. For thousands of years the people of India have used its leaves to keep stored food and clothing free of pests. It is extremely drought-resistant and makes an excellent windbreak. A neem tree can live for two to three hundred years. Its deep roots help prevent erosion and restore degraded land. Its wood is hard and naturally resistant to termites. It can even defend itself from an infestation of locusts.

It was for all these reasons, as Ruhan told me the first time we met, that the great emperor Ashoka had neem trees planted in every village and along all heavily traveled roads throughout his empire. In thirty places throughout India, Pakistan, Nepal, and Afghanistan, pillars of stone, each standing forty to fifty feet tall, still polished to a mirrorlike shine after 1600 years of exposure to the elements, bear the words Ashoka addressed to his people after his conversion to Buddhism, when he renounced war and devoted his life to improving the conditions under which his people lived so that they might be happy.

Born in 304 B.C., Ashoka was crowned around 263. Eight years later, the ambitious young ruler, known for his ruthlessness and cruelty, launched a bloody war of expansion to annex Kalinga to the empire he had inherited from his grandfather and father. It is said that while he was walking the battlefield after victory, overcome by horror at the death and suffering he had caused, he encountered a Buddhist monk walking quietly through the rotting bodies of horses and men, already being devoured by birds. Ashoka approached the monk and asked how he could be at peace in such a place. Was he happy? And if he was, how had he come to be so? And would he teach the emperor what he knew? In response to learning the precepts of Buddhism, Ashoka renounced violence and became an ardent convert, making a pilgrimage to the Buddha's birthplace at Lumbini and undertaking the lifelong study of Buddhism. In this way, as Sharon Salzberg, a leading Buddhist teacher in America, has written in her book *Lovingkindness: The Revolutionary Art of Happiness,* a nameless man with nothing but a robe and a bowl influenced the destiny of an empire. As a witness for nonviolence in the midst of carnage, the monk indirectly helped spread Buddhism throughout Asia, for Ashoka's son and daughter introduced Buddhism to Sri Lanka, Burma, and Thailand. The Buddhist Publication Society of Sri Lanka makes contemporary English translations of Ashoka's inscriptions available for free, hoping to continue sowing the seeds of nonviolence.

In one of the edicts still legible on an ancient stone pillar, Ashoka describes the carnage on the battlefield at Kalinga, where hundreds of thousands of men and animals perished. He speaks of his remorse for the great suffering he caused, recounts his conversion to Buddhism, and entreats his people to follow him in the way of peace.

As if it were not astonishing enough for an emperor to confess his remorse and devote his life to making amends for the appalling suffering caused by a war he waged simply to expand his power, Ashoka instituted a reign of peace that extended to all people, within and beyond his boundaries, and then to the land itself—plants, trees, birds, fish, and animals. He banned the hunting of many species of creatures and the sacrifice of any living being. In addition to creating thousands of monasteries, libraries, and hospitals, he set aside wildlife and forest preserves. In his second rock edict, quoted in the Buddhist Publication Society's translation, Ashoka made provisions for medical treatment for animals as well as humans, and "wherever medical herbs, roots or fruits for humans and animals were not available," he had them imported. The neem trees planted along main travel routes grew near the resthouses Ashoka had built along the roads. He also had wells dug and other trees planted for fruit and shade so that his people, especially the poor, might not endure needless suffering. The state, Ashoka taught, has an obligation to protect and conserve the entire living community.

In Ruhan's garden, the neem tree, with all its natural healing properties, commemorates this reign of peace and justice; its story is one of transformation and hope. In the context of the global marketplace, however, the neem is at the center of quite a different story.

In the past two decades, the neem tree has become the subject of intensive research around the world, as transnational corporations and governments of developed nations engage in a race to be the first to successfully patent and bring to market biologically friendly agricultural and pharmaceutical products derived from it. In 1992, an ad hoc committee of the U.S. National Research Council published its findings in a report called *Neem: A Tree for Solving Global Problems*. It concluded that neem has the potential to control many of the world's pests and diseases and reduce soil erosion, desertification, and deforestation. And if, as some researchers believe, neem is also the source of a natural spermicide, research could lead to the development of an oral birth control pill for men, thus helping regulate the growth of world population.

In contrast to other trees planted for reforestation, neem is more valuable for the byproducts of its fruit and leaves than for its wood, so it could be raised sustainably. Because it can be grown in poor soil, large-scale plantings necessary to harvest quantities of its seeds do not need to compete with food production. Large plantations of neem, given the cooling properties of its great crown of evergreen leaves, might even help slow global warming.

No other known plant or chemical possesses all of the neem's capacities for preventing and healing disease in soil, plants, animals, and humans. It all sounds so wonderful. Where, then, is the problem?

A short passage in the 1992 report's opening pages suggests the answer. The promise of the neem "is currently known to only a handful of entomologists, foresters, and pharmacologists—and, of course, to the traditional farmers of South Asia." It's that last phrase, which weighs a handful of specialists from technologically advanced nations against millions of traditional farmers in India, that gives so much away. What of these people—the world's largest remaining population of small farmers—and the millennia of traditional knowledge that is their birthright?

The creation of just one byproduct of the neem, an eco-friendly fungicide, requires twenty tons of seeds per day. Neem seeds are now being bought up by corporations in staggering quantities, driving the price so high that farmers in India can no longer afford to buy them. As a result, the neem is now the subject of a number of international lawsuits. Multinational corporations supported by developed nations are attempting to patent the tree's many byproducts. In May 2000, after a six-year legal struggle mounted by a coalition called the Neem Campaign, the European Patent Office revoked a patent granted to the United States Department of Agriculture and the multinational corporation W. R. Grace. India's leading environmental advocate, Vandana Shiva, who directed the campaign, speaks of the West's attempt to plunder the biological wealth and traditional knowledge of the rural poor of the East as "biopiracy." In this, she echoes one of her sources of inspiration—Sir Albert Howard.

"Why has civilization proved such a disastrous failure?" Sir Albert Howard asked in *The Soil and Health*. "The answer is simple. Our industries, our trade, and our way of life generally have been based first on the exploitation of the earth's surface and then on the oppression of one another—on banditry pure and simple. The inevitable result," he wrote at the close of World War II, "is now upon us." Sixty years ago, Howard argued that the way we grow our food—the way we till the soil in our own backyards—engages us with politics at the most fundamental level. "The real Arsenal of Democracy," he declared, "is a fertile soil, the fresh produce of which is the birthright of the nations. Does mankind possess the understanding to grasp the possibilities which this simple truth unfolds?"

As one of very few private gardeners in America to cultivate a neem tree in her backyard, Ruhan Kainth keeps alive the legacy of its sacred place in her native culture. And in her devotion to the community of the land she has helped to create by restoring the soil to life, she has taken her place as a citizen, not of the Punjab or America but of "the land." Here the seed and the tree are cultivated in a relationship defined as kinship—"adoption," as she puts it—a commitment to loving responsibility for the earth that is essential to the health of a democracy.

"It is my devotion," Ruhan says quietly, reflecting on what working in her garden means to her. "It teaches me. When I am out here, I am in the gardens in Delhi. I am visiting with the villagers on the farm in the countryside. That was a time of great peace, so when I work in my garden, I see those scenes and I remember that peace."

7

COMMUNITY

The Urban Gardens of Nuestras Raíces

HOLYOKE, MASSACHUSETTS

"I am seventy-three years old, soon seventy-four. The twenty-third of this month makes sixteen years I'm here."

For all his adult life Alejandro Marrero has tended food. Until he got this garden plot at La Finquita, Little Farm, the first of seven community gardens in Holyoke, Massachusetts, created by a grassroots organization known as Nuestras Raíces (Our Roots), it was always the company's field, the company's crops, and the company's profit. Alejandro came from Puerto Rico for six months in 1965 for his first job as a migrant farmworker, recruited by a labor contractor to harvest flowers in New Jersey. "Tulips," he says. I speak no Spanish and he speaks only a little English, so to help me understand, he illustrates, one hand shaping a cup, the other defining its stem. He signs with hands that know these flowers—he has picked them by the thousands, perhaps by the hundreds of thousands. For gladiolas, his fingers climb an invisible stem, rising into the air.

After the flower fields of New Jersey, Alejandro moved on to

Pennsylvania. "Asparagus," he says. "That was the worst. All day. The rows went from here to that building over there." He points to a clock tower on a hill across town. "You just go like this all the way down the row." He shuffles, bent double, one hand pressed to his lower back. After that, it was tobacco on the farms that stretch down the long exit road from Bradley International Airport, not far from Hartford, Connecticut. Shade-grown tobacco. It's called "stoop labor" by advocates of migrant workers' rights.

Then Alejandro got a job at a food-packing plant in Hartford. "I worked the train," he says. "A hundred thousand bushels a day sometimes. All packed in ice on a train. It comes in and we unload it. We rinse it, bit by bit, every bushel. We repack it, and then, you know, they sell it."

Before the hundred thousand bushels of broccoli or spinach get to the supermarket, someone has had to plant, tend, harvest, wash, and pack them. Alejandro used to be one of the workers, a community of men without women, living in barracks, traveling in buses, eating together, telling stories, making the loneliness of their lives more bearable. All day every day in the field, like all the other workers, he was exposed to the toxic chemicals used on factory farms: pesticides, fungicides, fertilizers. When I ask him if he knows what chemicals he was exposed to during the years he worked in agriculture, he says no. Sometimes the workers were provided with running water to wash their hands before eating lunch in the fields, sometimes not.

Alejandro worked at the far end of our food supply, the invisible end. Americans expect apples and tomatoes without blemishes, long perfect spears of bright green asparagus. This means that 85 percent of our fruits and vegetables must be tended by hand.

Before the end of the day, I will hear several more men with gardens at La Finquita describe their former lives as migrant workers—Heriberto Santiago, Israel Rivera, and Juan Lopez. I will hear them describe with pride how hard they worked, and

I'll learn about the contractors who recruited them from Puerto Rico. And the buses that took them back and forth between the fields and the barracks. The long hours, the short breaks, the exhaustion and danger and loneliness. And the bitter irony of their poverty and hunger: What does it say about our society that the people who grow our food are too poor to feed their own families?

In their gardens, listening to their stories, I will begin to learn the human cost of food. I will hear how, in the gardens of Nuestras Raíces, for the first time since they came to the United States, the fruit of their labor belongs to them.

On the clear summer morning when I arrive at his garden, Alejandro is planting beans. I must bow to pass under the lintel of his narrow gate, part of an enclosure constructed of wood and chicken wire. The fences of La Finquita are more symbolic than practical—it would take little physical effort to force your way through them. But no one does. All the symbolic marking-out of portions of public land for private use are respected.

Standing astride a long clear patch of dirt he has raked smooth, Alejandro leans down and makes a trough with a piece of wood, then drops shining white beans, *chicharos,* into the dark wet earth. They soon look like a row of giant's teeth. "Everybody plant different, you know?" he says. "Somebody make a hole, put in one bean, two beans. I put a line in."

As we talk, Alejandro continues to plant seeds drawn from a yellow plastic butter container with a shallow layer of fine black silt and water in the bottom.

"Alejandro," I ask, "what are you going to do with all these beans?"

"Give them away." He laughs, throwing his hands up, shrugging. What else? "This was all beans before." He swivels right, then left, his arm extended. "These beans, they grow like that." He pats a space three feet off the ground to show me how tall they get. "They're beautiful."

Alejandro has already harvested his first crop of the summer and given nearly all of them away. He loves to eat them with rice and chicken and the traditional Puerto Rican salsa known as sofrito. Now that Nuestras Raíces, with the help of the University of Massachusetts Agricultural Extension Service, has imported the seeds of *aji dulce,* "sweet pepper," the main ingredient for sofrito, he can make his own from everything he grows right here—tomatoes, onions, cilantro, and peppers.

In Alejandro's ten-by-twenty-five-foot plot, there is no room for weeds or waste. We are surrounded by fresh, safe food—vegetables, herbs, and fruit—in every stage of new growth and dieback. Though Alejandro can't grow the mangoes and sugarcane, the pineapples, bananas, and coffee of his childhood home in Puerto Rico, he has acquired a taste for the broccoli and eggplants maturing around us, and like his garden neighbors here at La Finquita, he grows his own strawberries and shares in the communal harvest of blueberries.

Several varieties of peppers and tomatoes hang thick and heavy down well-staked rows. At the end of one long row of newly sprouted seedlings, a specimen of cilantro has been allowed to go to seed. It stands tall and erect, covered with small round seedpods that look as if they're made of gold. Bright orange and yellow marigolds mark the corners near the gate. Pea vines have woven themselves through the wide squares of the fence that faces the long aisle between the plots, softening the lines of chicken wire with delicate curves and curling leaves.

"*Aji dulce?*" I ask, pointing to a row of shining red chilies shaped like acorn lanterns, ripe and ready for picking among stout green foliage. The sweet peppers have been planted among the hot and the bland, habaneros and cubanelles.

"Yes, *aji,*" Alejandro says, smiling, surprised that I know.

"What was that?" I ask of a row where nothing but thick dark leaves of basal foliage remains.

"Cauliflower," he says. Once he had harvested enough for his own needs, he gave the rest away.

Alejandro was one of the first gardeners to sign up for a plot at La Finq, as the gardeners call it. He knows everyone here, and he remembers the history of the place.

"Before Finquita, this was church property," he says. "It burn down. When they started the garden, one sister, you know, sister for the church, she stay in this house." He points across the gardens and past the parking lot. "She make a garden." Now La Finquita is home to more than thirty gardeners and their families.

"I get over here at seven-thirty in the morning, sometimes seven, every day," Alejandro says. "Then at night, six or seven, I put the water. It makes me happy." For many hours a day, every day, all summer, in the intense heat and humidity, he comes here to garden. When I ask if he thinks of Puerto Rico when he's working here, he answers with a shower of yeses. "Ah, yes yes yes yes yes," he says, radiant. Then he reels off the Spanish names of all the plants that make him think of home.

From the time Spain claimed Puerto Rico as a colony in the sixteenth century through today, this Caribbean island—the smallest of the Greater Antilles—has never been sovereign and free. Puerto Rican citizenship is not internationally recognized.

Since 1898, when the United States won control over the island at the close of the Spanish American War, Puerto Ricans have lived under the American flag without the full rights of citizenship. Though the shape of their land and their lives has been determined by American trade and agricultural policies, Puerto Ricans who maintain legal residence in their homeland have little voice in determining their own fate. They have one nonvoting representative in the U.S. Congress and do not have the right to vote in federal elections. Only if they leave their homeland and establish residency in the United States can they claim the full rights and privileges of a citizen—but not of their native land.

Under Spanish rule, the wealth extracted from Puerto Rico (which means "rich port") was gold and then, when there was no more gold, coffee. Under American rule, sugar replaced coffee, as investors from the United States bought up vast tracts of land on the coast for plantations. Enjoying years of special tax breaks in addition to a ready supply of low-wage workers who did not have the protection of the labor laws that shielded U.S. citizens, American companies grew wealthy while our government imposed strict trade policies on the island and did little to improve the quality of the natives' lives. When the American government banned the export of coffee, rural subsistence farmers were driven from their small farms, where the cultivation of shade-grown coffee had never precluded growing the food their families depended on. Without this cash crop, they could no longer live off the land, and without access to land, they could no longer feed their families. Drawn from the land into a wage economy, they crowded into urban slums and fell into poverty and hunger. By the 1940s, after fifty years of American rule, Puerto Ricans had one of the highest infant mortality rates and one of the lowest per capita annual incomes in the world.

As industry boomed in postwar America, a mass migration from the island began. By 1960, 400,000 Puerto Ricans—nearly a fifth of the island's population—had emigrated to the mainland, many recruited by agricultural employers who paid their way.

Holyoke, Massachusetts, became a destination for these immigrants because of its high number of housing vacancies, low rents, and proximity to farm and factory jobs. Seventy-five percent of the population of downtown Holyoke is now Puerto Rican. Most over the age of thirty were born in Puerto Rico, and many of the elders used to be agricultural workers and have had only a few years of schooling. The unemployment rate for Puerto Ricans in Holyoke hovers above 25 percent. The statistics for substance abuse and teenage pregnancy are four times the state average. Close to three quarters of the community's children live in poverty. There are no large supermarkets within walking distance of downtown South Holyoke, where, as Daniel Ross, the director of Nuestras Raíces tells me, half the city's available housing has either burned down or been condemned since 1970.

The meaning of the gardens of Nuestras Raíces has many layers. It begins with Puerto Rico's history as an ecological treasurehouse pillaged by foreigners. Next there is the history of Holyoke as a nineteenth-century industrial town built on the labor of successive waves of immigrants. Finally there is the story of what the gardeners of Nuestras Raíces have created here.

"Ecology is the science of communities," Aldo Leopold said in an address to the Conservation Committee of the Garden Club of America in 1947. "And the ecological conscience is therefore the ethics of community life." In their organic gardens, created from vacant lots they do not own, a disenfranchised, landless population teaches the wealthiest nation in the world what a restorative urban ecology can look like.

"From the beginning, our dream was to build a greenhouse. We wanted to create something that was sustainable for the organization, not something we'd always have to write grants for. We wanted to generate income and self-sufficiency—business opportunities, jobs, microenterprises."

Daniel Ross has been called "the Michael Jordan of community organizing." He has guided Nuestras Raíces from its early years, when there was only one garden, La Finquita, and few resources, to what it is now—a small complex called El Centro Agrícola, which includes two renovated buildings, a greenhouse, a restaurant, a bilingual library and computer room, a community kitchen, a plaza, and soon a working organic farm on four acres bordering the Connecticut River. With a greenhouse, the group is able to propagate its own plants from seed.

"In the early spring, every bit of usable space in here is dedicated to growing seedlings we sell to our community gardeners and at the farmers' market. Last year we grew tomatoes, peppers and eggplants," Daniel explains. The group's specialty is *aji dulce.* Until it was introduced here, this variety of sweet pepper had never been grown in the United States. The first year they grew starter plants from seed in their greenhouse, they sold five thousand seedlings in a matter of days.

Daniel was a fairly recent graduate of Oberlin College when he was hired as Nuestras Raíces' first director, but he had already had years of experience working for migrant farmworkers' rights. Born to Jewish parents living in Puerto Rico, Daniel first moved to New York City with his family and then to Massachusetts. As a boy, he grew up speaking more Spanish than English. Well-educated, politically astute, he knows how to move between cultures in this small New England town.

"Most people here in South Holyoke grew up on farms," he explains. "Many of them first came here as migrant farmworkers. The gardens are a way for the residents of Holyoke to put down roots here while maintaining the heritage and traditions of Puerto Rico. They're also a way for the elders to pass knowledge and traditions to a new generation.

"About five years ago, two of our elders and board members, Francisco Ortiz and Eusavio Ibera, started our youth gardeners program. On the first day, Francisco held out a handful of seeds and said, 'We're going to plant these seeds, and pretty soon tomato plants are going to grow. And then later this summer we're going to be able to pick tomatoes and eat them.' The kids didn't believe him. One of them even called him a liar. 'Tomatoes don't grow from seeds. Tomatoes come from the supermarket.' You've never seen kids so proud as they were six months later, picking their first tomatoes. It was amazing. They loved it. Francisco Ortiz was real proud, too.

"Now we work with over a thousand kids all over the city. We have one plot set aside for the kids in each of our community gardens. We work with after-school programs in all the neighborhoods. We involve them in projects and take them on field trips. We provide them with work during the summer."

A hundred families are part of the community gardens, each branching out to reach hundreds more, sharing food in the inner city, where there is no other source of fresh, organically grown produce.

Nuestras Raíces comprises eight gardens. Jardín la Finquita, Little Farm, is the oldest. Then there are Jardín Girasol, Sunflower Garden; Jardín de Piedra, Garden of the Rock; Jardín Ciudad Verde, Green City; Jardín Comunitario Jarvis Heights; the Boys and Girls Club Garden; the John J. Lynch School Garden, and the newest of the gardens, CuentaConMigo, Count on Me.

The first garden, La Finquita, came into being in the summer of 1991, when Seth Williams, a student from Hampshire College in nearby Amherst, began working with the residents of the neighborhood of South Holyoke to create a community garden as part of his interdisciplinary final project. Fluent in Spanish, Seth had worked with other Latino communities as a volunteer. La Finquita was the first project for which he assumed complete responsibility.

With a few members of the community, Seth organized the cleanup of a lot near the center of town. Raised several feet above the street, La Finquita was created on the site where Precious Blood Church, which had a long history in the immigrant community of South Holyoke, had once stood. Two buildings affiliated with the old Roman Catholic parish still stand—Broderick House, a beautiful old brick building that serves as a homeless shelter and has its own plot in the garden, and the old rectory, which houses a soup kitchen.

Led by Seth Williams, the "pioneers," as Daniel calls them, pulled bricks, trash, and hypodermic needles out of the soil. On one of the hottest days of the summer of 1991, Seth and a handful of men from the community used picks and shovels to dig a trench a hundred and fifty feet long and three feet deep so they could run a water pipe from the main pipe in the basement of Broderick House to the site. When the plumber who generously donated his time tried to connect the new pipe to the old plumbing, one of the original pipes burst, flooding the basement. When he couldn't turn off the aged, rusted valve, the water company had to send out a crew to resolve the crisis. Seth was handed a bill for several hundred dollars. His credibility—and the fate of the garden—hung on the good will of the Diocese of Springfield, which owned the land and the flooded building, and the people in charge at the water company, who finally canceled most of the bill.

Organizing this garden was Seth's education in the ethnic politics of South Holyoke. At every turn, he knew that it was his status as a white college kid that helped win support. What he most feared was that after he left, no one would come forward to provide leadership and the garden, like so many other well-meant projects, would fail. It had to become a true grassroots organization to survive.

Before leaving the area in 1992, Seth helped establish a board of directors that included members of the Latino community as well as several people from outside Holyoke. They worked together through 1993, managing La Finquita and working toward the goal of owning their own greenhouse. In 1994, just as they were gaining momentum, it was discovered that the president of the board had embezzled all of the organization's funds. Thirty thousand dollars was missing. It became a citywide scandal.

At that point, board members from outside Holyoke slipped away. "So it was left to some of the gardeners, Francisco Ortiz and Eusevio Ibera," Daniel says, "to step up to join the board of directors."

In 1995, through a small grant, Daniel was hired. "I made it my focus to rebuild our credibility from the bottom up," he explains. "That meant doing a lot of outreach work with the gardeners at La Finquita, building our membership base through developing new gardens."

To prospect for good garden sites, Daniel, Francisco, and Eusevio went out to visit available lots. Did they get enough light? Was there a nearby source of water? How visible were the lots?

Once they had selected good sites, they contacted the owners to work out a rental agreement. Then they put up a fence, built a *casita* for garden tools, hoses, and wheelbarrows, and began measuring out plots. People would stop and ask questions. Word got around.

Once people started digging and putting their plants in, Daniel says, the ones he calls the "nay-sayers," the ones who were sure it couldn't work, began to come by to ask if they could have a plot too. "That's the moment that's most important for us. Because people here have heard so many promises. You know, officials from government agencies that are supposed to be helping them, professors from universities who are doing studies. They've heard it all. And there have been so many years of displacement, disenfranchisement. You know, buildings being demolished, people getting kicked off welfare. They don't believe in their own power. They don't believe that anybody can do anything. So showing a community that they can work together and make a difference—having it be so visible and so real, you know —even *edible*—that's the most important outcome of our work.

"That's why I do it. To see that change in people's minds. And it's big—that's *big,*" Daniel says again. "And we've done it in every neighborhood across the city."

"When I started working here, I didn't see how important a garden could be," Hilda Colon says as we sit eating lunch in Mi Plaza, the restaurant affiliated with Nuestras Raíces. She is young, smart, motivated, and beautiful, a single mother and a passionate convert to community gardening. "It's amazing how much you can accomplish with a community garden, the impact it can have on the people in a community. Community gardening is powerful. It brings people together. It preserves the earth, it preserves good healthy nutrition, it preserves so many things—friends, families, cultures, values, traditions."

For seven years Hilda worked for Nueva Esperanza, a community service organization, trying to address the problem of teenage pregnancy in the inner city. Seeing the same problems over and over again, she found it hard to feel she was making any difference. A divorced mother of three, she realized she was burning out. So she came to Nuestras Raíces to work as one of the office managers, thinking she'd try something different for a while. She wanted to feel less exhausted and discouraged. But when she saw how few women and girls were involved, she couldn't help herself.

"I guess when you have a calling, it's kind of hard to stay away from it," she says, laughing. "Nuestras Raíces started with men, so it attracted more men than women. I needed to have more women involved, so I developed a girls' program. Soon after that I started encouraging the women gardeners to get involved with the girls, to help teach them how to plant the gardens. Then the women saw the need to meet by themselves. That's how the women's program started. We renamed the women's program this summer. Now they're called Raíces Latina.

"In Puerto Rico, whatever we use in the sofrito, we would grow at our own house. We did all our own cooking and canning." Through their kitchen gardens, through canning, drying, and cooking food, the women had always passed on their heritage. But when they came to the mainland United States, most entered the wage economy. Unless they had learned good English, they could find only minimum-wage jobs, and once they began to have babies, they couldn't keep their jobs—day care was nonexistent or too expensive. Living in the inner city without access to land, they lost the direct link between the garden and the family table.

"Here," Hilda says, "it's funny how much the girls didn't know. You know, I figured, they go to school, they study science. So on the first day I said, 'Okay, we're going to plant lettuce and we're going to plant tomatoes.' 'Really?' they said. 'They could grow *here*?' I said, 'In a few weeks, you will see.' Then I said,

'You know, if you take care of a plant, you'll see how much food you will get from it.' So when they saw the tomatoes, peppers, and beans that grew from the seeds they planted, they were just so happy."

What the founding male elders did for the boys in the gardens, Hilda has done for the girls and women. In the gardens, the girls and the women who guide them reclaim a vital part of their communal structure, passing down knowledge from one generation to another. "Even though the program was supposed to be for girls from six to twelve years old," Hilda explains, "the girls are now fourteen, fifteen years old, and they're still here. 'I want to do more,' they say. 'I could be a leader. I could teach the others. But please, I don't want to leave the program.' Now every time they see a vacant lot, they say, 'That's a big space—can we turn *that* into a garden?'"

Under Hilda's leadership, the garden has introduced the girls to a new relationship to South Holyoke. They have learned how to see—they have learned that what lies under the buildings and sidewalks and paved streets of this city and what is visible between the burned-out tenements is not dead blank space but dirt—soil—the medium of life. The real ground of their existence has become visible to them.

The girls of Raíces Latina can now imagine affecting the landscape of this urban center by turning empty lots into gardens. They have the knowledge, the skill, the desire, and now the power to affect the place where they live. The politics of urban space—the very idea of "real estate," the tension between public and private space—has been transformed for them through the simple act of learning how to plant seeds and grow their own food.

The women who are their mentors have also been profoundly changed by the discovery that gardening has the power to awaken their imagination and will. "As the women elders grew in number," Hilda says, "they also grew in ideas. They started getting more involved. Some became garden coordinators. One was the greenhouse coordinator for a while. One became president of the Nuestras Raíces board, and another is on the charter school board. I am really proud of them."

Nuestras Raíces, under Daniel Ross's leadership, offers its members training in participatory democracy, in the discipline of self-government and the building of consensus. Hilda has made sure this experience is extended to girls and women.

"That's one of the things that keeps me going—that I was able to bring women into Nuestras Raíces," she says, "and see their growth, see them decide to become self-sufficient. You know, the older women didn't get very far in school. Many of them are unemployed. Now they want to learn how to run a business. I tell them it's never too late to start. They don't want it just for themselves. They're thinking about their families, their community. How can they better themselves? It's unique, how through gardening they've been able to grow in all aspects of a woman's life. It's powerful that just by coming here to meet with these girls, we grew to become something else."

When I ask Hilda why she came to the United States, her answer surprises me. "I never wanted to," she says emphatically. "But my mom wanted to give us more opportunities in life. She felt she had to come here to do that. It wasn't my choice. If it had been my choice, I would have stayed in Puerto Rico. I wanted to be a pediatrician. I had the grades and everything, but my mom was always sick. She didn't want us to go away for school. My mother didn't really care for me to move forward. She just wanted me to go to work. When she saw how freely people lived over here, it scared the heck out of her. In so many ways, she was afraid we were just going to get lost in the world. That's the wording she used: 'I don't want you to get lost.'

"The women in the program have lived here long enough to see that you really need to educate yourself in order to be somebody, to have a good income and a good life. More and more they advocate for girls not to depend on men. Some of the women have been so abused. 'You know what?' they say to the girls. 'You need to learn, you need to study, you need to do something with your life, because you don't want to be depending on a man that's going to kick your ass and you'll have to take it because you're not educated and you have nowhere to go.' I see the passion in them, trying to get the girls up to the next level. Even though they're not related, the girls are their children too. In Puerto Rico we take care of each other's kids. My children were not only my children, they were the whole block's children. I see that in the women's group. 'You're not only a participant here, you're my daughter too. I want to mentor you, I want to take care of you, I want to advise you.' You see that passion.

"In Puerto Rico, having a garden is about growing your own food," Hilda says. "Here it's not only about food. It's your way out of your apartment if you don't have your own house. It's a stress reliever. And it's a way of screaming out, 'I want to keep my culture. I want to give this tradition to my children and leave them with this gift, this pride.' When you talk to the elders, you see the pride in their eyes."

To garden is to be drawn out of isolation. For the women, to teach girls how to garden is to reclaim an aspect of their role as esteemed elders.

I ask Hilda if she can remember when she first understood what the gardens of Nuestras Raíces are about. She knows precisely which moment it was.

"I went to the garden and took my shoes off. I touched the ground, I started planting for the first time. I remembered how in Puerto Rico I would walk around barefoot. And I started thinking, 'Well, no wonder these people enjoy this so much.'"

In the inner city, where else could you do this? You lose contact with the earth.

"At Finquita," Hilda says, her voice softening with affection, "you can sit down with the trees, and you can see all the beauty."

For Hilda, to sit down with the trees suggests a visit, as if with intimate friends or kin. To sit down with the trees, to rest from gardening and look at what the community has created there, releases the flow of memory, returning her to the feel of her native soil beneath her feet and offering her a new, more promising place in America.

Daniel Ross appears beside the table where Hilda and I are sitting, talking. It is market day, and he invites me to drive with him from garden to garden as he picks up produce.

In the middle of CuentaConMigo's fifteen gardens, Edwin Velasquez has laid his plants out in an intricate grid, with long rows of chilies several inches high alternating with seedlings. Daniel pours seeds into a tiny plastic cup, then reaches out to Edwin, who leans across a row of cilantro to receive it. "Slo Bolt Lettuce," it says on the package. There are enough seeds in Edwin's hand to put fresh greens on his family's table for the next four months.

"I love it here," he says. "I don't have to buy anything now. I got my lettuce, my cilantro, my peppers, my tomatoes. Everything's expensive in the store now. You plant, you don't have to buy. I got a wife and five kids."

Daniel estimates that one garden plot can save a family a thousand dollars in food in one season. Edwin has at least three under cultivation. He came from Puerto Rico in 1975 and found factory work in New York and Rhode Island before he settled in South Holyoke. "Now I'm working for demolition," he explains. "They knock the building down, we clean the bricks.

"Every year I have gardens. I got one in Jardín de Piedra in my name, I got one in Jarvis Heights in my daughter's name. And Nuestras Raíces lent me eighty dollars for plants and seeds, so whatever I get here, I got to sell, to pay them back.

"Excuse me," he says, turning from me to Daniel. "What you selling these for there?" He holds up a fat bunch of freshly picked cilantro.

"What do you want to sell them for?" Daniel asks him. "A dollar fifty? A dollar?"

"A dollar."

"Okay, a dollar."

"Yeah," Edwin says, grinning. "Make everybody happy."

It's a small but significant moment in the working of a local economy where every participant has a say.

Once Edwin has filled two boxes to overflowing, he leans over the fence of stakes and white twine to surprise me with a bouquet of cilantro. "For you to take home," he says, smiling.

I hold it with both hands and smell it, my eyes closed, the cool leaves against my face. When I am home, standing at the counter cutting up this cilantro for supper, I will know exactly who grew it, where, and when. I will see Edwin's face, radiant, and feel the strength of his generosity to me. I will remember the dark earth between the evenly spaced plants of his beautiful garden, how the herbs are sown in generations. I will savor the welcome this gift signifies, the gesture of acceptance Edwin offered me. I am the stranger here; for Edwin, this is an extension of home. When the gift becomes part of my evening meal, the ancient rite of gift-giving, the sharing of food to establish community, has been restored.

CuentaConMigo is the newest of the community gardens. The woman who made it possible was part of Hilda Colon's program.

"I have pictures of what this place was before," says Julia Rivera, whose idea it was to put a garden at the end of West Street Alley. "You should have seen it. Now people are here all the time, keeping it clean. Everybody has put their heart into these gardens.

"You see that garden for the 4H club?" she says, pointing to the far corner. "That's for the little kids in my program. They're learning to take care of plants. They come here every afternoon. You see that corn over there? One of the kids started that from seed in the community room. 'That's my corn,' he says. 'That's my *tree,*' he says. He's so proud of that corn." A row of tasseled corn six feet tall stands near the chain-link fence.

"I've seen how giving people something to do makes them change their mind about living in this place. We have a lot of problems with drugs and gangs. This is something different. The kids have the time to learn and play at the same time. They see the benefit that Mother Nature gives us. And then they're going to bring tomatoes and lettuce into the house. It will help them economically. Some of these people live on welfare. Here they have something for free. And they love it, they really love it."

The children have been given a portion of the garden along the fence facing the street, and each of them has marked his or her small part of it. WELCOME TO MY GARDEN, a sign buried deep in cilantro says. Nearby, a pair of pinwheels, one red, one blue, raise spinning faces above mounds of marigolds; a butterfly made of white and yellow netting seems to hover above a bed of ruffled lettuce. Someone has filled a white plaster swan with red penstemon. A plaster cupid emerges from a mound of green. The children have planted bright flowers all around it—yellow snapdragons, pink begonias, deep red geraniums, bronze coleus, multicolored pansies, yellow marigolds, and striped petunias. The path through their fairyland of lettuce and angels, through the inspired chaos of bright whirligigs and deep green herbs, meanders. So many things in this brick city are hard, forced to go in straight lines. Here the children can make the roads go any way they want.

"You know, this is my first garden in the United States," Julia says. "My mother didn't know how to read, but she knew a lot about the garden. She used to tell me, 'When you plant something, you put part of your life in it. You should give love to your plants. They give back to you.' So when I was making this garden, it reminded me of her. In Puerto Rico we have just a little space. But even if it was just an empty can, my mother would plant something in it. Because in PR, you know, people used to live on what they have out of the farm. That used to be all we had.

"Some of these kids, they've never planted anything before. But now they begin to see the idea my mother taught me—that once they've planted something, it will give back to them. The other day my kids were eating broccoli with dinner and they looked up at me and said, 'Mommy, we planted this.' And I said, 'Yes, we planted that.' Teaching my kids something that I learned when I was a little girl in Puerto Rico is amazing.

"I ask everybody, 'Can you come see my garden?'" Julia says as we walk toward the gate, where Daniel and Edwin have finished loading the van. "One of the tenants, she's my assistant, I got her to come too. And now every time she sees something she planted come up, she says, 'Aiyee! I have peas! I have tomatoes!' Yesterday she was crying here. She said to me, 'I plant this. This is mine. I never plant anything before. This is so beautiful, I love it.' So even though this is part of my job, it's part of my soul, too. I have faith in this place."

"You can use your imagination," Daniel said when I first visited, three years ago, as we stood in middle of a large room with tall ceilings and big glass windows across the front, where volunteer workers were installing the front door. "This is going to be the dining room of the restaurant."

We walked outside and stood in a bare courtyard surrounded by a sturdy chain-link fence. "There's going to be a fountain here." Daniel pointed to a crescent of rocks on the ground beside the greenhouse, which was attached to the little stucco building that houses the Nuestras Raíces offices. "We'll have planters there," he said, turning slowly to describe an arc from the Cabot Street side around to Main. "It will be full of species native to Puerto Rico, things that can survive the New England climate. And in that corner," he said, turning to face the brick building with the hand-painted sign, CENTRO DE AGRÍCOLA DE NUESTRAS RAÍCES, "some banana trees, bamboo, and sugarcane. And this will be seating space for the restaurant. People will come right out that door there.

"You know," Daniel said, "when Holyoke was a booming industrial town in the nineteen hundreds, this was all hotels and horses and buggies and trolleys coming and going. This was one of the hottest corners in America."

The clock tower Alejandro invoked to measure the distance he covered while stooped over to harvest crops is visible from all over town, including the corner of Cabot and Main, where Daniel turned from asking me to imagine the future to contemplating the past. Its four faces were originally meant to measure time owned by the mills. The workers' lives were ruled by that clock. Who built it? The same men who had made their fortunes from the textile mills of Lawrence and Lowell, Massachusetts. Constance Green tells the story in her 1968 book, *Holyoke, Massachusetts: A Case History of the Industrial Revolution.* In 1847 the men came from Boston to buy a thousand acres along the great curve in the Connecticut River, hoping for another windfall once they'd harnessed the power of a sixty-foot drop in the water level at Hadley Falls. But unlike Lawrence and Lowell, Holyoke was a planned city. In fact, Holyoke was the most important planned manufacturing center in New England.

When the investors calling themselves the Hadley Falls Company met with local resistance to their plan to buy up all the land and displace a Yankee community already disrupted by the shift from agriculture to industry, they recruited a local man to act as their agent. Once they had secured the land in the company's name, they mapped out a grid of tenement housing around a system of dams and canals, which would use the power of the river to drive the huge mills. As in the more established industrial centers just outside Boston, local women, the daughters of Yankee farmers, were replaced at the looms by the first wave of immigrants. In Holyoke, those were usually Irish families fleeing the potato famine.

Irish construction workers built the dams and canals, and Irish immigrants first worked in the factories. Many chose not to live in company housing, the three- to five-floor tenements that still stand, now boarded up and burned out. They built windowless shanties over holes dug in the earth until they could afford something more habitable. Within a decade, the Irish established their own parish churches and parochial schools, taking refuge from Yankee contempt in a well-defended enclave.

Though religion and class were powerful barriers to acceptance for the Irish immigrants of the mid-nineteenth century, knowing English made their transition to work and life in America far easier and faster than it was for the groups who came after them—first the French Canadians, then the Poles, all Catholic as well, and finally the Germans, who established the first immigrant Protestant enclaves, building Lutheran churches and keeping separate from both the native Protestants and the ethnic Catholics. German immigrants tended to be highly skilled industrial workers and moved into positions with better pay faster than any other immigrant groups. They were also more politically active. It was German Socialists who led the first successful strikes among millworkers.

When a recession undermined the plans of the Hadley Falls investors before all of the fifty-four mills in the original plan could be built, the Holyoke Water Power Company bought them out. The coming of the Civil War a few years later stimulated new growth in the economy, and the new mill owners, local investors, diversified quickly. They sold water rights and encouraged local businesses that would require their products, thus creating a more interdependent economy. Still, the economy was predicated on two kinds of exploitable resources: water and immigrant labor.

Holyoke became famous for the production of thread, silk,

cotton, woolens, and paper. At one point, over a hundred mills were in operation twenty-four hours a day, seven days a week. By the 1880s the city became the largest producer of paper in the world, earning itself the name it was known by well into the twentieth century: Paper City.

In the first decades of the 1900s, when eastern and southern European immigrants came to Holyoke in large numbers, the city was named the third worst in America because of the crowding and disease in its tenements. With the development of steam and electrically powered engines, however, it lost the advantage of its location on the Connecticut River. Through the twenties and thirties, the city's economy weakened, with only a few of the big textile mills remaining open. By the late fifties and early sixties, when the Puerto Ricans began arriving in significant numbers, they were the only immigrant group to face a city in decline.

And only the Puerto Rican ethnic community revitalized the inner city of South Holyoke by building on their agrarian heritage, creating a small-scale, sustainable economy based on organic gardening.

Late on the summer afternoon when Daniel and I went from garden to garden collecting produce for the farmers' market, I walked back to the original garden, La Finquita, to rest. The path down the center of the gardens has one small branch to the right, which leads to a grassy spot where a picnic table and two benches sit in the shade of a pair of maples. Red, blue, white, and yellow stripes spiral up the base of each tree, giving the quiet grove a festive look. A *casita* for tools and wheelbarrows has been painted midnight blue with deep yellow trim.

Up on this rise, I choose a bench and sit down. It's cool under the maples. The gardens are quiet and empty.

A man on a motorcycle races his engine, waiting for the light to change. Sirens wail in the distance. But here, near the gardens, a calm has settled. Pea flowers have opened in the afternoon sun, unfurling ruffled petals on the twining bright green vines. The gardens are planted thick and neat. It really does feel like a small farm.

Here and there a rake or a hoe has been left lying between the rows. Each marks a pause. The gardener will soon come back, lean down, take it up again, and continue to work. As I study the long avenue of garden plots, each with a tool carefully laid beside the row where someone left off to go home and eat and rest awhile from the intense sun, a question comes to me: Why are gardens so often presented to us with the fact of human work erased?

This morning, after I met Alejandro and before Daniel took me to see the gardens, I sat here on this bench asking some of the elders about their experience as migrant farmworkers. Candido Nieves, a thirteen-year-old member of the boys' group known as Protectores de la Tierra, Protectors of the Earth, sat beside me, translating.

The rows stretched from here to the clock tower. Alejandro said it first, when he tried to explain how far he had to go, stooped over, picking asparagus. Later Juan Lopez, Israel Rivera, and Heriberto Santiago all said the same thing. "Big big big farm," Israel said. The rows of onions, or mushrooms, or strawberries, went from here to that clock over there on the hill. The rows of cucumbers were so long that when they looked up, they could not see the sun.

Heriberto then got down on the ground, kneeling on the cool grass under the painted trees of La Finquita, and smiled with pride, miming how deftly he pulled back leaves with one hand and cut the stems with the other, shuffling forward the length of a row on knees and shins, left, right, swipe, swipe, shuffle, shuffle. He drew the curved blade of the knife he'd brought with him from Puerto Rico in the air. He couldn't find one like it here.

'You worked like that all day?' I asked through Candido.

Yes, for hours at a time.

Inching forward on his knees, as in some penitential rite of the pilgrim. Now I understood how Heriberto could not see the sun.

Once Juan, Israel, and Heriberto left, I packed up my things and followed Candido back into the gardens.

"Now will you show me your favorite part of the garden?" I asked as we turned into the broad aisle that runs down the center. It was hot and still, and Candido moved slowly. He kept walking, as if he had not heard me. But then he stopped and turned.

"I like this part, because you see flowers, white flowers, everywhere," he said. "They're from the beans growing up the fence." He put one large hand behind a leaf and lifted it gently so I could see the blossoms and the light shining through the intricate pattern of white lines on the sharply cut leaves. "This is where the fruit comes from, the bean. It comes from the flower. I like the color in the leaves. The white lines on the green. How it matches the white flowers and green stems. I like how the flowers are formed. They're like a little animal here. A little elephant, they look like. And the shape on the leaf is like an insect, like camouflage. It looks like a little kite right there. A butterfly too."

Candido is very tall. To look this closely at a leaf or a small white flower, he must stoop over the trailing vine. I looked with him, leaning into the leaves to see the opening flowers where his imagination, still capable of wonder, finds an elephant, an insect, a butterfly, a kite.

"I like walking here," he said quietly. "It's like a forest."

The word sounded formal, as if Candido were describing an august place, one best approached with the blend of awe and desire I heard in his voice.

"When did you learn that the flower forms the pea?"

Seven years ago, when he joined La Finquita. "It was my first time gardening here. We planted our own garden," he explained.

Seven summers of gardening, learning from the elders how to plant seeds, how to water, what to weed, and when to harvest.

"Look at those squirrels trying to eat," Candido said, smiling as we passed through the gate. "Look at the colors of the peppers," he added, at ease, gesturing toward the last garden plot on the end.

"What do you think you want to do when you finish high school?" I asked him as we stood at the corner of Cabot and Main, waiting for the light to change so we could cross back to the Nuestras Raíces office.

"I want to go to a culinary school," he said. We turned at the same moment, as people will who walk side by side, and Candido smiled as he said to me, "That's what I'm practicing in school now. I want to be a chef." An eighteen-wheeler lumbers by. "I'll probably work there," he said, nodding toward Mi Plaza, the community restaurant in the renovated building beside the Nuestra Raíces greenhouse.

"What's unique and effective about Nuestras Raíces?" Daniel says in our last few minutes before I leave. "Here's how I would put it. A youth worker and an elder start *aji dulce* seeds in the greenhouse. When those little seedlings grow big enough, they get sold to one of the community gardeners here or at the farmers' market. Then in August the pepper is harvested and sold to somebody in the community kitchen, who produces sofrito. That sofrito is then sold to the restaurant owner, who uses it in his cooking and sells it to the public. This summer we're going to complete the circle by composting some of the food waste from the restaurant. Then we'll mix the compost into the soil of the gardens and the greenhouse. So what we're doing at its most basic level is recreating a healthy community and economy. We're building it from scratch because it's been lost . . ." Daniel pauses, then adds, "if it ever did exist."

Nuestras Raíces is closing the circle, imitating nature in moving toward a sustainable, no-waste system that continually renews itself through the cycle of growth and decay.

"The only progress that counts," Aldo Leopold once said, "is that on the actual landscape."

In the end, it's a question of scale, the difference between the inhuman length of a row of tulips or asparagus on an industrial farm, measured by the distance from La Finquita to the clock tower, and the length of a row of Alejandro's beans.

If you could see South Holyoke from the air, the original plan of the men from Boston would still be visible: the dam on the great curve of the Connecticut River at Hadley Falls, the horseshoe of mills around the stepped canals that once drove their turbines. But then, all around the straight bar of silver light that is the calmly flowing water of the Race Street canal, you would see the green oases of the gardens of Nuestras Raíces. And there, on the corner where the coaches once stopped, you would see the ribbed arch of a greenhouse beside a fountain and a brick plaza surrounded by a raised garden. And on the wall above the entry to Mi Plaza, you would see, at the center of a huge mural painted by children, a blue-and-green globe displaying the familiar shape of the Americas linked by a slender belt of land. From it a great tree has grown—a flamboyan, native to Puerto Rico. Its blazing crown—the same color as New England trees in autumn—spreads wide, sheltering the land, its slender roots reaching down to encircle the earth.

8

JUSTICE

A Yankee Farmer and Sacred Indian Corn

STONINGTON, CONNECTICUT

"I'm the eleventh generation of the family to work this farm. And I may be the last. This is the last working farm in Stonington, and it was also one of the first. We haven't missed a crop here since 1654."

He's got the thickest Yankee accent I've ever heard, bar none. Tall, thick-chested, with clear blue eyes and a weather-creased face, Whit Davis comes to greet me in jeans and a blue denim shirt, red suspenders and a straw hat.

Whit Davis, a local gardener told me, was someone who had close ties with the Native American tribes of Connecticut, the Mohegans and Pequots. His English ancestors were the Stantons, one of the founding families of Stonington, a picturesque fishing village that is now an enclave of the wealthy and that was built on a sheltered headland between Long Island Sound and the Pawcatuck River, on land that had once belonged to the Pequots.

It had taken nearly two weeks to arrange to meet. The first

time I came, I found the farm, but no one was home. It was a clear, hot day in July, and all around me the waving grasses hummed with insects. Up on the knoll stood a dark brown house of great age and grace. It was rundown, with all the signs of a working farm in midsummer where no one had time to keep up the yard, yet striking for the dignity of its clean geometry and its purchase on the land.

I walked up the rocky unpaved driveway and knocked at the kitchen door. No one answered. I peered in the windows. A huge Glenwood stove sat back against one wall, cardboard boxes stacked all around and on top of it. Through the windows opposite, I could see clear across the road to the sweep of a great meadow and low-lying salt marshes. This must have been the summer kitchen. Despite the clutter inside and out, an air of stillness and tranquility inhabited the place.

I wrote a quick note, tucked it in the side window of a pickup parked in the driveway, and left.

When Whit finally called, I told him what I was looking for.

"Well, I've got a two-acre field of Indian white flint corn up here. When the Mohegan tribe has its annual Wigwam this August, I'll be going up there to make the johnnycakes for them," he said.

If I want, I can drive up and see the corn.

A few days later, we drive down hot mud tracks through the grass between the fine old house and a barn and then head toward the water. "Hold on now, this is only front-wheel drive," Whit says. "I've got to get through this mud pretty quick so we don't get stuck."

The corn is taller than we are. Whit stops the truck, jumps out, and disappears down a row. I hear his voice booming through the stalks and leaves and try to follow. The mosquitoes find me instantly and swarm.

"This is your corn right here, filling in pretty good." He strips back the husks on a long fat ear to show me the kernels. "That's the old eight-row Indian white flint corn. They all grew it—Narragansett, Pequot, Mohegan, Nehantic. And when that begins to get a little shadow, kind of a butterscotch color, a spot on the tips of the ear of the kernels, it's ready to pick and dry. We're going to let this go longer, we're going to let this dry on the stalk pretty much. When that dries, you run it through a sheller. And then you go to the corner of the barn and you pour it, one bushel basket into another, and the wind's blowing, and that will blow all that chaff right out of there." Winnowing, the ancient way. "This is the johnnycake corn," Whit says emphatically. "Yokeag corn. Right back from before the colonists came here."

Johnnycakes is a corruption of "journey cakes." In 1628, Isaack de Rasieres, an agent for the Dutch West India Company, described how the local Indians made them: "The finest meal they mix with lukewarm water, and knead it into dough, then they make round flat little cakes of it, the thickness of an inch or a little more, which they bury in hot ashes, and so bake into bread; and when they are baked they have some clean fresh water by them in which they wash them when hot, one after another, and it is good bread, but heavy."

"Do the Mohegans or Pequots still have this seed?" I ask Whit.

"No," he says. "It was a stone trap, a dead fall. They lost it when they lost their land."

Blunt and swift, the cruel surprise of tricking your prey into releasing the bone-crushing weight that will kill it, "stone trap" seems an apt figure for the history of the English, the Indians, and the land—the story held by this cornfield.

The story of corn in New England is the story of one idea of the garden supplanting another, as one culture set out to supplant another. Three hundred and fifty years ago, the seeds of white flint corn that the Algonkian-speaking Indians had carried east with them a thousand years earlier passed into the hands of their European conquerors. In a quiet gesture of restorative justice,

Whit Davis, who inherited the seeds with the land that came to his English ancestors in the decades following the Pequot Massacre at Mystic in 1637, now gives them back.

On the way back to the house, Whit describes his plans for this corn. "Once it's dried—that'll take about a year—I'll have this ground for cornmeal, johnnycakes, cornbread. Bring it up to Harry Here's Farm up there in Exeter, Rhode Island, where he has a water-driven gristmill, and have it ground. I gave him some of my seeds a few years back, and when I went up there to get some this year, why, he gave me some of my own seeds back. They've been in my family for generations. Now I hope that when we have a homecoming, a Wigwam Festival, we can have our own corn this time—we won't have to go buy the meal from another farmer that grows it and has a gristmill."

Something in this account, lodged in Whit's pronouns as he slides from *I* to *we* and back again, catches my attention, but I don't say anything.

When we arrive at the house, Whit invites me in. He launches his narrative before I'm halfway through the door.

"You see that table there? You ever heard of Uncas? He was the first chief of the Mohegans. During King Philip's War, Uncas sat at that table right there. If that table could talk, boy, she'd tell you some stories."

We sit there too, and I run my hands over the table's worn surface, relishing the eighteen-inch boards. King Philip's War, the costliest war in American history, broke out in 1675 and consumed New England like wildfire, spreading from Connecticut to Maine.

"My original ancestor, Thomas Stanton, was interpreter general for the United Colonies," Whit says. "He was a friend of Uncas. In fact, he wrote Uncas's will. We've been looking for that will for over two hundred years. Still haven't found it."

The Stonington Chronology notes that in 1670, "accompanied by a picked band of braves in full war regalia, Uncas visited his old friend, Thos. Stanton, at his home in Lower Pawcatuck to have him write and witness his will." They held "a 'big party,' with Indian dances, a great feast, and much smoking of the peace pipe." This house, and the field of corn we have just visited, would not be here if these two men, Uncas and Stanton, had not played pivotal roles in the struggle to determine whether colonists and Indians could live together in peace.

Whit stands up and asks me if I want to see the rest of the house. We climb all the way to the attic, and he shows me where the black slaves whose descendants now come to the Stanton family reunions slept around a huge brick chimney. "See those trunks over there?" He points to the far corner, where great wooden trunks with arched lids, their wooden ribs coated in dust, are piled on top of one another. "Those haven't been opened in three generations."

While I'm pondering the mystery of what those trunks from colonial days might hold, he turns and I follow him slowly past worn leather doctors' bags, birdcages, and dollhouses. We descend carefully down the stairs to the second floor, where he shows me his father's cradle, the Revolutionary War musket his great-grandmother saved, an eighteenth-century muzzle-loader, the seventeenth-century diaries of a ship's captain who sailed between Barbados and New England, and then a pair of silver spurs so sharp you can still pierce a finger on them. Once the house is turned into a museum, as it soon will be, it will never again be possible to visit each room and hear the story of each clock and lamp and photograph told with the intimate, knowing relish of someone who lived here.

As rich and deep as the Stanton family lode is, three centuries of dwelling in the same house feels thin beside the history of the land and the seeds Whit has planted there. Standing near a window composed of twelve over twelve panes of wavy and bubbled glass, he gestures toward his land. "We've got stone tools from a field down there that go back ten thousand years. And there's a village site that's five thousand years old. We've had archaeologists come down here three times since the 1930s, and every one of them has told us the same dates. That village site down there is just one tribe on top of another. They'd fight and drive each other out, then another tribe would live there. I didn't want to see all that buried up and blacktopped. I want it preserved as a farm." Whit and a board of directors have secured nonprofit status for the house as a future museum and have begun raising funds for its restoration.

"So anyway, I got it by the attorney general that we can pass the land on to members of the family, and well, I think that pretty well guarantees that the state isn't going to get a hold of it. There are five hundred Stantons out there, still living. Because the first thing the state does when they get a piece of land is scorched earth—they burn the house for a fire drill, bulldoze in the cellar, and that's it—cover it over and that's the end of that. That's the state's policy. That's been for as long as I can remember."

The theme of preservation, the need to be keen in foreseeing betrayals and foreclosures in order to outwit and outlive them, has been struck; it will resound, with deepening variations, for the length of the raveled story.

"The state cheated me," Whit says, his syllables clipped as he remembers. "We agreed on the price, but then they found a loophole and they got it for sixty cents on the dollar." He shakes his head in disgust. We've reached the front room, where dust motes hang in the light filtered through the old glass. This is where Whit nursed his father through his final illness, having set up a sickbed near the potbellied stove, which kept them both warm in the huge, drafty house. He sweeps his arms out, turning slightly so that my gaze follows his around the room—from the sagging beam and buckling wall where one of the original six chimneys threatens to give way to the long folding tables friends have set up, covered with the contents of old cupboards, closets, and drawers, so they can sort their way through three hundred and fifty years of family life.

"I'd have had this house all fixed up if they hadn't skinned me," Whit says. "So I'm in the Indians' corner. Broken promises. Broken treaties. You know? The greed of the white man."

I am so startled to hear this from a tall, robust, blue-eyed Yankee of such a pedigree that in spite of myself, I laugh.

It is strange, but true, that the justification for taking the Indians' land in New England—and so the resulting violence—grew out of an argument for the true nature of a garden.

"The whole earth is the Lord's garden," John Winthrop, Sr., wrote in 1629, in *Reasons and Considerations Touching the Lawfulness of Removing Out of England into the Parts of America,* ". . . and he hath given it to the sons of Adam to be tilled and improved by them . . . Why then should we stand starving here for the places of habitation . . . and in the mean time suffer whole countries, as profitable for the use of man, to lie waste without any improvement."

Preparing for the Great Migration of the English to America, Winthrop anticipated the objection that "we have noe warrant to enter upon land which has so long been possessed by others." He resolved the moral dilemma by arguing that because the Indians "enclose noe Land, neither have any settled habytation, nor any tame Cattell to improve the Land by," the only lands they had established title to were their cornfields. This meant "the rest of the country lay open to any that could and would improve it." So long as the English left the Indians land "sufficient for their use," Winthrop argued, "we may lawfully take the rest, there being more than enough for them and us."

The English described their coming to "the garden of New England" as a *planting,* not a violent uprooting of the indigenous peoples. Each settlement was a *plantation.* This made the English both *plants* (or, more properly, *transplants*) and gardeners, cultivating their culture in a new land. But what place in this extended garden metaphor did this leave for the Indians? Winthrop's invocation of the biblical mandate to cultivate "the Lord's garden" sanctioned a religious and political ideology of racial supremacy, lending credence to a form of economic and ecological imperialism that would give rise to incalculable suffering for Indians and whites alike and initiate a series of cascading biological and social changes that would do violence to the land as well.

Among the first biological consequences of European contact with the New England tribes were the epidemics of 1616 and 1633. Exposed to pathogens to which they had no immunity, Indians died in vast numbers. The rapid spread of infection emptied whole villages, reducing the Indian population so drastically that the tribes of northern New England states, including New Hampshire and Vermont, virtually disappeared. In 1632, Thomas Morton, the author of *The New English Canaan,* wrote that coming upon an Indian village wiped out by disease was like coming upon "a new found Golgotha," there were so many skulls and bones lying exposed on the ground.

Once the terrified and demoralized survivors of the epidemics fled, leaving their dead unburied—a sign of the extent to which disease broke down the traditional structure of their communities—the English took over their gardens, harvesting their cornfields and raiding their pit barns, using the carefully stored dried corn for seed and for food. They built their own villages where Indian villages had once stood, cutting more and more trees for the construction of solid wooden houses and strong fences to enclose private gardens.

"God," John Winthrop wrote in 1634, "hath hereby cleared our title to this place."

In 1635, just one year after Winthrop's startling claim that God had cleared the title to New England for the English, Whit Davis's ancestor reached the shores of America.

No one really knows why Thomas Stanton renounced his

patrimony to sail for the New World in January that year. It may have been his decision to become a Puritan, and as a result his withdrawal from Oxford University in July 1634, that put a wedge between him and his parents. Whatever his reasons, Stanton immediately shaped an extraordinary role for himself in a defining moment of American history. Arriving in Virginia aboard the *Bonaventure* when he was no more than twenty, he walked all the way to Boston, where he knew he would find friends from his home in Warwickshire. By the time he arrived, having been given food, shelter, and guidance by tribe after tribe on the long trek north, he was fluent in the Algonkian languages.

Once in Boston, Stanton quickly gained a post as a mediator between the English and the Indians in matters of trade, land disputes, and treaties—a role he would play, later with the formal title of interpreter general for the United Colonies, until his death in 1677. After he was accepted as a member of the Puritan congregation in Hartford, he was granted a monopoly on the fur trade along a stretch of the Connecticut River. He became known to the most powerful Englishmen of the Massachusetts Bay Colony, who needed his services as a translator. He also became known to the principal tribes along the Connecticut shoreline, including the Pequots and the Mohegans.

The Mohegans were in fact Pequots who had only recently broken away under the leadership of Uncas, a young and powerful sagamore tied to the royal family by both blood and marriage. It was Uncas's frustrated claim to the status of sachem —his rivalry with Sassacus, his father-in-law—that led to his rebellion and banishment from the Pequot tribe in 1635. Tensions arising from the recent extension of the Europeans' trade routes and the smallpox epidemic that had decimated the coastal tribes as a result in 1633 contributed to this split. The two factions of the tribe chose radically different strategies to deal with the European invaders: Sassacus chose resistance, Uncas alliance with the English.

In 1636, soon after Stanton's arrival in Connecticut, a series of heated skirmishes fueled in part by the escalating pressure of colonial trade on the Native American subsistence economy led to the outbreak of war between the Pequots and an alliance of English, Mohegans, and Narragansetts. This, the first of New England's Indian wars, culminated in a predawn attack on the Pequot fort at Mystic in 1637, led by John Mason. As William DeForest recounts in his *History of the Indians of Connecticut*, once Mason had succeeded in penetrating the palisaded fort that enclosed many hundreds of sleeping Pequots, including women, children, and old people, he shouted, "We must burn them" to his second-in-command, John Underhill. The fire they set burned so quickly "that in little more than an hour this frightful death-agony of a community was over." Between four and seven hundred Pequots perished in the fire.

The remaining Pequots fled southwest along the coastline and took refuge in a large swamp in Fairfield. Not content with having driven the Indians from the valuable coastal territory they wished to control, the English pursued them. Led to the swamp by Uncas, whose men had no trouble tracking the starving refugees through the wilderness by noting the signs of their desperate hunt for edible roots and tubers along the way, the English surrounded them. Though Mason tried to dissuade him, Thomas Stanton, attempting to avoid a second massacre, went into the swamp to explain to the Pequots the terms on which their lives might be spared.

Within two hours, two hundred Pequots—old men, women, and children—came out of the swamp. Only a group of warriors remained. The next morning, in deep fog, a fight ensued. Many Pequots were killed. The rest were taken prisoner.

"The colonists at first tried to make use of their prisoners as servants, or, more properly, as slaves;" DeForest writes, "but such was the uneasiness of these proud children of the forest, and so troublesome did they make themselves to their master, that very few of them remained any long time in servitude. A small number, as we learn from Winthrop, were shipped off by the

Massachusetts people, and sold in the West Indies." The surviving Pequots who were not sold into slavery were divided among the tribes allied with the English. The largest number, nearly one hundred, were given to Uncas, whose power grew in proportion to the suffering and dispersal of his former people.

The terms of defeat, it is clear, were meant not only to subjugate but to strip a whole people of their identity. "The Pequots," DeForest records, "were not to live in their ancient country, nor to be called by their ancient name, but to become Narragansetts and Mohegans. Lastly, the Pequot territory was not to be claimed by the sachems, but to be considered property of the English of Connecticut."

In the years following the Pequot Massacre, tensions escalated between Indians and colonists, culminating with King Philip's War, named for the great Wampanoag chief Metacom, called Philip by the English, who led a loose alliance of independent tribes against the colonies. This, DeForest writes, was "a war for freedom and existence, and when those were no longer possible, it became a war of revenge."

As William Cronon argues in *Changes in the Land,* it was the cascading effect of the colonists' transformation of the landscape, one change leading to many others, that unraveled the balanced subsistence ecology and local economy of the Indians and led to the violent collision of two distinct views of how to live on the land. The provocations for the outbreak of King Philip's War included an arrogant attempt by the government of Plymouth Plantation to force the Wampanoags into an agreement granting the colonists the exclusive right to purchase the land Indians had begun to sell in order to survive, and the continual destruction of Indian gardens by colonists' farm animals, for which the Indians sought legal redress, without success.

The war, DeForest records, "broke out in June, 1675, just about a century before the commencement of our own struggle for independence, and continued with uninterrupted fury until the autumn of 1676." This was "the last great struggle of the native tribes of New England against the race of foreigners which was gradually crowding them out of the land of their fathers."

In 1676, after a raid party captured King Philip's wife and children, Philip himself was also captured. The war ended soon after he was murdered while in custody, killed by an Indian loyal to the English. The losses on both sides were terrible. But for the Indians loyal to King Philip, the consequences were especially devastating. Those who had not lost their lives lost their land, and many more lost their freedom as men, women, and children were sold into slavery in the West Indies.

The Indians' fight to drive the English from the land was over. All across New England, Englishmen returning home recorded coming upon acres and acres of abandoned Indian cornfields.

Without this historical context—the abandoned corn as the sign of English dominance on the land—Whit's return of the seeds that were at the center of Native American culture before the English conquest can seem like an idiosyncratic or sentimental gesture by an aging farmer. Yet the meeting of Indians and the English is a critical moment for restoring history and politics to the American garden, and corn is the most potent seed of all for unearthing the complicated story of our tangled relationship to the land.

Corn. *Zea mays.* "If maize were the only gift the American Indian presented to the world," Alfred Crosby writes in *The Columbian Exchange,* "he would deserve undying gratitude." Indigenous peoples of the Americas domesticated two thirds of the staple foods the world eats today, corn so long ago that no one has ever found a specimen of it in the wild. As corn traveled north with peoples migrating from Mesoamerica into what is now the United States, it evolved into local land races—ethno-ecological adaptations of a seed not only to the place where it was cultivated but to the people whose hands planted, tended, and harvested it. Oaxaca Green, Hopi Blue, Pawnee Black Eagle,

Cherokee White Eagle, Iroquois White—the many names of Indian corns testify to millennia of intimacy between people and the seeds their lives depended on, seeds they held sacred, seeing them always as a gift of the Creator.

As Roger Williams noted in the seventeenth century, the oral tradition of New England tribes preserved the ancient origin of corn in their veneration of "Kautántowwit, the great God of the Southwest, to whose house all souls goe and from whom came their Corne and Beans."

One of the most detailed descriptions of Indian gardens in New England comes from John Winthrop's son, John Winthrop, Jr., who presented his paper "Description, Culture, and Use of Maiz" to the Royal Society in 1662 while in London to negotiate a formal charter for the colony of Connecticut, where he served as governor.

> The corn, used in New England before the English planted there, is called by the Natives, Weachin, known by the name of Maiz...
>
> The Ear is for the most part, about a span long, composed of several, commonly 8 rows of Grains... and in each row, usually above 30 Grains. Of various colours, as Red, White, yellow, Blew, Olive, Grenish, Black, Specked, striped, &. sometimes in the same field, and the same Ear. But the White and Yellow are the most common.
>
> ...It is Planted... most commonly from the middle of April to the middle of May. Some of the Indians take the time of the coming up of a fish, called Aloofes, into the Rivers. Others of the budding of some Trees.
>
> ...The manner of Planting is in Rows, at equal distance every way, about 5 or 6 feet. They open the Earth with an Howe, taking away the surface 3. or 4. inches deep, and the bredth of the Howe; and so throw in 4. or 5. Granes, a little distant from another, and cover them with Earth. If two or three grow, it may do well...

> The Corn grown up an hands length, they cut up the weeds, and loosen the Earth, about it, with a broad Howe: repeating this labour, as the Weeds grow. When the Stalk begins to grow high, they draw a little Earth about it: and upon the putting forth of the Eare, so much, as to make a little Hill...
>
> ...The Indians, and some English (especially in good Ground, and well tilthed) at every Corn-hill, plant with the Corn, a kind of French or Turkey-Beans: the Stalks of the Corn serving instead of Poles for the Beans to climb up with. And in the vacant places between the Hills they will Plant Squashes and Pompions; loading the Ground with as much as it will bear. And many, after the last weeding, spring Turnep-seed between the Hills, and so, after Harvest, have good Crop of Turneps.
>
> ...After 'tis gather'd, it must, except laid very thin, be presently stripped from the Husks; otherwise it will heat, grow mouldy, and sometimes sprout.
>
> ...The Natives commonly Thresh it as they gather it, dry it well on Mats in the Sun, and then bestow it in holes in the Ground (which are their Barns) well lined with withered Grass and Matts, and then covered with the like, and over all with Earth: and so its kept very well, till they use it.

Winthrop's is a careful account of the traditional intercropping of the "Three Sisters," corns, beans, and squash. He records the Indians' method of mounding up corn hills and the natural signs by which they knew the correct time for planting—when the *aloofs,* or alewives, are running, when the shadbush blooms. Winthrop records the evidence of an astonishing genetic diversity—a rainbow of corns, sometimes all in one field or even on one ear—and notes that the Indians could "load" the land so that it yielded several harvests without exhausting it.

The earthen mound of the corn hill made more air and moisture available to the corn's roots, while the corn stalks provided

support for the climbing beans, whose roots in turn fixed nitrogen in the soil, replenishing what the nutrient-hungry corn removed. And the squash plant's huge leaves and trailing habit provided a living mulch that kept weeds down and cooled the soil while trapping moisture. It was an elegant and sophisticated form of gardening.

John Winthrop, Jr., saw no contradiction between his father's claim thirty years earlier that the Indians did not know how to use land and so had no legal claim to it and his own testament to how efficient and productive their intercropped gardens actually were. The Winthrops could not, or would not, see how sound the Indians' use of their land was. Though Roger Williams argued eloquently that the Indians' methods of cultivation gave them legal rights to their traditional lands, his voice did not prevail.

"This is the field right here," Whit says. An expanse of timothy, a deep, rich green, stretches away from us toward an old stone wall. We stand at the edge of the field quietly, just looking. "Right over that knoll, that's where the Indian village was, right on the shore."

Years ago, Whit and his father found an old seashell midden on the riverbank. Oyster shells. "They were there, but we didn't know what they were. An archaeologist in the thirties came out here poking around and spoke to my father and asked if he'd show him around. My father says, 'Oh yeah, sure, I guess so.' He had a little pointy trowel with him. He dug down a little bit, just scooped away the shells a little bit, and he found a piece of a flint chip from making arrows. Then he found a little piece of bird bone that'd been thrown out, you know, when they cooked it, threw it in the fire—you know, the bones. So he asked if they could come down here and pitch a tent and spend some time digging. The agreement my father had with them was that my father was to have all the stone artifacts, they could have the pottery and bones. Well, they got some beautiful pots, and they're all up to the University of Connecticut. That's how we came to know how old the remains in these fields are.

"They were supposed to stop at the house every time they came out, the archaeologist was, the big shot that was sponsoring the dig down there. And leave all the stone artifacts, which we were supposed to keep, with my father. And they were to have the bones and pottery. Well, we didn't draw any distinction at the time, not knowing they were going to find any graves there. So they come out—now, this was just a dirt cowpath, a wagon road, trail—and they came out one time and they stopped at the house. They had to come up through the yard. So he showed my father the stone artifacts. I imagine a lot of it went out that he didn't see, that they just took. So my father sees a box on the back seat. And he says, 'Well, what do you have in that box there?'

"'Well,' he says, 'that's just some remains that we found of a child.' My father says, 'You found the remains of a child?' He says, 'Yes.' My father says, 'What are you doing with it out here?' The guy says, 'We're going to take it back for our collection at the museum up in Hartford.' My father says, 'Oh no you're not.' 'Well,' he said, 'you said we could have the bone artifacts.' My father says, 'That's right. All the animal bones you want. Those are human bones.' My father said, 'That child was born there, lived there, died there. And somewhere around there were people who loved the child, and that was his home, and you're not going to move them, you're going to leave them right here.'

"So he kicked them out right there. My father says, 'Tomorrow night, sundown, I want your tent pulled up and moved out.'

"Not knowing which pit they came out of, we weren't sure what to do with them. My father at that time had a cabinetmaker who was pretty handy at making wooden gadgets and things. So he had him make up a little coffin box with a glass cover, and we kept that in the case inside the door there under lock and key.

"Well, came along one day one of the state men was down. He represented the land preservation department in Hartford, I

guess it's part of DEP, and I showed him the Indian relics in the glass cabinet there by the front door that I showed you. And it came out as we talked that he was an Indian. He was at that time the executive director of the Connecticut River Powwow Society. So I showed that to him and he said, 'Did you ever think about a reburial?' I said, 'Yes. But I didn't know how, know who, nor when.' He says, 'I know how and I know who. You tell us when.' 'All right.' So we agreed on a date. I told him that I didn't want any newspapers, I didn't want any press or media down there of any kind, and no pictures. He says, 'Fine.' I says, 'You can invite whatever Indians you want to attend.' So he did. We had forty. Men, women, and a few children.

"The supreme medicine man of the Wampanoag Nation did the service. He's dead now. We were all down there at the gravesite. The Indians dug the pit. And all the white man did, and that was me, was to take a crowbar and stick it down in the ground and get down where there were no stones so they could dig. They took the dirt and put it on a tarpaulin. The Indians dug the hole, and they were all down there. The medicine man asked me, he says, 'Where are the remains?' I says, 'Up at the house.' I said, 'You get your assistant there, get right in my pickup there, we'll go right up and get it.'

"So we went up to the house and went in and I got the key that I had hidden in the house. I opened up the case. It was very touching. I didn't mean it to be. I was just surprised. But I took the little box out and I handed it to him and I says, 'Here.' I says, 'This is yours.' And he kind of looked at me, he looked kind of funny, you know, and then I saw the tears coming down his cheeks. He said, 'You know, people don't do this for us.' He says, 'What we find is that they've been ground up with the bulldozers and excavators, opening up roads and building houses.' He says, 'We don't get a chance to put someone back where they came from, where they lived.'

"So that was it. I wasn't trying to be demonstrative. *Here, this is yours, this is your people. Here, take it.* That's all. We planted that, we buried that child's remains, right between the women and the big guy they'd unearthed in the thirties. I didn't want to disturb them. The child was within fifty feet of either one, down between them.

"We took everyone down there with a pair of horses, in the hayride wagon, about twenty of them. Most of them were in regalia. The medicine man was wearing deerskins. My wife and I and her daughter and her two kids and my oldest son were the only non-Indian ones there. I never saw such an impressive ceremony in my life. In fact, I liked it so well that I asked the Mohegans when my time comes if they'll come down and do a service for me up there in the cemetery."

"You know, you come from good people," I say as we climb into the cab of his old pickup to head back up to the house.

"Oh, I don't know," Whit replies, not turning to look at me.

"That's a good instinct, don't you think?" I ask.

"I don't know. I treat people the way I'd like to be treated. That's all I can do."

One day while reading the history of the New England tribes, I discovered that in 1930, around the time Whit's father caught the archaeologists attempting to spirit away the remains of an Indian child from the ancient village gravesite, a young Mohegan woman named Gladys Tantaquidgeon published a piece about the enduring place of white flint corn among the Aquinnahs of Gay Head, Martha's Vineyard. A branch of the Wampanoags, the Aquinnahs, who still live at Gay Head, are a remnant of King Philip's people. The island of Martha's Vineyard was originally theirs.

Gladys Tantaquidgeon, now 106, carries the last of the authentic Mohegan names. She has been the Mohegan Nation's honorary medicine woman for many years, having played a crucial role in preserving the tribe's history in a small museum on Mohegan Hill in what is now the town of Uncasville, where she lived with her brother Harold, who was tribal chief for a time. Harold Tantaquidgeon was a friend of Whit Davis's father.

In "Notes on the Gay Head Indians of Massachusetts," Tantaquidgeon writes with deep respect of the Aquinnahs, describing them as "peaceful, conservative-minded people" who "have made every effort to maintain the rights bequeathed to them by their sachem 'Metaark' in 1681 . . . Despite the culture-destroying forces of Europeanization," she notes, "some few uncontaminated practices have survived at Gay Head," the most important being their abiding tie to their ancestral corn.

Unlike "the remnant groups on the mainland," Tantaquidgeon notes, a discreet allusion to her own people, the Aquinnahs had preserved a core community of two hundred who had never left their traditional lands. She lingers over the Aquinnahs' continued love of yokeag, the food made from white flint corn that has been parched and pounded—the fine cornmeal the Narragansetts shared with Roger Williams, the same food that Thomas Stanton must have eaten on his long walk to Boston three centuries earlier. Well into the twentieth century, the Aquinnahs still prepared yokeag, "a delicacy to be served on special occasions or when one's 'aboriginal nature or constitution' demands 'pure' food, sacred through being made from corn by an ancient process." They still used handmade wooden mortars and stone pestles, "purely aboriginal utensils," to grind their corn into fine flour, as their ancestors had for hundreds of years. The Aquinnahs' reverence for the rules governing the preparation of yokeag, Tantaquidgeon concludes, bear "the traits of an ancient religious rite."

Soon after I found Gladys Tantaquidgeon's essay, I contacted the Aquinnah tribe to ask if they still had the seeds of the white flint corn necessary for the ritual preparation of yokeag. They did not. Would they like some? Their response was immediate.

It's two days before Thanksgiving when I drive back up to Whit's place—bright sun, unclouded sky, and a light wind that carries a chill. But the grass is still green and the sun warms my hair. The corn has been harvested, sorted, and put away to dry, and I have come to see it. By now I know the way here so well that I arrive early. Since Whit isn't back from delivering eggs yet, I take advantage of my solitude to roam.

The house is so still and quiet that it seems as if it has already become a museum. Having seen the old main door only from the inside, I walk around to the front for the first time and sit down on the threshold, a dark half-moon of gray stone. One clump of tall black-eyed Susans is still blooming, sheltered by a stone wall, chest high, that reaches all the way around a gently sloping stretch of grass, enclosing it but for a space where a gate would have been. This must have been the original kitchen garden. I get up and walk its perimeter. The 'Red Sail' lettuce still looks fresh, so I reach down and tear off a leaf and eat it. Nearby is a row of rhubarb, its ruby stalks bright amid the dark green leaves. The dried pods of locoweed rattle when the breeze stirs, ready to scatter mud-colored seeds.

Three hundred years—that's how long there has been a garden here. The sun has warmed the rock just enough so that it's comfortable enough to sit, so I do, turning to touch the grain in the weathered clapboards. I know that just inside the wide door, its wood gray with age, hangs a ceremonial Indian pipe, its bowl made of deer bone still packed with tobacco. Above the door, alternating square panes of cobalt blue and clear old glass let daylight into the hallway. An old brass oil lamp, its glass chimney intact, hangs from a nail. It would have been hung high on the wall beneath the great staircase, its light visible through the clerestory to guide a traveler home.

In 1649, Thomas Stanton was granted a three-year monopoly on trade near the place where the Pawcatuck River empties into Little Narragansett Bay. First he had a trading post built about two miles from here, right on the riverbank, and a house near here; in time, work on this house began. Though a skilled carpenter, perhaps a shipbuilder from nearby Mystic, might have supervised, it was probably Indians, and perhaps a few African slaves, who actually constructed the house. Someone would have used an ox to drag the stone for the threshold out of a field all the way up this rise to the spot just outside the front door.

By the time this stone was set in place, Stanton held title to thousands of acres of what had once been Indian land. The beautifully carved railings and corner cabinets, the clocks, china, glassware, silks, draperies, and books that would make the great house in the wilderness a gentleman's home, were all carried to America by ship. Stanton would have moved his large family here from New London when the house was ready. Here, he and his wife, Anna, raised ten children, one of whom eventually sailed for Barbados, where he supervised the supply end of Stanton's trade in molasses and rum—one leg in the triangular Atlantic slave trade.

In this house, Whit Davis grew up during the Depression and raised his own children, during the long years after the family fortune was gone and farming was in decline. He tended his dying father in the room where Uncas had once sat, and left this house only when he remarried and moved to Groton, after years of living here alone following his first wife's death. But this is still where he comes to work every day.

From my perch above the old garden, I can look across the marsh to a stand of trees—hickories, oaks, and maples that have shed their leaves. I can see light glinting off the waters of the bay. There is more history there, in the field of timothy that runs undisturbed to a massive stone wall at the far limit of Whit's land, than there is behind me. Here is where two cultures met and clashed and one displaced the other—but not completely, and not forever.

The wheels of a pickup crunch on the gravel in the driveway. Whit has arrived. When I leave an hour later, I take with me seven ears of dried white flint corn.

As Whit shows me the burlap sacks crammed with ears of corn, I begin to tell him about finding Gladys Tantaquidgeon's essay about the Aquinnahs and their corn. I tell him how members of the tribe have been moving back to their communal lands at Gay Head on Martha's Vineyard and how they want to create gardens as part of their efforts to renew their heritage. Listening but saying nothing, he looks for and finds a special few sacks of corn, then unties the mouth of one of them. Inside are ears that Whit has carefully separated from the hundreds of others suspended in mesh bags from the rafters of the old summer kitchen behind the house. The ones he shows me now are not meant to be ground into meal for making johnnycakes at the Mohegan's Green Corn Festival next August. These are the seed corn for next year's planting.

"If something comes from somewhere, it should go back," Whit says. "That's why I gave it to the Mohegans. I'll give you half a dozen ears for the Aquinnahs. That should give them a good start." He rummages through his sack and picks them carefully, handing them to me one at a time, explaining that these are the prized ears, each with a double cap. "Tell them they should plant two, three fields of it," he says, "and to keep them separated. After three, four years, they should take the best seed from all three and mix them together and start again. That way they keep the corn strong."

Whit is the keeper of the corn—and of the land and all it holds—and as he sees his long, good run on this land coming to an end, he is visibly moved to be invited to extend his generosity.

I gather the ears of corn in my arms. They are hard and golden and heavy. I don't know what to say other than thank you, which I keep repeating. We walk slowly toward the back of the house, where Whit's truck and my car are parked. It promises snow tonight, and he needs to get on the road to Maine to visit his kids for the holiday. I put the corn in a cloth bag in my car.

"Tell them that I wish them well," he adds. "Tell them that I wish them good luck in all their endeavors."

"I will," I say.

I drive away thinking about the husked and dried seed corn on the back seat. How can a gesture as simple as the gift of seeds be a meaningful answer to centuries of injustice?

Because it makes possible the restoration of the seed's place in a structure of meaning. The English imposed on "the garden of New England" the idea of land as commodity, the wilderness as a fund of natural capital at their disposal, and seed as a form of currency. Whit's return of the seeds refuses those meanings.

When John Winthrop, Jr., sailed to England to give his report on maize to the Royal Society in 1662, the English had already transformed sacred Indian corn into a cash crop traded in a global marketplace. Corn had also become an essential source of food for provisioning the slave ships that traveled between the windward coast of Africa and the shores of Rhode Island and South Carolina. The trip to London to clarify Connecticut's status as a colony marks an important moment in the history of writing about American gardens. Winthrop was careful to omit the politics and economics—the blood and money—that defined the colonial approach to the cultivation of maize in the New World.

What Winthrop missed entirely was the meaning of corn for the Algonkin peoples. He missed the corn's *story.*

Stories, like seeds, hold the power to sustain a people. A seed without its story will still produce a tall green stalk of corn, a weighty harvest of beans, a fat, ripe *pompion,* or pumpkin. It might still satisfy a merely physical hunger. But it cannot by itself preserve a culture, though it will hold in genetic memory the history of its relationship to the hands that first cultivated it. The story of corn without the actual seed speaks of a different kind of sadness—a cultural heritage ungrounded, a myth of food for a real but unanswered hunger of the spirit. When the seed and the story of its place in the life of a people are reconnected, a part of the original violence that sundered them may be mended.

The fact of the seed's survival, like the fact that Whit Davis, eleven generations after Thomas Stanton and Uncas, also mediates between the white man and Indian culture, suggests how hopeful even a symbolic act of justice can be.

One ear of corn yields more than a hundred seeds; six ears yield many hundreds. If even half of them were to grow, one season's harvest would multiply the possibility each seed represents to many thousands. Generations of seed will come from the return of the ancestral corn. Out of the distant past will come a future, a garden.

EPILOGUE
A Garden Democracy

The garden of the world
is one huge democracy.

RUDOLF BORCHARDT

When Maska Pellegrini said, "It's our life, you know," reaching down to pick me something to eat from her garden, she thought she was merely stating the obvious.

The earth is the actual ground of our lives—we grow out of the soil too. If it dies, we die. If it lives, we eat and live. You know this when you grow your own food.

Maska didn't see this as special knowledge. There was nothing romantic about it. In her experience, it was a simple fact, learned as a girl in Italy. But so many of us in America don't know, or if we once knew, we have forgotten. So little in our culture asks us to remember our dependence on nature.

Maska's all-embracing phrase, "It's our life," included the whole garden—soil, plants, worms, birds, insects, water, sun, wind, and *her*. In her marvelous, encompassing, humble phrase, "our life" extended to include "their lives." Her garden was an interdependent community, a democracy.

Like Vanzetti's garden, which kept alive in him the memory

of a place where he belonged as a citizen of a world that transcended any mere nation, Maska's garden was as much a place of the mind and heart as of the actual earth. Her garden, like his—like all the gardens whose stories have been gathered here—answered needs at once practical and symbolic.

For so many of the gardeners whose stories we have heard, as for Vanzetti, when the human community failed them, the community of the land did not. The garden is where they have claimed, or reclaimed, a just and good relationship to the earth. It is where they affirm a sense of who they are and where they come from. When they were compelled to make a new life in a place where no one spoke their language or knew how to pronounce their names, the earth responded to their knowing hands. In their gardens, as Sokehn Mao explained, the earth doesn't speak to them "in a foreign language" but speaks to them "in their own language," a universal tongue. In their gardens, they are home.

ACKNOWLEDGMENTS

First and last, my greatest debt is to all the gardeners, my teachers. I especially want to thank the many people whose stories I could not include here—their words inform every page. My apprenticeship in the art of listening began with Liesbeth Slosberg and Sansericq Mathieu, the first to open their doors to me.

I thank my agent, Sarah Jane Freymann, for her wisdom and grace in shepherding me through the many stages of creating the book; and my editors, first Joanne Wyckoff, for her insight, for her patience and sense of humor as she helped me find its shape, and then Brian Halley, for his warmth and skill in bringing the finished manuscript to publication.

For enlarging my sense of the possible, I thank everyone at the Sitka Center for Art and Ecology at Cascade Head, Oregon, and the Island Institute in Sitka, Alaska. Each provided me with a time and a place to work out my ideas in a spectacularly beautiful and serene setting. They also gave me the chance, at last, to meet my audience, for which I also thank Rachel Epstein of the Alaska Center for the Book at the University of Alaska in Anchorage. A scholarship to the Wildbranch Workshop in Outdoor, Natural History and Environmental Writing at Sterling College in Vermont introduced me to an inspiring group of writers and one of the finest teachers I've ever met, Ted Gup, whose words and example gave me courage in the early stages of the book's life.

Penelope Colby of the Guilford Free Library put *The Letters of Sacco and Vanzetti* into my hands for the first time, and so altered the direction of my life. Paul Hawken read the earliest version of the prologue and introduced me to the work of Aldo Leopold. Deborah Madison responded to the idea of the book with extraordinary generosity, understood the meaning of food in the stories from the beginning, and introduced me to Michael Ableman, whose unwavering enthusiasm for the project helped to sustain me during the years when I had no external support of any kind—for time he could not spare from his family, his farm, and his own writing, I will always be grateful.

How I met the gardeners is a story in itself. Stanley Crawford led me to Clayton Brascoupé and the Fresquez family; Marquetta Goodwine introduced me to Ralph Middleton; William Clack was the first link in the chain that connected me with Gerard Bentryn and Akio Suyematsu; Nancy Lowry brought me the news clipping that led me to the Khmer Growers and Ronnie Booxbaum, who shared generously of her knowledge of the Khmer community; it was Ronnie who connected me with Daniel Ross, who in turn urged me to contact Tullio Inglese; Penelope Laurans gave me the part-time job that supported my travel and research and put me in New Haven to meet Ruhan Kainth; and Chris Careb sent me down the road a piece to find Whit Davis. Joan Little and Marty Ragno, to whom I owe so much, connected me with Maska and Mario Pellegrini, and, together with Page Allen, and Dave and Nancy Leedy, offered me a place to stay and a vehicle as I traveled the country, doing interviews.

Many librarians, archivists, and scholars shared their expertise and made helpful suggestions along the way, particularly Barbara Doyle, historian at Middleton Place Foundation in Charleston; Ben Kiernan of the Yale Program in Genocide Studies; Jason Mancini, senior researcher at the Mashantucket Pequot Museum and Research Center; Faith Damon Davison, archivist for the Mohegan Tribe; and independent scholar, Jane Edmundson. Martin Bailkey, Steven Grafe, Kenneth Helphand, Joseph Inguanti, Philip Klasky, Claudia Lazzaro, Clifton Olds, Thomas Sclereth, David Slawson, Sam Bass Warner, Jr., and Laura Wexler spared me hours of fruitless wandering by sharing books (including portions of works-in-progress) and ideas about gardens and ethnic landscapes.

For help in crises large and small—from taking notes on paper bags and placemats so that I would remember what I'd just said during the periods of inevitable writer's block, to showing up at my door with arms full of food or providing financial support in moments when I couldn't have gone another step without it—my heartfelt thanks go to Susan Bianconi and Bob Voght, Lynne Bundesen, Mark Burde, Susan and Ira Fogel, Mary Beth Golja, Christi Keller and John Timpane, Alice Linder and Steven Siegel, Lawrence Lifshultz and Rabia Ali, Stephen Lloyd, Patricia McNerny, Alfred Mahan, Wade and Corinne Neubegin, Mary Keohane Pelliccia, Laura Prusof, Darrell Ripley, Julie Rivkin and Michael Ryan, Johanna and Michael Rosen, Nicole Schless, Galina Vromen, Alice White and Richard Beck, and Robert Wilkins. I am also indebted to Richard Beck for his unfailing grace in providing computer support, and to Richard Warren, who salvaged a torn and pleated tape so that I could finish Tullio Inglese's story. To all the others, family and friends, who were with me every step of the way: *I remember.*

I am glad to have the chance, at last, to thank those who read and commented on portions of the manuscript: Emory Campbell, William Clack, Mary Felstiner, Geoffrey and Renée Hartman, Margaret Homans, Dori and Johanna Laub, Melody Lawrence, Larry Lifshultz, and Kim Stafford. I am especially grateful to Theresa Vara-Dannen for the sensitivity she brought to reading the entire book in draft; and to Joseph Opala, one of the most generous scholars I have ever encountered, for sharing his knowledge of Gullah culture and the slave trade and for reading and commenting on every draft of the second chapter.

Finally, two friends whose presence lit up the darkness whenever doubt and exhaustion seized me remain to be thanked. To Anthony Riccio, for countless hours of conversation, for translating from the Italian, and for believing, with me, that oral history has the power to render justice to those whose voices are rarely heard, *mille grazies*. And to Sharon Kessler—indispensable friend and most demanding reader—for the fullness of her response as she took time away from her poetry and her family to read and comment on every draft of every chapter, and for continuing to believe when I could not, I owe more than words can say.